Design for Shopping Centres

Nadine Beddington, MBE, FRIBA, FSIAD

Butterworth Scientific

London Boston Durban Singapore Sydney Toronto Wellington

First published 1982
© Nadine Beddington 1982

British Library Cataloguing in Publication Data

Beddington, Nadine
  Design for shopping centres.
  1. Shopping centers   2. Shopping centres
  Design and construction
  I. Title
  711'.552   HF5430

  ISBN 0-408-00357-X

Photoset by Butterworths Litho Preparation Department
Printed in England by The University Press, Cambridge

Foreword

by Edward D. Mills, CBE, FRIBA, FSIA

Facilities for shopping are as old as civilization itself; in the remains of every civilisation and in the remains of every ancient city all over the world, can be seen the ruins of the shopping streets and markets where food and every day commodities were bought and sold.

Nadine Beddington's book is not a history of shopping but one on the specific subject of *Design for Shopping Centres*. It is based on British practice, but retailing principles remain constant in all conditions and in all countries. The expressed intention of the author is to bring together for the benefit of the architect and designer a comprehensive presentation of design information directly relating to the comparatively new building type, the managed shopping centre.

First the book examines the philosophy of shopping and the different types of shopping and then in considerable detail deals with the planning of a shopping centre starting with the design brief, and discussing alternative solutions; then follows a detailed examination of some of the important design problems such as servicing, provision for the handicapped, cleaning and maintenance, etc. The role of the architect is given proper prominence and the increasing impact of legislation, regulations and controls on architectural design solutions is discussed. The rapidly changing technology not only of building but also of actual shopping techniques is not overlooked, for the influence of the computer and the microchip is an important factor in the design of any distribution system.

Nadine Beddington has been concerned with the design of shops and shopping centres for a large part of her career as a practising architect; she contributed the section of *Planning (Ninth edition)* on 'Department Stores, Supermarkets and Shops' and has written widely on the subject.

It has been said that the English are a nation of shopkeepers, and although the idea of the shopping centre originated in North America, it has developed rapidly in the UK in the last decade and, indeed, is still developing. The shopping centre in various forms has proliferated all over Europe, often as the result of large scale rebuilding of war-damaged city centres, and in Australia and North America the Greenfield, out-of-town shopping complex, often combined with community facilities, provides comprehensive buildings for the car-owning shopper. In this book the author considers the possible future direction of shopping centre design and whether escalating fuel costs, micro-technology, the increasing popularity of domestic deep freeze and mail-order shopping and other factors will influence the future trends in design for shopping.

This comprehensive study of shopping centre design is essential reading for all concerned with shopping – developer, architect, designer and tenant. It is of interest to note that in the United Kingdom the nationalized industries pension funds have invested heavily in shopping centre development, both at home and abroad – one of the most surprising examples being the purchase by the National Union of Mineworkers, for £17 million, of the mammoth private enterprise luxury Pompano Fashion Square in California, USA.

Nadine Beddington's book follows the established pattern of the *Butterworth Design Series*, and includes many case studies illustrated by diagrams and photographs. The shopping centre as a building type is new and complex, and it is constantly changing; the author has therefore included a glossary of terms to enable the reader to understand the vocabulary used in connection with retailing activities.

There is no doubt that the traditional corner shop and general store will always have a role to play in British urban and country life, but it is clear that new forms of shopping complex will develop, and this book has been written as a practical guide for all those concerned with the design of such facilities in the future.

Contents

Acknowledgements

I would like to acknowledge and thank the following to specialists in many fields for their help and co-operation in preparing this book:

The many architects and others mentioned in the text for supplying drawings, photographs and information.

The developers and management who are referred to in the text and who spared their time to give me valuable advice and opinions and . Specifically I would mention Mr. Ian Northen of Capital and Counties Property Company, Mr. Ron Jennings of Town and City Properties; shopping centre managers Mr. Clive Kaye (Victoria Centre, Nottingham); Mr. Gordon Allanson (Eldon Square, Newcastle); Mr. David Peek (Managing Director, Hempstead Valley, Kent); Mr. Michael Brown (Centre Director, Brent Cross) and Mr Allen Duff (Commercial Director, Milton Keynes Development Corporation).

Also Mr. Paul Beaufrere, FCA, (Investment Analyst) and Mr. Keith Crawford (Property Analyst) both of W. Greenwell & Company, Stockbrokers; Mr. Chidlaw (Company Architect to Marks & Spencer) and Mr. Gerry Writer of Edward Erdman & Company.

The (Specialist) Consultants: Bylander Waddell Partnership, F. C. Foreman & Partners, Ove Arup & Partners, Mr. Murray Cameron of S. W. Barbanel, and to the many specialist commercial firms who placed their expertise at my disposal, amongst whom are Colt International Limited, Concord Lighting International Limited, Philips Lighting, Phoenix Electrical Company Limited, Lennox Industries Limited, Mather & Platt Limited, Total Fire Protection Company Limited, Marryat & Scott Limited, Lampson International.

The representatives of various bodies, Governmental and Advisory; the Unit for Retail Planning Information, the Fire Protection Association, Mr. Frank Robotham of the British Multiple Retailers Association and other specialist organisations listed in the text.

My very special thanks are due to Mr. Nigel Woolner of Chapman Taylor & Partners for his untiring and patient help and co-operation, to Mr. Dermot O'Brien who undertook the preparation of the illustrations and production of drawings as well as much valuable research and to Mr Frederick Willcox for reading the proofs.

Last but not least Miss Melanie Blackman for deciphering and typing my manuscript and tapes.

The uncredited photographs were taken by myself.

Nadine Beddington

*Eaton Centre, Toronto. Part of the Galleria or main mall showing
decorations. (For a complete description of this centre, see page 160)*

Introduction

The concept of the 'shopping centre' is by no means new. Wherever communities have grown up, 'shops' or markets have developed and over a period of time have become 'shopping centres', the focus of every town and village.

With the development of sophisticated technology in actual building and in the distributive trades, and with increased population, higher living standards and a whole host of social and technical advances, designing for shopping has become complex and specialised. Thus, following the 1939–45 war, a new building type emerged – the planned shopping centre. This is not a static form but is still developing in a number of directions.

In order to keep abreast of, or to initiate new developments, and produce successful solutions to what is still a 'fluid' problem it is essential for the designer faced with the prospect of 'a shopping centre' to understand and sympathise with the principles behind this movement. It is necessary also to understand the requirements of the shopper and of the retailer as well as of the developer, and the implications, physical and social, of shopping design.

In this book I examine practical execution of shopping centre design in the context of the principles governing successful retailing, specifically as it affects the work of the architect concerned with this new building type. The principles are equally valid in the organic High Street centre, the Planned Central Area Redevelopment, the Greenfield or the 'Hypermarket' concept. The book concentrates on British shopping centre practice as affected by overseas influence and examines the way in which this is being, or may be, translated into solutions suitable for local conditions, controls, population distribution and customs. Retailing principles remain constant in all conditions. These UK solutions in their turn are having an effect on design elsewhere, as conditions change and new problems develop. Trading principles governing shopping centre design also involve an understanding of unit shop design, which will be considered where appropriate.

The first part of the book is devoted to those preliminary activities relevant to the development of a shopping centre. These may not necessarily involve the designer, but he must understand them in order to work with the developer and his team to produce an effective solution. The remaining chapters are concerned with the physical design of the centre. I have dealt specifically with the 'managed' centre forming a complex of tenant retailers, considering in particular the concentrated mall type, single or multi-level, open or closed.

The shopping centre had its origin in North America. The USA, being the cradle of this emerging new idea, has produced a stereotype for a sucessful centre. With new trading techniques and a changing social pattern this concept has spread internationally to all continents and countries, adapting to local conditions in the process. It is not generally appreciated to how great an extent the concept has been adopted in the UK. At the present time there are said to be 19 000 shopping centres in the USA and only about 250 in the UK. The list of UK established shopping centres (1980) given in the Appendix will indicate the magnitude of the UK movement. Unfortunately not all have been marked by high quality and design standards, or maximum results in terms of successful trading and satisfied retailers and customers.

In a building type as new and as complex as a shopping centre there are no standard solutions. Each project will need fresh thought, thorough and painstaking research, and from major policy to technical detail will have its own unique and individual problems to be solved. The picture is constantly changing, and will continue to do so, as the retail trade reacts sensitively to immediate conditions; legislative patterns alter, technical knowledge increases, economic and physical conditions change.

The designer new to this form, nevertheless can do with some guidelines – at least to point him in the right direction – to alert him* to the specialised and

* For the purposes of brevity in this book, the word 'he' embraces 'she' and 'him' – 'her'.

not yet much publicised problems of retailing, and to help in development of appropriate solutions.

I cannot offer a recipe for instant success in shopping centre design and this book is not a 'Bible' of mandatory design information. The building type is so rapidly evolving that each new project in what is still an experimental field must be researched fully in terms of current and specific conditions, but with benefit of accumulated experience to which I hope these pages make their contribution. This book is based on research, with help and information from many varied sources of which the opinions and deductions are my own interpretation.

I have concentrated on those aspects peculiar to shopping centres which appear to me to have received less attention than they deserve. I have emphasised demand of shopping centres which may seem to be an irritation to the designer, often justifiably, sometimes through a misconception of the true function of the managed centre. I have also been, during my studies, mystified and exasperated by an apparent absence of communication in many instances between those whose co-operation is essential to the project. Planners and legislators can be blissfully unaware of the ABC of trading, while developers and retailers can be 'philistine' in their insensitivity to the visual impact of what they do.

The temptation for some retailers or developers to accept the 'second best' is a deterrent to inventive design and successful fulfilment. A shopping centre must have **style**; without this it remains a boring repetition of a standard formula. With style comes a new dimension – to transform the routine task of shopping into one of interest and pleasure to the shopper. This 'customer-orientation', defined as the need to attract and please the shopper, is surely what it is all about! To achieve this, eagerness for high quality and good design must be harnessed to a comprehensive sympathetic understanding. Successful examples throughout the world demonstrate that enterprise and high risk capital investment show adequate returns. I suggest this is a challenging motto for those concerned with shopping centre design.

Nadine Beddington

Glossary of terms

The following is a short glossary of terms which the reader will find repeatedly mentioned in the following text. The definitions given are those which have developed in common usage.

Shopping centre Planned shopping complex under one central management, leasing units to individual retailers, with a degree of control by management who are responsible overall for the centre. (Author's definition)

Catchment area Area expressed in terms of distance related to travel time and population served by the centre.

Mall or plaza Traffic free pedestrian precinct serving the retail units, linked to transport discharge points.

Court Focal point linking malls.

Turnover Total trading receipts of a retail unit – usually measured annually.

Gross margin Difference between turnover and total cost of goods and materials received annually, less stocks at the start of the year, plus stocks at the end of the year.

Mark-up Unit profit on article sold i.e. the difference between the cost of the article to the retailer and the price received from the customer.

Percentage rent Rent based on a given percentage of gross sales of the tenant.

Guaranteed rent Minimum rent guaranteed by the tenant irrespective of the level of sales.

Impulse buying The purchase of goods 'on impulse' not as a result of a previous decision.

Stock Goods on hand for sale in a retail unit, including materials for repairs to customers, goods and provision of meals.

Stock turn The length of time an item of stock remains in the unit between delivery and sale.

Multiple Retail organisation having ten or more branches. A retailer having fewer than ten is considered as 'independent'. (Board of Trade definition, 1971)

Department store The most complex shop type, offering full service throughout a full range of specialist merchandise and services, including restaurants, food hall and franchise operators. Minimum sales area $20\,000\,m^2$ (though there are 'Junior' department stores of $10\,000\,m^2$ sales area or less).

Variety store Sells wide range of non-food and food goods in open sales areas, mainly by self selection. Sales areas range from $200\,m^2$ to $15\,000\,m^2$ with total gross area of larger stores in excess of $20\,000\,m^2$. A catchment area of $80\,000$ to $100\,000$ population is needed to support the larger units.

Small shop A shop with a sales floor area not exceeding $280\,m^2$ per floor or not more than three floors – one of which may be a basement (From BS Code of Practice CP3. Chapter 4. Part. 2).

Supermarket Mainly self-service food and convenience store, trading with a limited range of non-food items occupying not more than 15% of sales area and varying in size between $1500\,m^2$ and $4500\,m^2$ gross. Sales areas usually between $1000\,m^2$ and $2500\,m^2$ with minimum sales area $400\,m^2$.

Superstore Single level self service store offering extensive range of comparison and convenience goods, with sales area minimum $2500\,m^2$ and gross area of 5000–$7000\,m^2$.

Hypermarket A store operated by a single retailer handling a wide variety of convenience and comparison goods, food and non-food. Mainly self-service with minimum capital and running costs and consequent competitive pricing. The basis is a single level single

the outside of the external perimeter walls (and centre line 'gross floor space').

Net sales area   (net floor space or net rental area). Internal floor space of a retail unit, used for selling and displaying goods and services, including floor area to which public have access, counter space, checkout space, window and display space. (Normally used by retailers to calculate density of their trading turnover.) It excludes lobbies, staircases, toilets, storage, food preparation, warehousing, staff accommodation and other support areas which are regarded as non-selling areas (From BS Code of Practice CP3 Chapter 4 Part 2).

volume building envelope, usually, though not always, a 'one-stop' out-of-town enterprise with extensive car parking, often with restaurant, tyre, battery and car accessories bay, and filling station. Sales area $5000\,m^2$ but more usually $10\,000\,m^2$ with gross area 7000 to $15\,000\,m^2$ requiring a large site, say 5 to 10 acres, in a prominent position and easily accessible by car.

Retail areas   Varying methods are used in describing retail areas. Two generally-used definitions are given below.

Gross leasable area   Total enclosed floor area (for exclusive use) occupied by retailers, measured up to

Chapter 1
Philosophy of shopping

The shopping scene

Before investigating contemporary design requirements a brief survey of the shopping scene is needed. Shopping is a primary human activity in which almost every individual in civilised society takes part, inevitably almost daily. Buildings and services for shopping are as closely related to housing as those for education, health, administration and entertainment.

From the point of view of the shopper, i.e. the consumer, shopping may be either a chore, a social pleasure, a relaxation, or a stimulus. One has only to think of tourists. What do they do first when landing in a major new town or country? Almost invariably they go and 'look at the shops' leading them inevitably to the heart of the city. Thus, for many people, shopping is a leisure pursuit, a relaxation.

As a resident, one is responsible for the welfare of one's family, and there is a continuous commitment to keeping the cupboard stocked with a vast range of commodities. This can be the tedious aspect of shopping being never-endingly repetitive. Here, the shopper wants ease of accessibility, flow, economy and convenience.

Now, what of the retailer? Trading involves today a vast range of activities – manufacture, storage and distribution of an enormous variety of goods before they reach the retailer. So the retail function is to provide the commodities demanded by the consumer, to obtain, store and stimulate demand for them, to react to stimulus by producers and manufacturers and introduce alternatives; therefore to attract trade, to display merchandise, to facilitate purchase, to provide an efficient service, and to provide the right merchandise at an acceptable price. All this must be done by selling at an acceptable profit, which is why the retailer is in business. Profit may be related to either large turnover with small 'mark-up' (i.e. profit per item) or large 'mark-up' on limited range of luxury goods. But, obviously, the buildings and infrastructure concerned in shopping contribute largely to the process.

It is worth noting that retailing is the only industry which expanded during the recession of the past decade. Discussion with retailers shows an enthusiasm and general enjoyment in their occupation, particularly the self-employed small shopkeeper. There is an attractive 'entrepreneurial' aspect of shopkeeping. Perhaps the British are after all by inclination a nation of shopkeepers?

We will be looking at the retailing functions in detail later on in this book but first we need to consider the design principles on which shopkeepers rely to attract custom and business. Obviously, an appropriate atmosphere is needed to create interest. In any shopping area there must be not only a feeling of bustle, excitement, sparkle, competition and variety, but also a sense of familiarity and of confidence in where to go and what to look for. Monotony of design, repetition and regularity are the enemies of trade. Moreover, people flow much like liquid, tending to follow the line of least resistance (and greatest attraction). They can be deliberately 'funnelled' into certain flow patterns and this is a trading axiom. Therefore the siting of every shop directly affects its value, as the greater the traffic past the shop and the more arresting the way the greater the trading potential. So to make best use of siting, impact is needed. An attractive shop-front, shop-sign, window display, lighting and correct planning of entrances to entice customers are integral to the design.

Inside, merchandise must be displayed in a way which will encourage the buyer. This sounds like an aphorism but is a skilled exercise, related to the particular type of goods, method of trading, shop character, price-range, intended customer flow, etc.

This is a matter needing considerable expertise on the part of the designer. The capital cost of providing shop envelopes must be directly related to estimated profit to be successful. The type, quality and quantity of merchandise must be related to the available custom – i.e. population within reach – and to 'mark-up' and turnover, i.e. to scale of project.

Historical development of shopping centres

The earliest, and still surviving, concentrated shopping centres were the open or covered markets and bazaars. These developed in one direction into sophisticated 'arcades' (the Galeria in Milan, Burlington Arcade London and Kyoto, Japan) and on the other, into today's street markets which still operate throughout the UK.

The alternative to the market was the shopping street. This was generally an organic development as seen in our High Streets, where often the ground floors of domestic buildings were gradually transformed into shops. We will look at this further when examining 'shop design' in detail.

Simple local shopping started to change in the 19th century. There is no need here to describe the whole series of social and technological changes the effects of which transformed retailing, but main headings must be referred to if we are to understand the present pattern of what have now become the 'distributive trades'.

Population growth and concentration have produced mass demand. When the railway and the motor car brought mobility to both goods and the consumer, the development of packaging, food preservation, direct advertising from manufacturer to consumer, accelerated the growth of the big manufacturer and the consequent problems for the retailer (i.e. stockholding, cashflow). This led to the development of the wholesaler who provided a distribution system between the manufacturer and the retailer.

Open 'bazaar', Cairo

Covered arcade shopping, Kyoto, Japan

Open street market, Stratford-upon-Avon (Photo: Dermot O'Brien)

This growth also led to the development of the larger unit, the 'multiple' and the department store (late 19th century). Thus companies set up their own central buying and distribution system and warehousing, helped by the development of such technical advances as computers and the 'fork lift truck' and, today, the 'silicon chip'. This latter is likely to contribute as a future essential element in distribution systems. When embarking on the design of any shopping project it is useful for the designer to have some knowledge of how goods arrive at the retail point.

The growth of the multiple was also encouraged by the development of the Institutions as ground landlords buying and leasing prime sites as an investment. The stagnation of trade during the 1939–45 war and resultant obsolescent buildings not matching up to their development combined with increasing involvement of married women in part or full time work, increased car ownership, the deep-freeze, increasing traffic problems in existing towns, involvement of major marketing and retailing companies, increased population and increased demand, all led to efforts to find solutions to 'shopping problems'. These culminated in Urban Developments on one hand and 'Greenfield Shopping Centres' on the other. Both developments gradually came to favour the pedestrianisation of shopping – and the planned shopping centre.

Today's shopping centre

The shopping centre started, with the benefit of land availability, as a conceived project in the USA where 80% of the population live on 2% of the land!

The increase of traffic and its problems in the 1950s and 1960s, resulting in the call for 'pedestrianised' shopping, led to an international movement towards the planned centre. Consequently with the growth of motor car ownership, good roads and an availability of greenfield sites, shopping centres proliferated and a stereotype emerged, which is still existent today. This is, inherently, a managed complex of trading units, served by controlled pedestrian circulation routes and fed by a transport system from the surrounding catchment area.

It assumed the incorporation at inception of 'magnets' or 'anchor units' – department stores, food supermarkets, chain stores, strategically situated, with smaller specialised shopping units between. The centre would have convenient car parking, but no vehicular traffic within the centre, attractive landscaping, a high amenity standard, restaurants, perhaps sports centres, cinemas, art exhibitions etc. and other ancillary attractions. All these, together with long opening hours, produced profitable trading conditions. This was the typical out of town American centre, varying in size and extent of facilities, and dependent for its success on its 'catchment' area. With developments in 'environmental engineering' – i.e. air conditioning and advanced artificial lighting systems – came the covered centre or 'closed mall'.

Fasta, Sweden

Meanwhile Europe was giving attention on one hand to rebuilding its bombed cities, and on the other to serving an increasingly urbanized population. Thus the classic early examples of planned European shopping were produced of which the Lindbaum, Rotterdam is the celebrated pioneer pedestrian centre.

The Swedish small shopping centres developed, and were planned as part of neighbourhood units related to stations on the new transport system into Stockholm. In West Germany, Dusseldorf rebuilt its bombed centre as a glittering shopping complex, and Cologne pedestrianised its main shopping streets while rebuilding on its bombed shopping sites, and retaining the existing street pattern. These are typical examples of what was happening all over Europe.

Lindbaum, Rotterdam

Pedestrianised shopping street, Cologne

In Great Britain, early attempts at rebuilding our town centres were less successful. Plymouth, Portsmouth, Bristol were rebuilt with shops on both sides of wide traffic thoroughfares with no appreciation of the significance of shopping sites other than that of relating existing sites to existing owners.

Gradually the transatlantic influence and European experience penetrated into the UK. The first substantial planned covered shopping centres were the Elephant & Castle in London and the Bull Ring, Birmingham. The Elephant & Castle can only be described as a failure – due primarily to its siting on an apparently inaccessible island site with a forbidding exterior. The Bull Ring, although adequately successful, seemed to be an economy version of the American Centre. Neither centre has very much resemblance to its transatlantic cousins lacking what were considered in the UK as 'trimmings', but in their shopping centre concept were the essential ingredients. These latter were sophisticated and high quality design, high quality low maintenance finishes with attractive and comfortable surroundings and convenient access for shoppers and servicing. However this was a start and much was learnt from these examples.

There followed in the 1960s a procession of central area redevelopment schemes some of which ruthlessly cut into the traditional elements of the town, replacing residential buildings, and individual shop sites with financially viable high rent office blocks over standardised shopping units. Elsewhere local authorities were busy 'road widening', making individual owners set back as a condition of redevelopment and in some cases allowing temporary 'bungalow fronts'. Some of these very authorities have since pedestrianised these very same High Streets! Thus we see the pendulum swing – a warning perhaps to over-enthusiastic planners and the need for flexible thinking.

Following the oil crisis of the 1970s, there was a pause in UK shopping centre development, while the movement towards urban renewal led to reconsideration of shopping centre siting. There was also a trend towards owner occupation, development by major retailers either as a consortium or singly, for their own use with subsidiary lettings of additional units as well as the one-retailer 'Hypermarket'. The latter not being a true shopping centre needs consideration on its own.

The UK is over-shopped, but obsolescent and uneconomic units stimulate demand for organised and financially viable shopping to suit modern retailing methods and 'life style'. There is as yet no central organised planning policy for shopping, it being left to Local Authorities and private enterprise to sort out problems and satisfy demand.

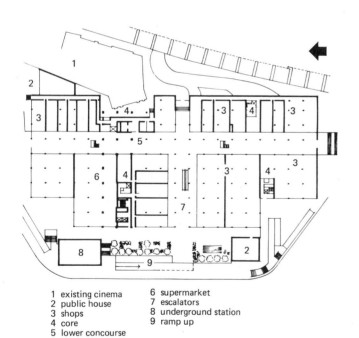

1 existing cinema
2 public house
3 shops
4 core
5 lower concourse
6 supermarket
7 escalators
8 underground station
9 ramp up

Elephant & Castle Shopping Centre. Site plan. The earliest of the British centres on a cleared existing island site with no obvious pedestrian access and of a forbidding elephant grey exterior (recently changed to a sickly green). No atmosphere of gaiety or frivolity here, no welcoming messages, no obvious or inviting entry, a new site but isolated and unfamiliar (Photo: Nicholas Halton)

Elephant and Castle Shopping Centre, London. External view

In spite of the pause, the impressive list of projected or completed UK centres demonstrates the still continuing need for planned shopping facilities. Fifteen new shopping centres were opened in the UK in 1980, together with the final phase of six developments accounting for 2.9 million ft^2 gross. Smaller centres (50 000–90 000 ft^2) account for 43% of these openings.* These centres are visualised as a total concept planned for an anticipated and calculated demand, related to the estimated catchment area. This is the building type we are discussing and which we will now examine in greater depth.

Future directions

We are now in 1982 at a point of possible change of direction. The energy crisis and escalating fuel costs, the rising popularity of the domestic deep-freeze, micro-technology, the increase of mail order shopping, the need to conserve agricultural land resulting in rising land values, the swing towards urban rehabilitation, all indicate new developments. In addition the growth of violent crime, demonstrations, vandalism and inflation, point to new attitudes, controls and systems while public participation adds a further dimension to planning decisions.

Will centres grow much larger in order to reduce prices and to serve the car-borne shopper who, energy conscious, will shop less often for convenience goods but stock up for longer periods to fill the deep-freeze? These centres would also cater for the 'car-less' public who will demand public transport into the centre. This is one theory, an alternative being towards more smaller centres within easy reach of the shopper with less mileage. Also it is a possibility that fuel scarcity will encourage a return to rail transport for major goods servicing, with a consequent rethinking of site planning, perhaps to rail-head termini?

However, in spite of gloomy predictions, some earlier successful USA centres are looking for ways of expansion – this sometimes even being possible as a result of the energy crisis, the popularity of the 'compact' car freeing car parks area for extension, without decreasing the number of car park spaces!

Meanwhile inflation, escalating costs and possible fuel scarcity and restrictions, with resulting high and increasing service charges, are possible reasons for signs of resistance by retailers to taking expensive space in closed centres. This could result in the experimental return to the open or part open centre or reduced environmental control. It is certain, however, that for 'consumer durables' and luxury goods, personal shopping in comfortable and convenient surroundings will remain the main shopping demand. Moreover in certain towns and cities there is an obvious need for increased shopping to relieve pressure on the existing 'High Street' with its obsolescent shops and congestion due to vehicular traffic, delivery problems and general excessive use of inadequate facilities. Consequently extension of shopping may not transfer existing magnets but, by attracting new traders, may extend the shopping area in scope and variety, consequently increasing the convenience of shopping in the existing as well as the new area. This would have the effect of 'up-grading' the retailing potential of the town and city as at the Friary Centre, Guildford (see Chapter 10).

There are also recently developed alternative types of shopping, such as the one stop 'hypermarket' or discount store. This differs from the true shopping centre in being operated by one single retailer instead of being a complex housing a variety of tenant retailers. This being a distinctive building type is not covered specifically in this book, though many of the factors governing shopping centre design apply equally to it.

Mail order also deserves a mention in its possible future effect; it is bound to take a share of the potential market for certain types of goods, though it has not 'taken off' in the UK to the extent that it has in the USA.

* From a report published by Hillier Parker May & Rowden, June 1981.

Chapter 2
Types of shopping

Major factors in shop planning

Although the shopping centre designer may not be involved in the detail design of individual unit interiors he has to provide satisfactory trading conditions, and must understand the main principles of retailing techniques, in order to provide suitable retailing units. Moreover the principles of retailing govern in exactly the same way the design of the units relative to the centre, as does the merchandise relative to the unit. Unless the centre provides essential services and convenient facilities to retailers it will not attract the required tenant 'mix' and will not ultimately be successful.

Main shopping activities

There are two main shopping activities – known technically as 'convenience' and 'comparison' shopping. Convenience goods comprise daily, or recurring, shopping needs, food purchases and certain weekly and less frequent consumer durables which need to be bought 'conveniently'. Comparison goods (also known as consumer durables!) are those when customers compare quality, variety, design, prices, service offered, etc before making a choice of purchases which may last a considerable time.

Merchandise in any category can also be classified as 'demand', 'semi-demand' and 'impulse' goods. The latter will be placed at eye-catching level – demand goods need not be so conveniently and so obviously sited.

Selling methods

Any goods in either category may be sold in a number of ways as outlined in the following paragraphs.

Personal service. This is the traditional method, where the customer is served by an assistant, sometimes from behind a counter. At completion of sale, the assistant takes the cash to a cash point and may give a receipt and pack the goods. This method suits high value and technical goods needing technical advice, such as jewellery or cameras, and exclusive salons or small specialist boutiques and certain types of food shops, delicatessen, cooked meats, etc. The customer is influenced by the advice and sales technique of the assistant and although display is necessary, all available merchandise need not be on display.

Self-selection. Here the customer may handle and select goods, and take them to a cash point for payment and wrapping. There will be some staff assistance available. This system is general in variety stores and many departments of department stores and specialist shops. Customers must be able to identify and handle merchandise, all of which must be available for sale, and can often try on clothing in fitting rooms. Merchandise may be grouped and laid out for maximum indentification; flexibility also being of prime importance.

Self-service. The customer walks around the store, filling a basket or trolley with goods from shelves, etc. and takes them to a check point for payment and wrapping; 'in' and 'out' entrances being separated and controlled. This is the principle of supermarket and hypermarket trading and is basically suited to convenience goods. Here the internal shop layout, arrangement of entrances and check-out points must encourage customers to follow as continuous a route as possible from entrance to exit, exposed to the maximum amount of displayed merchandise. This must be achieved without monotony or congestion, and with an impression of spaciousness which will depend on design and disposition of circulation aisles and of sectional planning.

Layout must provide for general surveillance from key positions, i.e. office, check-out points, service desks, preparation areas, etc. The amount of shelf or display space to be allotted to various products is of key importance. The relation of floor space, shelf display area, commodity location and turnover is delicately balanced and part of the traders' expertise. Therefore, maximum flexibility in design of the interior is essential.

Stock

Stock, its amount and disposition, is also a key factor. Stock is classified as 'forward' stock displayed and held in the sales area, and 'support' or 'reserve' stock, held in stockrooms ready to replenish sales areas as required. The method of replenishment is a vital element – varying from a sales assistant going and fetching something from a stockroom in a small boutique, to the fork lift truck of the hypermarket. The modern trend is for maximum 'forward' stock. The amount of stock will be related to Stock Turn – or the length of time an article can profitably remain in the shop before being sold – as well as to weekly turnover, delivery frequencies and methods of stock control. These are important considerations in planning service access.

It will therefore be obvious that the selling techniques of any retail unit must inevitably govern its shop design in principle and in detail.

Chapter 3
The managed shopping centre

The concept

The essence of a managed shopping centre is that of a total concept, anticipating demand and meeting all the shopping needs within parameters set according to the size and type of centre it sets out to be. It will be planned to serve a predetermined catchment area with a full range of goods, services and amenities to a prearranged standard.

The centre must be connected to an adequate transport network, private and public, both for customers and for efficient goods delivery and servicing to the retailer, not forgetting the transport needs of the centre staff. It will affect and be affected by, the infrastructure of the surrounding area, with heavy demands on supplies of electricity, gas, water, telephone systems and sewerage, as well as on the transport system. The main constituents will be individual shop units, interconnected by totally pedestrianised walks, or 'malls', open or covered; the centre will be fed from car parks and public transport discharge points, by lifts, escalators and walkways as necessary.

This is a megastructure, and not a single building. Although to the architect the physical planning and design of the centre will be paramount, he will be brought in at decision stage, preferably before the site is assembled, as part of a team of many specialists who will have to be consulted at all stages. Therefore all considerations governing the development of the centre must be understood and appreciated if the architect is to produce a successful solution; this is not a project which can be designed in isolation.

It has been fashionable in studying shopping centres to classify them into identifiable categories but the boundaries are becoming blurred as shopping centres develop in different ways. Examples of such classifications are as follows:

Catchment area i.e. neighbourhood, district, regional centres.

Plan e.g. mall and anchor store siting (strip, cluster, dumb-bell, triangular).

Physical characteristics e.g. open or closed mall, multi-level or single level, greenfield, urban redevelopment, urban expansion.

These are some of the major factors which will, as decisions are made, govern the emergence of the concept into a final, individual design. We will proceed now to consider some of these factors.

The developer

There are many types of development. The project will start with either a developer looking for a site or a site looking for a developer. The skilled developer who has assembled a team and is looking for sites is concerned with the production of a shopping centre in order to provide by use of his expertise a satisfactory return on capital investment, this being achieved by adequate rental return from tenants. If, as is sometimes the case, the developer is also a contractor, he has the advantage of achieving a substantial building contract as part of the package.

The developer will provide within the total design concept, shells of shopping units, for tenants who will be responsible for shop frontage finishes and internal fitting out. It is possible that buildings housing the large units or 'magnets' may be designed not by the developer's architect but by their own design teams, the whole being subject to overall landlord and design control.

The private developer
It must be appreciated that a considerable body of expertise has been built up by successful private development companies in the UK as elsewhere. These developers continue to adjust, develop and adapt transatlantic and European practices to local conditions.

In the UK and in most countries in Western Europe, the opportunity to provide shopping centres on greenfield sites is extremely limited, the main potential being either central urban redevelopment, or extension and/or redevelopment in suburban or edge of town areas.

The local authority

In the UK climate of comprehensive planning control exercised by consequently powerful local authorities the private developer has frequently joined forces with the local authority to produce schemes for central area redevelopment. Local authorities in the UK are favourably placed for site acquisition, with compulsory purchase powers and local knowledge of retailing patterns. As freeholders they may invite bids from developers to lease sites for shopping centre development accepting that long term managing developers will be able to continue along their own well-tried lines of shopping centre design, advising the consortium partners accordingly.

The competitive bid

Schemes prepared by developers with specialised design teams and backing finance, are submitted in financial as well as physical terms for competitive consideration. These projects should of course be assessed in terms of quality, excellence, durability, viability, and long-term – not short-term – financial return. Successful judgement will be largely dependent on the experience and expertise of the assessors in balancing these factors.

Sadly this does not always work. It is not difficult to identify projects which fail in one or other of the major conditions, the extremes of temptation being either short-term financial gain or inappropriate over-emphasis of specific or sometimes idiosyncratic design standards. The local authority may even assume the developer role completely, (as have the New Towns), an essentially British concept.

Whoever the developer, he has to find the capital. Earlier USA shopping centres and many European examples have been financed by big institutions. These – the insurance companies, banks, pension funds, etc. – have turned their attention from the Stock Market to alternative methods of investment.

The institutes

There is an increasing amount of institutional money such as from pension and insurance schemes seeking high capital growth with an element of control lacking in equity investment. Property development offers an attractive long-term alternative to Institutions, perhaps with the acceptance of comparatively low starting returns, (until the centre matures) thus form-ing a major source of shopping centre finance. In the UK the big nationalized industry pensions funds such as the National Coal Board, the Electricity Board, the Post Office have entered this field of investment not only through the professional developer but by extending their interest into construction and management, building up their own teams of designers, advisers and managing agents.

An interesting extension of institutional investment into shopping centres is investment abroad as instanced in the following new items in the Daily Express (7.2.80):

'Britain's miners have paid £17 million to buy one of America's largest and most luxurious shopping centres. Their mammoth new monument to private enterprise is the Pompano Fashion Square, near Fort Lauderdale, California. Bubbling fountains play outside its main doors, and 106 shops line its cool marble halls. They sell everything from hamburgers to Dior gowns. It lies just two miles from the white sand beaches of the millionaire retirement belt, and its stores grossed a staggering £500 million last year.'

Here is a vivid description of a typical USA centre. Could it honestly describe any single development in the UK? It illustrates a different attitude. British shopping centres have not so far been adventurous enough to emulate this picture of lavish appointment, quality of finish and amenity or its sheer magnitude of investment and return.

However, here is a significant move introducing additional appreciation of transatlantic practice and its potential into the design vocabulary of an increasingly influential British developer. Will this trend to foreign investment give impetus to more innovative and imaginative thinking and consequently quality upgrading of new British centres? It certainly illustrates the financial attraction of tried shopping centre trading as a sound investment.

The owner-occupier

As apparent activity in the late 1970s decreased owing to lack of available investment risk capital and to increased legislative controls, a new incentive arose amongst the large retailers. Wishing to expand, singly or as a consortium, they became increasingly interested in developing shopping centres which could provide outlets for their own use. This brings us to another major initiative for shopping centre development, the owner-occupier. The involvement alters the emphasis of financing motive, the whole centre being designed primarily with the requirements of the major use in mind. This is not only a UK development; in Japan for instance the department stores, as a major financial and powerful influence, have from the start projected and financed shopping centres.

The new generation of owner-developers is breaking new ground, though with less available feedback and using in some cases less experienced or even unspecialised consultants. So another participant, the letting agent, is frequently closely involved in the whole project from inception, his function being the successful letting of space together with advice to this end. Some letting agents specialise in this type of commercial letting and even offer a management service, which has been used to good effect by a number of UK developers.

The letting agent

Certainly it must be acknowledged that the letting agent can exert a powerful influence on the developer's brief and the design – from the selection of site onwards. There is a warning here. The temptation towards selling in the open market, with the consequent accent on easily lettable units of standard size, trading levels and character, may be a misguided policy and an inhibiting factor in the design and ultimate success of the centre. This is acknowledged by the experienced developer who exerts firm control over the tenant mix.

The vital factor in a successful centre is the carefully related, correct and convenient location of various traders, to encourage variety of choice and interest, and maximum pedestrian flow.

Management

A further key factor which has to be considered from the very start and all through the design and briefing process is that of management. By far the most satisfactory method, by consensus view and as demonstrated by results, is for the developer to have a continuing interest in the centre and to be responsible for management. Perhaps in no other building type does management play such a critical part in the successful operation of the project.

Every design decision taken needs to be considered in these terms and the least likely way to success is for a completed scheme to be handed over to a management team who have had no contribution to make to the brief or towards its execution, or whose experience is limited to budgeted maintenance of utility buildings for captive users. This is particularly the case with some local authorities who unfortunately but not surprisingly, have no concept of the need for 'glamour' – the entrepreneurial outlook, the power to gamble with ideas in promotion of the centre, and the need for a generous maintenance budget. Unfortunately, it is also the case that where schemes are on offer to developers in competition, inexperienced authorities

may select a lower bid rather than quality and performance, without full consideration of these implications.

So, initiative will come either from a developer with finance available looking for a site, from a retailer looking for outlets in this specific area, or from an owner with an available or potential site, i.e. local authorities, new towns, private owners or consortia.

Multi-use centres

The developer may have to combine with other uses, for instance as a co-operative venture with a local authority. Thus it may be necessary to incorporate housing, public service buildings for leisure, social or educational use, or commercial offices. This may be a financial or planning requirement, to maximise site use and reduce land costs, but it will certainly need caution in negotiation and design.

The local authority is frequently concerned with public transport. Many British urban centre developers, in negotiating with the local authority for sites, have agreed to the incorporation of a major bus station into the complex. This is in itself a building type with its own problems, needing skill to link it satisfactorily into the shopping centre project. In the right context, and done successfully, it can contribute significantly to the viability of the centre.

The multi-use centre imposes additional design constraints, not only on delivery, circulation, traffic, transport and car parking considerations but also on construction. This includes such things as a constructional transfer system, column and beam sizes at crucial levels, grid dimensions, wind pressure, storey heights and services, e.g. refuse disposal, drainage, plumbing, water, electricity and gas supply distribution. All of these ingredients will have to be designed for multi-use, and will have a major effect on the design of the centre and decisions affecting capital and running costs. They will need full and careful analysis of their likely effect, which will probably involve feasibility studies by the architect at negotiation stage.

The argument presented by local authorities that housing or office provision will contribute to successful trading has not been wholly convincing in the light of experience. A large regional centre may attract a weekly maximum throughput at peak seasons of between 200 000 and 400 000 shoppers. Even a large housing scheme is unlikely to make much impression on figures such as these, and anyway its main trading potential will be in convenience goods, not comparison goods, and the comparatively small additional input is likely to be offset by high constructional costs and management problems.

The design team

We will now look at the technical members of the design team. The early appointment of all technical consultantsis most important. This applies not only to the architect who is almost bound to be concerned with feasibility studies during the assembly of the site, but also the mechanical, electrical and structural engineers the graphic designer and landscape architect.

It is likely that a Project Manager will be appointed for such a large constructional undertaking and he also, if in post, should be in at the design stage. Another key figure may be the Centre Manager who will be responsible for the centre once it is in operation, and if experienced in this field, he will have a valuable contribution to make to the development of the brief.

All consultants need to be able to contribute with experience and initiative to the development of progressive solutions to what may be unfamiliar technical problems; these will require research or inquiry into precedents in other countries with different conditions and their application or adjustment to local conditions. Therefore whoever the client and wherever the site the architect must ascertain and influence the composition and nature of the team, realising that the design of the centre will be a co-operative exercise utilizing the expertise and judgement of all its various members as appropriate. Ultimately the success of the centre will depend on maximum exploitation of every available design possibility related to the site, with input from all concerned. Of all building types perhaps none is more difficult and complex to execute than a shopping centre.

Finance

The fundamental factor in production of a shopping centre is finance. It is not necessary in this book to make a complete analysis of the detailed financing of shopping centres. The architect's involvement is peripheral, but an understanding of the principles involved, and their implications, is essential if he is to offer correct advice and information and design a financially viable scheme.

It is helpful that trade associations and other government and non-government sponsored research bodies in many countries maintain records and information on retailing profitability for different trades – e.g. turnover related to gross retail area – which are invaluable in this context. In addition the big institutional stockbrokers maintain research departments employing property, retail and other analysts, who have the expertise to advise on investment.

As we have seen already, the developer's interest is return on investment. The share of equity will be relative to the tenure and the freehold and leasehold interests. For example it may be three-pronged – the local authority receiving ground rent and perhaps a modest proportion of rental profit, the remainder being proportionally shared between financier and developer. The capital investment comprises the cost of the site, including the work of negotiation and assembly, probably lasting over a period of years, the cost of building, promotion and letting related professional fees, interest on tied-up capital, all amortised over an agreed period. There will then be the continuing costs of management, promotion, servicing and maintenance (both short- and long-term) to which retailer's will contribute out of profit. The return will be in retailers rental, and for the owner/part occupier, or developer depending on percentage rents, also profit on turnover.

The typical USA financial concept has been for rental to be variable, on a graduated basis related to turnover, with a minimum turnover to be agreed and guaranteed by the lessee, i.e. 'percentage rents'. Thus the developer maintains a continuing interest in the successful operation of each unit, the retailer and the developer having a continuing common purpose. This system is more difficult to operate under the British landlord/tenant legislation and the usual UK system is the conventional one of a fixed rental for a given lease period. Often this is long term with periodic rent reviews at stated periods considered in relation to profitability and may provide for increase up to market levels. The rent will be adjusted to take into account commissioning costs (including shopfitting) and establishment period. Service charges will be imposed separately. This has certain disadvantages; not only is the developer at greater risk in view of inflation if his profit is not directly related to turnover but without specific safeguards the centre management long-term may lose control of the tenant mix, and the ability to make adjustment in cases of unsatisfactory traders.

These are the two main types of tenure, though there may be variations, as some UK developers manage a compromise tenure system incorporating a measure of percentage rental. Other ideas may emerge in due course, following changing trading conditions and methods. In all cases there will, in addition to rental, be service charges to be paid by the lessees, related to outgoings, and usually a tenants' association is set up to contribute to management control.

Regardless of the tenure system adopted, the developer's trading policy for the centre will be decided on the basis of the financial analysis, incorporating findings of traffic and market surveys carried out at inception of the project. From this will be drawn up a merchandising plan to form the basis of the brief. This will produce a target or turnover per square metre of sales for various units – which having been determined will affect siting, unit areas, and trading 'mix' in planning the layout.

If leases are executed with major 'strong-credit' tenants in advance of construction and as part of the financing arrangements, there will be a relatively low investment risk, as not only will well-known names attract better customers and other tenants but also these major operators will produce a substantial income base. Whatever the type of tenure, once such commitments are resolved interim financing can more easily be achieved. However, with this knowledge, added to their accepted attraction as a major element in the success of the venture, the strong-credit tenants will inevitably negotiate favourable leasing terms.

It is evident that correct design and planning of the centre is crucial to financial viability. The proportion of gross lettable floor area to site area is vital, as will be the proportion of net sales area to gross lettable area for each tenant. Calculations at design stage will need to relate number, type, area, cubic capacity and frontage of units to capital costs and likely trading potential. Allowance must be made for allocation of space and development costs of car parking, servicing, ancillary facilities, both non-profit making and profit making, which may be included as a result of negotiation with local authorities or other contributing bodies.

Capital costs will be balanced against maintenance costs, i.e. higher capital expenditure on materials, services, and sophisticated control systems will very likely be justified in lower short- or long-term maintenance charges, high quality maintenance standards and economy of labour together with promotional appeal.

All this needs planning skill, ingenuity and experience to produce viable solutions. The architect will be involved at the preliminary stages in setting all the factors into a physical layout in terms of feasibility studies and sometimes in the context of a competitive bid by his client, the developer.

The site

An important factor is whether this is to be a 'greenfield' site or a redeveloped (urban) site. In the first case, the designer's job may begin before selection of the site and, in the second, in making the best use of and advising during assembly of an existing area. In both cases, similar factors operate, but with very different emphasis.

New sites

The 'greenfield' or isolated out-of-town 'one-stop shopping centre' which is the standard transatlantic shopping centre solution, has hardly emerged in the UK (though hypermarkets are still exploring the potential). Brent Cross, and Hempstead Valley shopping centres are successful UK one-stop examples.

The UK is heavily populated, perhaps overshopped, and short of undeveloped land available for building. What is often needed is rejuvenation of existing shopping facilities rather than additional shops. In contrast to the virgin greenfield site, the 'edge of town' new centre, regional or district, in various sizes, is now established and successful as a viable concept, while numerous smaller new precincts up and down the country are emerging as part of the established shopping scene. Where a historic town centre cannot, without disaster, accommodate new modern shopping there may be a strong argument for accepting the situation and seeking a suitable 'greenfield' or peripheral site to supplement the High Street without 'tearing the heart out of it'.

What are the essentials needed for a 'new site shopping centre'? To quote a foremost successful developer they are 'position, position, position and position!' So how do we make sure the position is right? Careful and extensive research will be required by specialists in considering the primary factors which will determine the brief. The first of these factors is adequate catchment area, related to gross sales area and proximity to other centres; this will determine the size and type of centre, e.g. neighbourhood, district, regional, the main considerations being those of population and communication.

A *population survey* will discover the type and density of population and likely population growth as well as analysis of *per capita* expenditure on comparison and convenience goods both present and projected and related to the proximity of other major shopping foci.

A *traffic survey* will also be required and the length of journey to the centre by car or public transport related to radial distance from other major centres must be established. The indication may be 25 minutes from the outer zone, 10–15 minutes from the inner zone of either personal driving time or public transport time, from shopper's home to centre, for a large regional project. New sites generally have been expected to rely for custom on car owners, but car ownership by the shopping public is less in the UK than in the USA, and shoppers rely to a much greater extent on public transport. Other factors such as the length of opening hours and the extent to which the centre must rely on weekend shopping also affect shopping by car, and the results of the energy crisis may also require revised thinking. It may for instance become profitable to provide a free bus shuttle service between the centre and convenient public transport pick-up points (as operating for instance at Nice, (cap. 3000) which will need designing into the scheme. With the relaxation of the transport monopoly, there would seem to be a widening opportunity for serving greenfield sites by a bus or 'minibus' system.

Primary considerations are:

Proximity to main trunk road systems and their feed-in to the centre. This is vital, for servicing the traders with stock will inevitably be by road transport. The feed-in connections from the trunk road system must allow free and continuous entry for, as well as division between, customer transport and goods delivery at the main entry points.

In the UK the Ministry of Transport will need to be consulted in cases where trunk roads may be materially affected, directly or indirectly. This will control the planning, design and siting of access points.

Availability of mains services (electricity, telephone, water, gas, sewers). Developers must either look for sites with these facilities or, if presented with a site, must see that all facilities are available. There will be a heavy demand on all services for a megastructure project of this kind and negotiations with all the major supply companies must be undertaken and supply safeguarded. Siting of transformer stations, sub-stations, intake positions, existing supply runs and depths and levels will affect the whole planning and thinking of the centre from the start. The attraction of the greenfield site is that these can be economically planned into the centre without expensive diversion or alterations of existing installations.

Site character

New sites must be prominent, easily seen, attractively landscaped and easily accessible from the main road network which serves them. The USA shopping centre sign and elevational design of the one-stop centre has become a major design factor often an attractive as well as an arresting one.

In the UK one of the problems of giving sufficient attention to this feature is the reluctance of the planning authority to accept signing and identity as a fact of life and possibly even as an aesthetic contribution. Certainly the identification of shopping centre megastructures is a design element which needs more sympathetic understanding from the planning authorities, since they are able to exert such close control.

Physical characteristics

The normal investigation into physical site conditions needs no special identification here. Obviously these

Detail of shopping centre sign, Randhurst, Chicago

will cover geological formation, sub-soil loading, the presence of streams, springs, wells, sewers, other services, made-up ground, archaeological remains or existing foundations, etc.

The topography needs special examination. The determination of levels must allow visibility, and if the centre is situated relatively low to the surrounding 'feed-in' structure the roofscape will need careful handling as it will be a major design element. It may be that the contours of the site lends it to 'cut-and-fill' with redistribution of spoil to provide, for instance, wind-breaks against prevailing wind or just a levelling of site to allow entrances at varying levels from car park or public transport discharge points (see Hempstead Valley, Chapter 10).

The variation of entrance levels can be a major advantage if a multi-level centre is envisaged. A 'split level or mezzanine' may even eradicate the need for escalators and lifts if ramps can be planned into the centre.

Certainly the cost of 'correcting' unusual site conditions, if taken advantage of to help the design, may be absorbed by the lesser land value cost in the first place but must be assessed at the time of site acquisition.

Trader magnets

The availability or, in certain specific cases, proximity of the large trader magnets or anchor stores, i.e. department stores, chain stores, supermarkets, must be explored. These retailers must consider operation in the area viable as they will be needed as an essential function of the centre. (It is estimated, for instance, that a catchment area of 70 000–80 000 of population is needed to support one large store.)

UK planning policies regarding shopping centres are fragmentary, there having been in the past no overall national planning policy for shopping. This lack of direction has resulted in a tortuous and lengthy process in assembling and obtaining approval for new shopping centre sites some of which were first promulgated ten years or so ago, in a 'boom period'. The Brent Cross scheme took seventeen years from inception to opening! It has also blurred essential calculations regarding catchment areas, by the method of control within geographically artificial statutory boundaries.

However, the possible effect of additional new outlets on prices have become matters of public concern and in December 1977 the Department of the Environment issued Development Control Policy Note, No. 13 on *Large New Stores*. This gave guidance to all those concerned with planning control and is still recommended reading in the context of siting shopping centres. Local authorities were asked in an accompanying circular to inform the Secretary of State of planning applications for shopping developments outside existing city, town or district centres involving gross floor space of 100 000 ft^2 or more, so that applications could be called in for decision if planning issues of more than local importance were involved.

Development costs on a virgin site may be 20% less than in a built-up area; but, in spite of the potential of the one-stop centre, with the absence of suitable British greenfield sites, the reluctance of planning authorities to release agricultural land, fear of diverting trade from town centres, and the understandable difficulty in offering financial inducement to major department stores and other big retail companies to invest large capital sums in out of town and edge of town ventures; redevelopment is seen as the preferred successful UK and perhaps also European solution.

Redeveloped sites

In this section redeveloped sites are being taken to mean those within the urban context, though this may not necessarily mean redeveloped shopping. Frequently a 'change of use' is involved.

Redeveloped sites need architectural and visual definition just as greenfield sites do; they need to be integrated into existing shopping and related to it where possible. Many of the considerations for new sites apply, but there are some more specific consid-

erations. A new centre may be redeveloped if in the existing central business district (e.g. Eldon Square, Newcastle). But extending rather than replacing existing shopping may involve redevelopment of redundant sites previously used for other purposes (such as the Victoria Centre Nottingham, previously railway property, and the Friary Centre, Guildford). If it is intended to create a 'second down town' it should, to be successful, be within the axis of growth of the city and truly connected to it (e.g. La Part Dieu, Lyons).

Wherever sited the new centre must fit into the townscape, not as an isolated structure, but integrated both aesthetically and socially.

A redeveloped site may have to be assembled by negotiation with a number of different freeholders, and may include alterations to existing road patterns, requiring for instance 'road closure orders'. Public inquiries and public participation exercises may have to be held, and the whole process of site acquisition may be a lengthy and complicated one resulting perhaps in irregular boundaries, and retention of certain existing features or buildings and other design constraints unlikely to be met with on a greenfield site. It may be that major or subsidiary mains services running through the site may have to be diverted. Gas, electricity, water and Post Office mains, existing transformers, main soil and surface water sewers, may all be affected. Where diversion is inevitable this will have a very signficant effect on the cost programming and phasing of the contract, involving a long process of negotiation and execution.

In redevelopment, familiarity is important, for an established area has certain shopping landmarks such as the department store and the chain store. Disorientation may reduce trading potential, even if only temporarily. Extension linked with existing siting will help and a continuous flow of pedestrian access between the centre and existing important shopping foci must be maintained. Careful alignment of shopping routes to connect with existing or outside centre major attractions is needed where these exist. In some cities, for example at Victoria Centre at Nottingham, and the Brunel Centre at Swindon, the new shopping centres are integrated into a whole pedestrianised town centre.

'Rehabilitation' is another recent contribution. Rehabilitation or 'recycling' the transformation of existing structures into shopping centres, has one considerable advantage in that it avoids the problem of unfamiliarity by rejuvenation of familiar buildings and spaces into a new and interesting experience. However, physical limitations will control the scale of the operation which is likely to result in a 'specialist centre'. Examples are the Ghirardelli Square, San Francisco; Covent Garden London; the proposed

London Pavilion in Central London; and the Faneuil Centre, Boston.

Enlarged or extended shopping sites will usually increase trade to existing units if on main trading routes and not bypassed by new vehicular or pedestrian throughways. However a word of warning here – it is all too easy to kill trade, or a unit or of a complex, by altering the emphasis of access, visibility, etc.

Shoppers tend to flow like liquid, and obstructions will divert them while 'funnels' suck them in. Correct pedestrian flow is the main element of success in retail trading and must be a major consideration in planning the centre, relating the smaller trading units to the major magnets outside and inside the centre, and to specific physical and geographical features affecting the site. It is here that design skill and expertise, allied to experience and research, must be exploited to their fullest extent. The visual aspect of urban redevelopment is very specialised, needing sensitivity to the aesthetic of the existing urban fabric and character blended with appreciation of local trading patterns and habits.

Essential elements of the street are punctuation, interest, and progression. Residential streets are immediately recognisable, punctuated by front doors, windows and forecourts which give interest and measurable dimensions to the pedestrian walking along them.

The High Street has traditionally consisted of a continuing line of shop frontages of appreciated scale offering interest, encouragement and a known dimension to the pedestrian. This should not, except after much deliberation on its effect, be replaced by large masses of continuous blank walls at eye level. However attractive the elevation may be architecturally it will fatigue pedestrians faced with what may appear long unbroken walks, and will take the life out of the street. Thus if giving onto streets in urban centres, the elevations should give at least glimpses into the interior, indicating what is going on within, and stimulating interest. Secondary street entrances, or shop fronts or even peripheral shops facing outwards may be necessary to avoid a deadening effect on the urban scene.

Chapter 4
Planning the centre

The brief and its design implications

The centre as we have already seen is a building type on its own and from now on I will refer to the architect as the operative physical designer of the centre.

As we have seen, the architect will be concerned in the early stages of the project in co-ordinating production of feasibility studies and alternative layouts depending on a variety of factors, the solutions to which will be based on the results of specific research.

Decisions largely controlling the character and viability of the centre and consequently the major physical characteristics will have to be made at the outset.

The mall

Whatever the type of centre it will revolve around the mall, the natural sucessor to the High Street as expressed in the planned centre. It may be a single pedestrian thoroughfare or a series of major and subsidiary malls of varying or constant widths and height, either single or multi-level. These will probably open out on to one or more plazas or courts forming major foci of the centre, the arrangement being inter-dependent with the planning of the centre, and a major component of the design.

The mall is therefore the predominant element setting the scene and providing at the same time safe, relaxed, comfortable, easy-to-follow circulation routes for customers between the entrances and the shops, and leisure and pleasure as well as window-shopping. This offers something more than, and different from, the traditional High Street. Obviously a design character must be adopted and co-ordinated throughout.

Requirements of the mall
Malls must identify the shopping areas without confusion; the shopper must not be disorientated by symmetrically duplicated designs with no recognisable landmarks, but should readily be able to identify his/her whereabouts relative to entrances, exits and major units. Devices will be required to break up spaces, and to give interest. This will lead to consideration of major plan types e.g. the Y, the dumb-bell, and the cross plan, which will open up into wide span courts at intersections. Too much variety of route will dilute the pedestrian flow to the detriment of some unlucky traders; an overall retail balance must be kept, providing 'maximum flow' past all shops. But a too direct and obvious a route between entrances and exits must also be avoided. The layout should be kept simple and easily identifiable and it must not be monotonous. The rule of a maximum 200–250 m (600–800 ft) between points of interest and pause should be observed, as it has been found that shoppers will not travel further than this without losing interest. Blank wall surfaces will also deter shoppers and there should be continuous shop fronts between one focal point and another.

The open mall centre
The earlier transatlantic and European planned centres, usually single level, were served by open air malls. Frequently they were elegantly landscaped and restrained in design; always they provided covered walkways between all shops from entrances and car parks, and were pedestrianised.

Many highly successful centres in the UK and Europe have continued on this pattern, offering a spread over a large ground area – either where greenfield sites are available at an economic price, or in central redevelopment schemes – giving scope for urban design on a wider scale than is possible within the technical and economic restrictions of a totally enclosed centre. Climatic conditions will affect the solution. In extremes of temperature it is more conducive to successful retailing to provide for customers a controlled environment in which to shelter from temperatures – too hot, too cold, too humid or too wet. But in a temperate climate, there is an argument for the pleasure of strolling in the open air, which may prove convincing in terms of energy conservation and minimum service charges! Even in open malls, semi-sheltered short-stay areas, i.e. cafés, bars, etc. can be comfortably heated in spring and autumn moderate climatic temperatures. However, it must be accepted that the open mall is without the excitement and climatic protection of the fully enclosed centre.

The internal faces of the surrounding buildings comprising the complex, whether of shop units only or supporting other buildings above, will form the perimeter of the open malls and arcades. This is, as it were, the street, and must be considered accordingly as part of the larger problem of the elevational treatment of the centre in its relationship with the surrounding area – whether open site or existing buildings.

Character of open malls. Whether a restrictive feeling of enclosure, an open parkside, an urban street, village or even 'film set reproduction' as in some USA specialist centres, the design needs full attention in providing an individual character of the open mall centre. This is co-ordinated with all the 'open air' street furniture, soft and hard landscaping, lighting and signing.

The basic characteristic of the open mall is pedestrianisation in a planned shopping area; the provision of clear, attractive and untiring circulation routes along sheltered walkways past and into the shops offering stimulus and relaxation, with seating refreshment and toilet and other facilities available, and interesting features punctuating the routes. This is contrasted with the bustle, disturbance and traffic congestion of the High Street. The shape, design and dimensions of the malls are totally variable, but certain specific design requirements must be met.

Wind. Wind must be guarded against. The behaviour of wind is particularly unpredictable in the vicinity of high buildings or on short lengths of walkway between open courts. In these conditions, if malls continue in a straight line from the entrance in a direction away from the prevailing wind, the effects can be devastating on the users of the centre. This will be especially important where the centre is combined with a tall building. Even with a building having a height four times the height of the lower building, a high pressure area develops on the windward side and a low pressure area, i.e. suction area, on the leeward side. Meteorological data should be consulted, and aspect related to prevailing winds; the effect of high rise adjoining buildings, the shape and direction of the malls, position of entrances, must all be examined with this in mind, possibly even to the extent of experiments using models and wind tunnels.

Covered walkways

An essential feature of the open mall shopping centre is the provision of covered walkways. These may be provided by setting back the shop frontages behind the main building face of upper storeys or by some form of canopy. The design of the canopy offers an opportunity to the designers to create a main design feature, but the relationship of width of mall to width and height of canopy, presents a perennial problem.

An average height of glass line in a shop front is approximately 2.75 m (8 ft) from pavement level although different trades will require differently-shaped windows. The retailer will expect space above this 8 ft line and below the canopy height, whether in the traditional form of a fascia or otherwise, for display of signing, and lettering and to design and identify his shop. If variety and interest are the aim, variation from the traditional fascia pattern is to be encouraged. Therefore, to allow scope for individual design a shop front height of, say, 3.5 m (11 ft) below canopy is desirable. A canopy at this height on a south elevation theoretically needs a totally impractical throw to protect goods from solar damage and will not protect customers from driving rain. One solution is the shaped canopy but there is the danger of claustrophobic loss of scale and a deterrent effect if a solid canopy edge is too low – 8 ft considered as being the minimum.

A further constraint on canopy design may be vehicular and/or Fire Brigade access. Canopy height, if maintained along fire fighting routes, may be controlled by the type of fire fighting appliance to be used. In the UK Fire Brigade vehicles require minimum clearance of 3.6 m (12 ft) with an axle load of 10 tonnes although it may be possible to negotiate with the Fire Brigade for the use of special smaller fire tenders. Continuous canopies may, if too low, be considered a fire hazard, as they could trap smoke at a level allowing it to enter adjoining shops, so some form of smoke ventilation must be introduced at intervals.

Canopies will almost certainly need support from the main building face unless columns on the pavement edge, forming an 'arcade' are acceptable. A cantilevered R.C. canopy will need to be pre-cambered to avoid 'droop' and the dimension at canopy edge will need to be one-twelfth of the canopy projection. Whatever the design, it is obvious that it must be part of the character of the complex, both in scale and design.

An alternative solution for protection of shoppers, and of merchandise, is the sun blind. This is not satisfactory in the managed shopping centre as it leaves decisions concerning its operation to the retailer and permanent protection to the shopper is not secured. However there may be an argument for drop

SOME EXAMPLES OF COVERED WALKWAYS IN OPEN CENTRES

Rockside Shopping Centre, Montreal. General view of walkways

Rockside Shopping Centre. Close up of arcade

Oakbrook, Chicago

Brunel Centre, Swindon. Open mall

Brunel Centre, Swindon. Covered way

Tapiola, Finland

Swan Walk, Horsham Surrey

blinds from a high canopy edge on south or otherwise exposed elevations, for protection of merchandise; the colour and design of these can provide additional sparkle and gaiety to an open centre.

Sloping sites have special difficulties – pavement levels must be related correctly to shop levels and entrances. Traders dislike sloping malls, which they think deter shoppers, though practical experience shows this is not necessarily so if the area offers sufficient attraction on the 'up slope'. However, shops should not be entered by steps, which as well as being a deterrent are dangerous to window shoppers. The co-relation of canopy levels to change of shop floor levels also needs careful handling to maintain correct relationships, avoid extremes of height difference, and provide satisfactory detailing at change of level of canopy.

Mall widths. The controlling principle of mall and arcade widths is that there must be room for window shoppers to pause, while allowing circulation past them, but an excessive width will deter them from crossing from shops on one side to those on the other. Thus a minimum width for minor and connecting malls could be 5–6 m (15–20 ft) which may result in them finding themselves fully covered by the canopies and forming covered arcades! In the UK there is a recommendation in the appropriate Fire Code that open mall widths should not be less than 5 m (16 ft) wide between the shop fronts to minimise the risk of fire 'jumping' from one shop front to that opposite. Main malls may need a width of up to 13–15 m (40–50 ft) to allow for central features, pause areas, with seating, planting, kiosks, play sculptures, etc. while complying with the regulations regarding circulation routes. There is also a danger, if malls become either too wide or too obscured, that shoppers will use one side only to the detriment of traders on the other.

Design of units. The open centre tends to offer more scope for individual design of units than the closed mall, and this is to some extent desirable in that it provides variety of treatment and satisfaction to the retailer. Careful overall control is necessary, however, to ensure a consistent standard of design and quality while avoiding standardisation and promoting and affording scope for interesting and original shop design solutions. Schedules and design guides will need to be prepared and carefully negotiated with the retailers concerned, without unnecessary restriction on trading pattern and original thinking. Choice of materials will be more limited than in the closed centre, needing to afford proper weather protection from extremes of temperature and climate at both ends of the scale.

Streetscape. The streetscape is a vital design component. Escalators, staircases and lifts are not the easiest of elements to design into multi-level open or part open mall centres. They need to be easily accessible, visually attractive and weather resistant, but must not obscure the mall features or interrupt the flow to shop units.

Street furniture, i.e. kiosks, lighting standards, bollards, litter bins, paving materials and patterns, hard and soft landscaping, seating, balustrading, sign posting, and amenities generally must be unified with careful study into an integrated design. In particular the 'floorscape' is important; texture, colour and pattern being a major contribution to the overall scene, both aesthetically and as an 'indicating' guide to the use of space. There may be cases in central urban areas for permitting limited vehicular access for deliveries at restricted times, and provision will probably have to be made for fire brigade appliances. Where this occurs walkways will need to be constructed to take the required wheel load, and possibly paving patterns identifying limits for vehicular access.

Broadmarsh Centre, Nottingham. Deliveries in pedestrian area

Control and administration will affect the layout. The open mall managed centre is likely, though not of necessity, to be closed at night, needing gate closure positions and careful design of entries and exits including those discharging into car parks, and also allowing for occupation by security and cleaning staff, stock movement by traders, etc. Whatever the circumstances and design of the managed open mall centre, continuing control by management must be incorporated into the maintenance programme and physical provision made for staff and equipment.

The composite mall centre

Conditions may sometimes favour what, to the proponents of the total concept, is a compromise solution – the part-open, part-closed mall. Following a period in the 1970s, during which interest was concentrated on the covered centre, the energy crisis and escalating capital and maintenance costs are resulting in what many retailers are finding to be unacceptable service charges. Today there seems to be perceptible swing back towards the concept of the open centre or compromise.

One compromise solution is the 'open ended' roofed-over single-storey centre, operating as a protected street, with extract ventilation and perhaps winter heating but without summer cooling. This, not defined as a closed centre, is therefore not subject to the stringent UK fire regulations on smoke control, means of escape and structural fire precautions of the truly enclosed centre. An example of this, as first built, was Milton Keynes.

The disadvantage of this solution is the unpredictable effect of wind and weather on the centre when completed, as once committed to this type of building, the major change to a fully enclosed centre may be difficult to implement.

It may be the site is too large, to straggly or too interconnected with existing shopping or other buildings to be considered wholly as one covered unit, though justifying a covered central controlled environmental core. Should this be the choice it is imperative for design and management to ensure that the closed section, if so intended, remains the centre of gravity of the development. Should too much be happening outside or the trading emphasis moved away from the covered centre, this element will lose its essential purpose and become a meaningless and unprofitable white elephant.

A solution is for the centre to be planned so that existing outside 'magnets' are situated to draw shoppers through or into malls clearly designed for specialist or limited trading. The closed centre may also itself have a modicum of perimeter shopping, incorporating covered walkways. Such perimeter shopping may give opportunity for tenancies to be allocated to Building Societies, Banks and Travel Agencies and other ventures not strictly relating which while offering a useful service to the public, might interfere with the run of shop front display within the malls and may need specific planning approval in the UK.

The closed mall centre

There is certainly evidence that while a new open mall centre may not significantly increase pedestrian traffic flow, and consequent increased trading potential, a new closed mall centre demonstrably provides a dramatic increase. There is, also little doubt that the closed mall centre successfully designed will attract highly concentrated use. So the true one-stop shopping centre of today has become almost by definition 'closed mall'. This is the complete building concept, where traders and shoppers are protected within an enclosed and controlled-climate envelope – main access to shops (which can be open-fronted) being from within the centre.

The enclosed mall may be the focus for social occasions, display, exhibitions, promotional activities, refreshments etc. as desired, as well as forming the circulation routes between shops. In climatic extremes, whether of heat or cold, the centre becomes a retreat where the public can enjoy comfortable environmental conditions, strolling, window shopping, enjoying refreshment and other leisure facilities, and where they will congregate even if not on a specific shopping expedition, but with the added opportunity of 'impulse buying'.

This type of centre is a highly serviced and technically appointed complex, the design, planning, appointments and servicing of the malls being integral to the scheme. It may range in size from a small specialist or neighbourhood utility centre to a vast many acre project and whether greenfield 'one-stop' or urban redevelopment, certain specific factors emerge.

The centre could be operating perhaps up to 24 hours a day – restocking, cleaning and maintenance taking place outside opening hours – and security will be necessary at all times. Late night shopping may require two shifts working with consequent additional staff and staff facilities. The centre may need to be physically closed to the public at mall access points out of shopping hours. Special arrangements may be needed for access to ancillary facilities such as restaurants, sports centre, cinema, etc. with appropriate security provisions. An enclosed shopping centre without perimeter shops facing the street can be closed after hours and consequently offers protection against one of the more recent escalating dangers to retailers, rioting and consequential looting.

Some form of climatic control will almost certainly operate in enclosed malls, involving full or partial air conditioning and sophisticated use of natural and artificial lighting. Problems will need to be solved regarding open-fronted shops and their effect on mall air conditions. Onerous structural fire precautions, smoke control, and Means of Escape conditions must be met while maintaining a high standard of amenity and maintenance and high quality durable and attractive finishes. Special decorative features, play sculptures, fountains, landscaping, sculpture, are desirable and must be integrated into the design.

Single or multi-level

Many specialised problems of the shopping centre apply chiefly to the closed mall – one of the few totally new building types to emerge since the 1939–45 war – and its specialised problems need to be identified. In relation to mall design they include technical considerations which are examined in other chapters in this book such as structural systems, column position related to shop front lines, extent and control of natural lighting and air conditioning, systems of escape and smoke control.

One early consideration that needs to be determined at briefing stage is whether the centre is to be single or multi-level? The number of shopping levels will depend on site area related to planning and economic factors. Multi-level trading may be necessary to produce sufficient G.L.A. for adequate financial return.

This will be part of the site selection process dependent on careful comparative costing studies of capital and running costs, floor areas and rentals involving the architect. The exercise is to relate the size of the site available, with car parking, servicing, malls, plazas and other functions, to gross lettable area, recouping site, building and interest costs, and providing sufficient shopping to produce adequate turnover, rentals and trading profit.

Design skill as well as expenditure is needed for success of multi-level trading, as to encourage shoppers on to upper mall levels is not easy. This is a fact well recognised by the retailer, who tends to resist upper level lettings. Lower level malls may be of sufficient width to incorporate full height central wells with perimeter balconies revealing upper storeys, and their shop fronts.

Alternatively closed ceiling lower level malls may open at intervals into full height courts revealing as a surprise element, upper storeys, reinforced by attractively situated escalators and staircases offering inviting passage between levels. A sloping site will help, access being from different external ground levels. It is easier to persuade people to go downwards rather than upwards – the 'flow' principle again – so upper level entrances are an advantage if they can also lead from through routes easily to other levels. In any event multi-level malls must indicate interesting and enticing views of other levels, with easily accessible open-view escalators or passenger lifts, servicing all floors with direct approach from car parks. These too should discharge onto various storeys. Clear directional signing and location plans strategically placed will facilitate access and circulation between the levels.

UK Fire Regulations inhibit the straightforward design of an open-well centre of more than two storeys

Peninsular Plaza, Singapore: view of concourse showing five trading levels (Photo: Alfred Wong)

though it has proved successful elsewhere. Solutions are being examined to meet objections and solve the problems of smoke control and fire safety in the UK.

Multi-level 'magnet' units such as department stores, which by reason of their required floor area need to be themselves multi-level, can assist if planned to discharge into the malls on various floors. If compartmented from the malls they can also be designed to meet Fire Safety Requirements.

Fairview, Montreal. A simple and successful treatment of a single level mall

Where multi-level construction is needed only to suit the larger unit, such as the department store, it may be advantageous to use upper storeys over one level shops, for stock and staff accommodation, service areas, etc. where multi-level trading is not needed. Smaller units neither need nor like the considerable floor to floor height required by the large store and the design needs to take this into account wherever possible. (It may even work to allow for shop mezzanines within a minimum of, say, 14 ft clear floor to ceiling height.)

The single level centre also needs skilful handling. Imaginative design and maintenance of upper elevations above shop fronts will maintain scale and unity while avoiding monotony on the one hand or detraction from the shop fronts and their identification on the other. Some traders welcome an opportunity for expression of their units at upper levels by use of display signs or logos, thus avoiding an unnecessary adherence to the traditional 'fascia' treatment which may well be irrelevant. This is a facility worthy of consideration when designing the elevations.

Design character of malls and of the centre

This is largely the product of an intricate resolution of ideas and requirements, between the developer, agent, architect, other consultants and ultimately the tenant-traders, as carried forward by continuing management. It is the amalgam of these skills that will lead to a successful outcome and it is here that the architect's contribution is paramount – using imagination, balancing the multitudinous physical planning, financial, and legislative constraints and alternatives to produce a commercially as well as aesthetically successful solution

There is no standardised formula – fortunately there is an almost infinite variety of solutions – but one rule certainly operates – the design must not be overdominant but must form a framework, unifying the retail interests and emphasising their attraction throughout.

The shopping centre has for its main object the achieving of profit in trading. Without this result, however pleasing the concept, the project is not performing its function. This has been the achieved motive of classically successful shopping centres world-wide, and to alert the designer to the possibilities and potential is one of the objects of this book.

The exercise is quite different from that of designing an individual building, and it is a sad but salutary lesson that some British award-winning designs have been less than totally successful commercially as a result of ignoring this factor.

It is therefore essential for the investor, developer, agent, architect and management to operate throughout an agreed concept of the character of the centre. This design and merchandising concept will control the trading mix.

Is the centre to be 'utility' or wider ranging, including luxury trading? There are many (too many in the writer's opinion!) centres in the UK and elsewhere which are largely 'utility' where, although with a reasonable range of convenience and comparison trading, shops sell within fairly limited price ranges, the 'multiple' is predominant and luxury and special interest goods, and private traders are virtually non-existent. Lacking the contrast of individual spontaneity of design in the retail shop units, these centres are in danger of expressing either a bland lack of identity or an over-dominant design character understandably imposed by the designer to offset the effect of indifferent and pedestrian standards of shop design and shopfitting.

Avoiding these pitfalls a varied trading mix will produce a lively centre, having individuality and sparkle, and offering maximum attraction to the widest possible shopping public. This suggests a minimum of enforced design control within the tenant's premises and at shop front point other than that of durability and high quality. It also pre-supposes that imaginative and enterprising shop designers will be employed by individual traders and encouraged by the developer and architect.

It is in the mall design and communal areas that the centre architect will have full scope. I have already alluded to the treatment of the mall perimeter above and around shop fronts, the height of malls, and the daylight factor, which will be major design elements. Also contributing to the mall character will be the constructional system, selection of materials, the colour combinations, lighting levels and the features and furniture to be incorporated into courts and main malls.

Ghiradelli Square, San Francisco

South Woodham Ferrers, Essex. A newly erected village? No, a shopping centre. (above) Mall view; (below) Central court

The design of large centre covered malls can range from an 'indoor street' concept – with its consequent indications – street lamps, 'outdoor' type landscaping, etc – to the almost 'drawing room' or art gallery atmosphere of the luxury fashion centre.

A rehabilitated centre may make full use of the character of the original buildings, contributing to urban revitalisation, as at Covent Garden London, Ghiradelli Square, San Francisco, Faneuil Hall, Boston and London Pavilion Piccadilly, London.

There are innumerable international examples of sophisticated shopping centre design revolving around the design character of the mall. They include not only the very large scale enclosed multi-mall concept but also such bizarre solutions as the 'reproduction village'. There are also, it must be admitted, some highly successful versions of dominant design which absorb and incorporate retailers requirements.

The external elevational design will have a serious visual impact on the surrounding environment. In redevelopment, central or peripheral to town or suburb design, good manners are needed to impart an emphasis but not a jarring one. If within a 'conservation area' or historic town, even more skill, tact and

imagination are needed to insert this modern concept without on the one hand offending the existing environment, or on the other losing the advertising strength of the new centre.

While the 'trading face' of the complex must express the shopping message and invite interest, the shopping centre backs for instance, where facing a residential area, can with sensitive design unite it with the new development. This can be done using scale carefully with suitable elevational treatment in local materials reconciling local opinion to the new intruder!

Layout of centre

In conjunction with decisions on mall types, character and number of levels, there are other primary planning factors. These will include:

(i)   Number, size and disposition of 'anchor' or 'magnet' stores dependent on the type of trader who can be persuaded to take space in the centre.
(ii) Distribution, number and size of standard shop units and their relation with the above, and their servicing requirements.
(iii) Ancillary attractions and facilities.
(iv) Mall entry and exit points relating the malls to public transport, car parking, general circulation.
(v)   Extent and disposition of car parking.
(vi) Extent and/or availability to tenants of environmental control with its consequent effect on the plan.

These matters need, at the start, to be determined in terms of the shape of the site and the surrounding areas, with the 'feed in' network integrated into existing shopping when appropriate. Having determined the mall type, levels and storeys, availability of anchor units, and considered the general character, these must be reconciled into a satisfactory layout.

As we have already seen, a major consideration will be pedestrian flow, direct circulation amongst units, from and back to, suitable entry points, remembering the need for visual impact – particularly that of the anchor stores. These will be the department store(s), chain store(s), super store/supermarket(s), the area, volume and siting of which are likely to control the shape of the centre.

With plenty of opportunity to consider new plan types and developments, it is nevertheless worth reviewing past examples based on what has been considered good and successful practice. Typical of these which are illustrated in Chapter 10 are:

1. The one anchor store – integrated into rectangular site.
Example: Hempstead Valley, Gillingham, Kent.

2. The Dumb-bell plan – 'magnet' or 'Anchor' stores each end of main mall.
Example: Brent Cross, North-west London.
3. Four magnet.
Example: Wood Green, North London.

Fire Safety Regulations will fundamentally affect the planning and relationship of large and small units. In the UK it is assumed that a minimum of 60% of a shopping complex will be composed of small units (each maximum $280 \, m^2$ or $3000 \, ft^2$ floor area).

Large units of $3700 \, m^2$ minimum facing the mall will need full compartmentation (i.e. fire shutters across shop front opening). Two large units over $2000 \, m^2$ must not face each other across the mall unless frontages are protected by automatic shutters or a back-up wall. If they adjoin, there should be back-up walls behind shop windows at least $3 \, m$ each side of the division wall or separated from each other by a small unit maximum $280 \, m^2$ area. In the case of internal angles between large units, protection between open frontages of $3 \, m$ ($9 \, ft$) one way, or $1.5 \, m$ ($5 \, ft$) each is needed.

Special conditions are leading to the rethinking of generally-accepted tenets of centre design. In the Far East for example, pressure to provide closed mall shopping centres on constricted sites is producing new plan types, such as a series of large open courts or 'atria' serving five, six or even more shopping levels. Major magnets may take all units on one floor; for example, a department store at 2nd floor level, and a supermarket in the 'basement'. In such cases escalators and lifts become a major design attraction emphasising and encouraging vertical flow while vertical design features such as dominant freestanding columns of 'wall climber lifts' lead the eye upwards. This type of multi-level design requires, for economy's sake, minimum floor to floor height. This is easier when fire precaution requirements do not encompass the type of smoke reservoir required by British Regulations and where the method of air conditioning reduces the need for deep service ducts.

With the emphasis, at the time of writing, on shopping in urban centres, the system of planning the centre around magnet positions may vary. There will be cases when some of these magnets are already established adjacent to but not within the centre, or where an irregular site requires unorthodox solutions as in the specialist centres. Close co-operation with existing traders will facilitate clever and careful routing to channel shoppers into the new centre, such as between transport points and existing external major attractions. These conditions will need to be observed in planning the arrangement of major units. Consideration of the component units of the centre is now necessary.

Major units

A major department store is likely to require a minimum sales area of $20 \, 000 \, m^2$, which by definition presupposes a multi-storey building or a whole floor of the centre, although the 'junior' department stores sometimes taking space in a centre may need less.

A superstore, chain store or supermarket will require $2000–2500 \, m^2$ sales area minimum, (preferably planned on one floor) relative sales area to ancillary accommodation being, say, 60% sales to 40% ancillary.

Food shopping tends to serve a smaller catchment area than that of a major regional centre, but, on the other hand food shoppers pay more frequent visits. In the long run the arrival of the deep-freeze may persuade car shoppers to make larger purchases of convenience goods at longer intervals combined with visits to large regional centres for comparison shopping; on the other hand fuel shortages and energy conservation may lead to more local shopping for convenience goods.

Whether this option, balancing freezer and running costs with fuel costs of less frequent journeys, as opposed to a return to local shopping, will affect shopping patterns, remains to be seen, though the convenience and attraction of the major centre seem set to remain. The tendency of the big food chain is towards fewer and larger outlets, achieving lower prices and the sale of non-food items with a gross profit margin to justify capital outlay and running costs.

Smaller units

Correct siting of smaller units is just as important as that of larger ones. The UK guideline that small units should compose 60% of the floor area of a shopping centre avoids over population by large multiple units. Their disposition along circulation routes between access points and anchor stores must aim at getting major customer flow past the greatest number of units. Shops bypassed by general flow will lose out.

However, variety of treatment along main and subsidiary malls will add interest, and break up apparent excessive distances which may deter shoppers. In arranging the centre the possibility of varied shop front lines giving variety to a long mall should be studied. This is more desirable with open fronts, which do not mask one shop by another. Interest must be introduced at key points to lure customers along the full length of the shopping facades, without forming a barrier to the areas beyond.

An appropriate 'mix' of trading types in the smaller units, in different price ranges related to catchment area and sales potential, is an important ingredient of the successful centre. In preparing the layout plan the designer may be helped by the considerable information available, produced and updated by Trade and Reasearch Associations on recommended promotions of sales areas of various trade types needed to serve a given catchment area. Figures relating sales areas to turnover for various types of sale are also available.

Flexibility for the trader is of utmost importance and should be encouraged. It is important to allow as much latitude as possible to the retailer in expressing the size and character of his shop within the total unifying envelope.

Unfortunately many retailers in the 'utility' range do not appreciate the asset of carefully designed high quality shop units and their contribution to the overall success of the centre; although this design and quality is recognised as a feature of luxury or specialist trading.

In the UK the consultant designer is too often concerned only with luxury and specialist 'boutiques', many other individual retailers depending on shopfitting companies for the design and fitting out of their units. In many cases the design can be criticised for conservatism and lack of imagination. (For instance, weather drips and mat wells still appear as elements in enclosed mall shop fronts; indicating a thoughtless repetition of standard elements without regard to particular circumstances!)

The growth and power of the multiples has, as I have already indicated, tempted some developers, and in particular their letting agents, to take the easy way out by going into the open market and letting standard units to the highest bidder, irrespective of trading mix, – an attractive prospect with the traditional UK rental system. However, this method is likely to lead to a weak trading balance and consequent lack of variety and attraction. There may be also an overemphasis on the standardised solutions of the 'in house' design departments of the multiple firms, though due regard must be given to their specialist requirements, recognised 'logos' etc, which will be looked into in a later chapter.

It is usually accepted that service trades, e.g. cleaners, shoe repairers, opticians, rental services, will accept secondary sites. This is on the basis that customers have already made up their minds to visit them and will make the effort and also that turnover will only justify lower rentals. But this does not mean that these units can be tucked away and forgotten; they need to be brought to the attention of the public as an additional attraction of the centre.

A now well-established development is the 'fast food', 'picnic' or gourmet area where management provides servicing and seating surrounded by concession food 'bars' serving a variety of 'snack' food. Disposable cutlery and dishes will decrease service problems but will create one of waste disposal. To make this type of venture successful and a social asset to the centre, attractive design combined with absolute cleanliness and maintenance of a high standard must be provided by the management.

Variations of type of centre
In the past it has been an axiom originating in the USA that a 'managed' shopping centre must be built around at least one, if not more, magnet stores. Preferably this should be a department store. However, there are a number of examples emerging in the UK and elsewhere of enclosed mall shopping integrated into existing traditional 'High Street' central areas in which the magnet stores remain in their existing High Street positions while the new enclosed mall centre houses a supermarket and/or speciality shops, possibly also an enclosed market and other features. In the Brunel Centre, Swindon, for example, a number of the established units such as Debenhams department store and other multiples are sited on the 'perimeter' of the centre, and at Wood Green 'Shopping City', chain store multiples are outside the centre.

In urban centres exactly the same principles need to be followed as those of the out of town or completely redeveloped site. Thus, they must be carefully sited in relation to the existing magnets; they must not be off location but on the main pedestrian traffic routes. In fact they need to be planned as an extension of the existing shopping. In some cases they will be part of an already pedestrianised thoroughfare, while in others they will form the only pedestrian part of the main shopping area.

There has now appeared the speciality centre, containing only certain types of unit, e.g. restaurants, cafés, fashion and luxury shops. Three recent interesting examples of integrated shopping centre units (see Chapter 10) are in Central London – 'West One'; Covent Garden and the proposed London Pavilion. All these have individual characteristics, demonstrating the potential of integrating new or existing features as major shopping foci, and appealing particularly to the tourist.

Ancillary attractions/facilities
The extent of ancillary services will have been determined in the brief and could include at least one of the following:

Sports centre
Cinema/theatre
Community hall
Swimming pool
Skating rink

Skating rink at Omni Centre, Atlanta (Photo: Nigel Woolner)

Library
Tyre fitting, service garage and petrol station
Garden centre
Medical centre
State services (social security, employment centre, etc.)
Art gallery
Public house
Children's supervised play centre for shoppers
Fast food area, restaurant
Coffee bar and café

A shopping centre will almost inevitably contain at least the last two; without these it will not attract long stay shoppers. They should be planned into suitable positions, easily visible and convenient; the restaurants perhaps taking advantage of any available views. Both may overflow into, or be designed as, part of the mall. The remaining ancillary units need not be in prime trading positions, though they must be clearly indicated and easily accessible. If to be used separately from the centre, access, servicing, car parking and security will need special attention.

Customer facilities
These must include adequate toilets for both sexes, conveniently situated for shoppers in the centre – but not too accessible for passers by – and preferably supervised. Public telephones are also needed – sited where least vulnerable to vandalism – hoods being preferable to cubicles.

A play centre is a useful and popular adjunct, encouraging mothers to a longer stay in the centre, but requiring staff and space.

Provision for the handicapped to use the centre fully is a 'must', remembering those who may be temporarily incapacitated by illness or accident, as well as the permanently disabled. There must be conveniently placed lifts, no changes of level without ramps, adequate width of circulation areas and openings, and accessible specially-equipped toilets.

Circulation

It is salutary to realise that the whole of the goods delivered in bulk to, and stocked within, the shopping units in the centre will (with the exception of certain heavy items delivered to the customer's home by the retailer) be removed from the site individually by the customer within the stock turn period. This is in itself a considerable logistical problem and explains the basic importance of siting access points in relation to convenient car parking and public transport. The success of the centre will inevitably depend on these arrangements.

Thus we come to the circulation component in planning the mall. This covers access and egress related to car parking, public transport and security. Entrances are also exits and are seen from inside as well as outside. If too prominent and inviting as seen from within they may sweep the unsuspected shopper from the centre and so must be subtly and carefully arranged and designed as a background rather than a focus.

The height and width of entrances need relating to the external and internal elevations. If too low and with too subdued a lighting level they may not readily pull-in the public; they need strong external demarcation. The detailed design will need to take into consideration the type of climatic control, effect of wind and smoke control. Automatic doors may be needed, and/or an air curtain to prevent negative pressures on the one hand, or excessive wind velocity on the other.

We have seen already that the principal and subsidiary malls, single- and multi-level, form the 'streets' along which customers walk to the shops and to enjoy themselves, and how they need to be broken up by central or intermediary courts forming foci and offering various facilities to shoppers. Shoppers can be exhausted by long travel distances between focal points; a maximum to be aimed at is 200–250 m (656–820 ft). It should be possible for all parts of the centre to be covered by one shopping expedition and 'pause points' must be skilfully sited to allow this. Vertical circulation in a multi-level centre is equally important. Escalators, lifts and staircases must be strategically placed and readily identifiable to invite shoppers onto the various levels, with minimum obstruction and without creating 'dead-leg' areas.

Mall design

In covered centres the daylight factor is crucial. If daylight is to be utilized to light the mall, it will be either by clear-storey or by roof lights or both, with or without diffusers. This will affect the design of the vertical section of the mall, whether multi-level or single level shopping, and must take account of solar gain, by specialised ventilation and choice of material, incorporating necessary smoke reservoirs, vents, etc. and by maintaining sufficient height, volume and cleverly arranged angles of turn for dispersal. Natural lighting may involve a complete change of atmosphere and lighting when night-time conditions transfer daylight into artificial light. This is of considerable importance in winter time and northern latitudes. The introduction of some daylight, even if subsidiary, contributes to the attraction of the centre by maintaining contact with the outside environment and gives glimpses of points of reference and of special interest.

The fully artificially-lit centre will have a constant image, regardless of external conditions, implying a protected environment. Further aspects of this decision – daylight or full artificial lighting – are examined later as they affect energy conservation and insulation, heating, cooling, maintenance and cost.

An artificially lit centre may have a solid roof and intermediate beam or slab, probably with false ceilings below service ducts. Naturally-lit malls also offer a wide variety of design solutions from open glazed roofs with services incorporated, to translucent suspended ceilings. In all cases, smoke vents will be needed with adequate facilities for cleaning and maintaining glazing and servicing smoke vents.

The height of main and subsidiary mall will be a dominant feature of the design – whether minimum height or multi-level, with large open wells or dramatic high level enclosures. The cross-sectional area i.e. height related to width, is important, the height increasing in proportion to mall width. The minimum storey-height at shop front level in order to allow full scope to shop front design may vary between 3 and 5 m (10–16 ft) and must avoid any claustrophobic tendency. Opinions as to minimum mall widths vary. Width of major malls in major centres, as we have seen, should be 15 m (49 ft) to meet peak period load, while allowing for mall 'furniture'. Subsidiary malls and arcades need to be a minimum of 6–7 m (20–23 ft) to allow clear walking space of 3 m (10 ft) past shops on both sides. In the UK 6 m width between shop fronts will be a minimum, demanded by the Fire Authority.

Malls will need ingenuity in design of vertical access bringing at various levels, treatment of escalators, stairs, lifts, etc. all relating to entrances, exits, main Magnet Stores, car parking and usual attractions to entice to other areas. Punctuation of long malls can be achieved by opening out into rest and recreation areas, with seating, cafés, planting, and kiosks.

Thus there is interest and variety for the shoppers in using the mall as introduction to the shops – landscaping, seating arrangements, features, sculptures, fountains and other focal points – perhaps information or selling kiosks, with easy recognition of vertical and horizontal circulation points and directional location plans. All these must be integrated into a pleasant, comfortable, stimulating but non-tiring environment as the matrix of the shopping centre.

Care of the centre

Supervision in the UK, as elsewhere on private property, is not a police duty, and special arrangements have to be made, for security, involving call systems and security patrols. Day-to-day and long term maintenance and supervision are also of vital importance and involve every design decision as will be examined in this context in later chapters.

The degree of use of malls, as restaurants or coffee bars, fast food areas, exhibitions, trade fairs, promotions, etc. will have implications for supervision, staffing and maintenance, as well as, in the UK, on rateable values. These latter are determined by degree of public use other than circulation by those not engaged in shopping activities, maintenance and security.

Car parking

The design of car parking for a shopping centre is very specialised. Parking should be sensitively designed as part of the retail image of the centre, welcoming and easily identified at entry points from incoming traffic routes.

Ground level car parking must not result in vast asphalt deserts – a deterrent to shopping and a scar on the landscape. It must be carefully landscaped, broken up if necessary, planted, with clear and attractive marking, signing, and forming an attractive setting to the centre.

External parks, access roads and footways must be kept clear of snow and ice, and protected against excessive rainfall. Surface water drainage and 'falls' must be carefully designed to eliminate the possibility of standing water.

Clear and simple circulation from car parking bays as well as from public transport points must be carefully planned, well lit, providing interest, and wherever possible, under cover.

Carefully designed and easily negotiable pedestrian walkways, if provided, will add to the interest and safety of shoppers. Well designed waste bins, conveniently situated both for deposit and removal of waste, will add to car park amenity.

In calculating the required extent of car parking, unit car space multiplied by the time of occupation must meet normal weekly peak shopping demand based on, for example, $100 \, m^2$ of gross retail area. This will have been determined at briefing stage allowing for each bay to be used between two and ten times a day so the vital factor in achieving maximum car park space use is ease of turn around.

Siting
Car parks must be clearly visible from main routes and feed into and out of them without congestion. The maximum distance between shoppers car, or public transport pickup point, and principal shops should not exceed 201 m.

Ground level car parking is obviously preferable, subject to this proviso, and to sufficient land being available. However the amount needed to provide the requisite parking space for a large centre at one level may be uneconomic and better use can be made of it for ancillary or retail use where land values are high. Thus multi-level, subterranean or roof deck parking may have to be considered, particularly when feeding multi-level malls, or conveniently utilising ground slope.

Roof parking is likely to be a more economical solution than basement, as not requiring mechanical ventilation, smoke control, sprinklering and other fire precautions, and perhaps offering additional parking space at ramp levels. Shopping centre car parks must not be available to non-users of the centre, though arrangements may be needed for their use outside shopping hours to serve ancillary facilities forming part of it such as a sports centre, cinema or restaurant. Also if car servicing, petrol station, tyre bays, motor shop, etc. are to be provided they must be available to the users of the car park but not to passing custom and all this must be planned for.

We have been looking only at shoppers' car parking but it must be remembered that the shopping centre will need to cater for considerable staff, of both its own management and that of tenants. A decision will be needed at commencement as to whether car parking should be provided for staff separately or not at all; staff must not be allowed to take up valuable space allocated to shoppers.

Staff car parking must be quite separate and entered from service areas and not from customers access points. It is more likely to be needed in one-stop out-of-town centres than on urban sites and certainly a modicum of car parking for visitors to tenants and centre management will need to be provided as part of the service areas.

The arrangement of the car parking spaces is crucial. The function of shoppers' parking bays is different from that of the garage or an all-day commuters park in an industrial or business centre. With such a potentially large turnover a vital factor is ease of turn round and rapid and easy parking, and this must allow for imperfect driving skill! Complicated manoeuvring into narrow spaces between columns, for instance, may hold up parking or exit for other vehicles besides shortening tempers, thus reducing the potential sales turnover within the centre. Moreover the shopper may return to the car loaded with merchandise probably on trolleys; some of this will go into the boot and some possibly into the car interior. For this reason access must be possible both to the rear of the car and to the side with door fully opened without interfering with passing traffic. So ample width and length for parking is essential.

Suggested minimum dimensions are 2.4 m (8 ft) wide for 45° parking bays and up to 2.7 m (9 ft) for 90° bays. A minimum cross dimension for one lane and two bays should be 18 m for 90° parking and 14 m for 45° parking. Clear marking of bays is needed and, if the bays are wide enough, this will avoid the congestion caused by straddling. Parking is easier, quicker and more accurate when bays are arranged at 45° angles, rather than 90° though taking up more space.

As far as possible parking aisles should be directed at right angles to the shopping centre, reducing the distances and giving clear direction to shoppers.

Identification
Good quality surfacing and clear and well designed marking are a must; clear signing, indication and identification of individual parking bays will be needed, not relying on pavement writing. Adequate illumination is essential. As height of standards is related to distance, an effective use may be made of few high elegantly-designed standards, as an alternative to closely spaced shorter ones. A minimum lighting level of 50 lux should be aimed at in an open park; more in subterranean or multi-level parks.

The multi-storey car park
Multi-storey car parks can, without design control, dominate the centre and destroy its character and scale. This must not be allowed to happen. They must discharge occupants easily to the main mall as well as to ancillary facilities; lifts and perhaps escalators will be required. Lifts must be adequate to accommodate customers and trolleys with trolley collection points at each level, giving easy trolley access from check-out

points at self-service food and other units to car boot without traversing the malls with arrangements for trolley recovery by shopping centre staff.

Multi-level covered car parks for shopping centres will in particular require adequate supervision and should be connected to the control room at the heart of the centre in order to avoid or deal with congestion at peak periods and other problems. Without such supervision congestion can build up losing valuable shopping time, reducing the turn-round time and deterring shoppers from future visits.

Numbers of staff required must be agreed and staff facilities, i.e. toilets, locker rooms, etc. provided. If car parking is charged for, check in and check out points, with attendant kiosks and security facilities, must be planned for.

Trolley park, Hempstead Valley

Where serving food stores, planning for trolleys must be considered carefully. There are many solutions – none of which is perfect! Trolley bay disposal points should be easily identifiable and accessible but separated from car parking spaces either by raised curbs, planting or variation in paving surface. From these points staff will return empty trolleys to trolley parks adjoining the store entrances where they can be picked up by shoppers. Trolley disposal points too far from point of discharge into the shoppers car will not be used causing problems of vandalism theft or obstruction and shortage of trolleys.

In all car parks a high standard of routine and long term maintenance is required, and particular problems arise in multi-storey covered parks. A higher

level of lighting then in open car parking is needed and adequate parking bay and manoeuvring space. None of these attributes is conspicuous in the typical multi-storey car park which is often a vandal-inviting, gloomy and deterrent cavern.

Ideally, multi-storey car parks forming part of the shopping centre should be designed and built within the control of the developer and handled as part of the general management by the management team rather than let or built by concessionaires or local authorities who are likely to be familar only with a more general type of car park use.

If car parking is to be charged for, the method chosen is important. A maximum period will need to be enforced (or discouraged by escalating charges) to avoid long-term parking by non-shoppers (4 hours for instance is too long). A supervised barrier method of intake, exit and charging is satisfactory, but not the 'self help' unsupervised ticket system. Systems allowing discarded tickets are to be avoided as encouraging litter.

Roof and subterranean car parks

Construction problems in providing access ramps and road ways to roof or subterranean parks are not such a problem as for service vehicles in view of the lighter loading. Ramps should not exceed 1 in 10, surfacing should be non-slip and jointing of the road ways requires careful detailing. Good wash-down facilities must not be forgotten and petrol sumps may be required. Owing to the restrictions by the size of parking bay and circulation routes, column spacing of subterranean car parks or any car parking integrated into the construction will need very careful handling. Column spacing at lower levels may need to be closer than on upper levels, if carrying the additional load of the main decks, to avoid excessive beam depths but this needs interpolating into grid spacings in both directions if it is not to inhibit comfortable parking of the kind we have been looking at. This problem is multiplied when the centre also supports office blocks or flatted housing and, in all these circumstances, very careful research and investigation is required before deciding on the grid dimensions at parking levels.

As the one-stop shopping centre emerged from the demand by car shoppers for easy parking and 'one-stop' shopping in vehicle-free conditions, the success of any centre is very closely bound up with successful design and operation of its car parking facilities which are bound to be a major element in the overall design.

Chapter 5
Servicing

Population of centre

In any successful shopping centre the 'through-put' of shoppers will be fast and continuous, resulting in an intensive use of all parts of the buildings. Determination of space standards, accommodation, materials and servicing must be considered accordingly.

The maximum use of a shopping centre cannot accurately be calculated, but a useful guide to occupancy of units is offered in the BS Code of Practice, Chapter 5, 1968 – in relation to means of escape. It suggests the following calculations:

1 For shops trading in the common types of consumer goods (e.g. food, hardware, clothes, cosmetics, fabrics, etc.) – $1.9\,m^2$ of gross sales floor area per person.
2 For specialised shops in more expensive or exclusive trades, (e.g. bespoke tailoring, furs, furniture, jewellery, carpets) $7\,m^2$ of gross sales floor area per person.

These are peak period figures. By assuming the length of time of an average visit in each unit, say 1 hour, and averaging throughout the centre (it is over-optimistic to assume maximum occupation of all retail units simultaneously) some idea of the total maximum throughput at peak trading hours may be achieved. This will be affected also by the attraction of the centre to 'window shoppers' and users of other available facilities.

Another quoted rule of thumb statistic is that the area of malls and courts may approximate to 10% of the total centre area. This is a starting guide only; the actual economics of detailed research into each particular venture will determine the extent of G.L.A. and common areas which will be viable for that centre.

The size of the likely staff population must also be considered. As a guide, in considering the large space user, an area of $3000\,m^2$ sales area might require up to 200 staff, while standard retail units would range from minimum of 3 upwards depending on area and type of trade and selling methods. Added to this will be the staff of the Centre Management – administration, security, maintenance.

Servicing and administration

Delivery and despatch of goods to individual units are the life blood of the centre. Servicing vehicles must have easy slip routes from main transport throughways to unloading bays, with adequate temporary parking, communication to units, and easy get-away when empty. All these must be separated from, and if possible unseen, by customers and customer access.

It is useful to understand something of the methods of computerized marketing. Automatic deliveries based upon sales returns or computerised records may rely on a strict routine of return and refill. Heavy vehicles may be arriving at regular delivery time from central warehouses to feed major or multiple units and a calculation of number and size of these is needed to relate to service roads, axle loading and type of handling. Major units may even house their own computer centres and are likely to require loading facilities within their own site curtilage.

Unit shops usually rely on direct deliveries from various manufacturers in a random fashion at all hours and from various types of vehicle. Timing of these deliveries is likely to be haphazard and during shopping hours.

Adequate provision for physical handling of goods, i.e. unloading and delivery to units, with notification to unit (by 'intercom') that delivery vehicles have arrived, is part of the delivery process. The intercom system should be of the 'banned access' type, between shop and entry point only. In the UK the GPO monopoly position prevails and provides the service on its own conditions; the customer having no choice!

Thus all types of delivery vehicles must be expected and service routes must cater for articulated vehicles of maximum size. Useful dimensions are:

Maximum length of (articulated) goods vehicles 15 m
Maximum width of goods vehicles 2.50 m (8 ft 2 in)
Maximum height 5.3 m (17 ft 6 in) for tippers
Ministry of Transport recommendation under bridge 16 ft (5 m)

Dimensions for Fire Brigade vehicles:
Minimum width of access road 3.66 m (12 ft)
Minimum clearance height 3.66 m (12 ft)
Minimum turning circle 16.76 m (55 ft) dia.
Laden weight 10.160 kg (10 tons).
[*Note.* For refuse disposal or Fire Brigade vehicles, allow a maximum reversing distance of 30 ft (9.2 m). Maximum turning circle 16.76 m, (55 ft) dia].

There will also be a considerable amount of 'behind the scenes' traffic to be catered for. This includes vehicles concerned with sales 'reps', management and supervision, staff recruitment, etc, staff circulation and transport.

All goods and staff vehicles must arrive by clearly defined routes separated from customer access, and leading goods vehicles into unloading bays. These routes must be designed to allow for free clear lanes, weaving lanes and temporary parking, with clear through routes or adequate turning spaces clear of through routes.

There may also need to be facilities for customer dispatch of heavy consumer durables, i.e. furniture. From the delivery point, communication with individual units will be needed and access delivery points to rear service entrances of individual units must be direct and convenient. This may have to be provided vertically by goods lift (or hoist) and horizontally by service corridors suitable for trolleys, small fork lifts or pallets. Electric fork lift buggies, if provided by units or management will require battery charging points in the service area.

A major decision will be the level of discharge for goods vehicles. Where space allows , discharge points will ideally be at ground level. Service courts at ground level need to be carefully designed into the scheme, concealed from the public (at the same time giving easy access to all units), and separated from customer vehicular traffic. The difficulty of achieving this agreeably is the reason why service courts are not liked by some local authorities, though if site area is available, this is the preferred solution on grounds of cost, ease of access, maintenance and convenience.

However, on restricted sites consideration must be given to alternatives, balancing additional construc-

tion costs against freeing of valuable ground level areas for other uses. Obvious alternatives are subterranean or roof level. Whatever the decision, basic requirements will be:

Two-way access, throughout the vehicle route a loop way system.

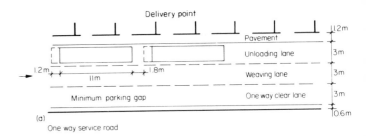

(a) One way service road

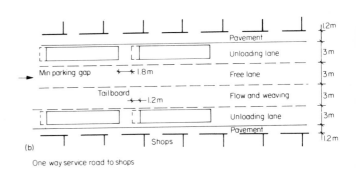

(b) One way service road to shops

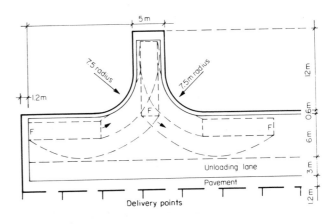

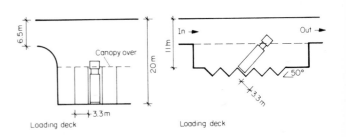

Service entries

Standing for vehicles, clear of the service road.
Parking for vehicles free from interference with service routes by physical design or adequate administrative control planned into the system.

Levels of service road must relate to finished levels of goods reception areas of individual units. Some large users may require loading platforms.

Where service roads areas are above mall, units and stores, the design and construction of the roof and roof finish are of utmost importance to avoid any possibility of roof leaks, either through expansion, failure of expansion joints or a failure of roof finish. (It does not seem that a foolproof solution of the expansion joint on heavy lorry routes has yet been achieved!)

Ventilation, sprinklering, smoke control, means of escape, permanent adequate lighting and fire precautions generally for all delivery routes and standing spaces, as for car parking, must be to required standards.

Adequate access for fire fighting must be incorporated into the planning of the centre, the likely solution being to take advantage of the service roadways. Generally access can be round the perimeter of the development, or, if this is not practicable, at 90 m centres, where connections will be needed to vertical access points.

Where service roads are to be used as escape routes, pavements or areas designated for pedestrian use must be provided, and segregated from the vehicle roadway. They should be at least 2 m wide and continuous to the external air. They will need to be protected from adjoining internal spaces by fire resisting doors. Magnetic door closers operated by smoke detectors may be justified if doors are likely to be in constant use. Care must be taken in the layout to discourage any possibility of escape routes being used for or blocked by surplus storage or accumulation of waste.

Service roads and standing areas must conform with the following requirements.

(i) To be of adequate loading strength for heaviest vehicles serving the centre (see MoT requirements and Chapter 6).
(ii) Width, height and turning space must accommodate the largest vehicles operated by the tenant, haulier, local authority and Fire Brigade.
(iii) Gradients of ramps must not exceed 1 in 10.
(iv) Satsifactory non-slip finish to MoT standards, including protectional measures against snow, ice and excessive rainfall.
(v) Overhead weather protection while unloading is advisable and may be demanded by some retailers.

A further precaution in basement vehicle service areas may be carbon monoxide monitoring by CO detectors, connected to the central control room.

Waste disposal

There are a variety of methods available to deal with the disposal of the large volume and variety of refuse generated within a shopping centre. Whatever the method of disposal, removal facilities will be required from collection points within the servicing areas. Removal may be either by the local authority or by a private contractor or even a combination of the two.

Consultation at design stage is essential as the choice will depend upon facilities offered and constraints imposed, such as the frequency of collection related to the volume of refuse, method of removal at point of collection (from compactor skip or paladin), method of loading, capacity of container/compactor, and Union conditions. The system and collecting requirements must be agreed early and specialist advice will be needed as to what system to adopt.

The more usual systems are:

1 Deposit of untreated waste into containers (probably skips) for direct removal by container lorry and in series. Success will depend on frequency and reliability of refuse collection.
2 Compaction. This reduces the volume by a calculated ratio, in compactors suitably sited, with arrangements as before for removing compacted waste but with greatly reduced volume.
3 Incineration. This method is not often favoured, due to difficulty of meeting anti-pollution standards in populated areas.

Whatever the method, separation of dry and wet waste may be decided on, depending on the amount and character of food waste to be disposed of.

Large users may provide their own refuse disposal units, probably compactors, and possibly shredders for dry waste and with arrangements for separation of saleable waste. So, service areas must be planned accordingly.

Each method will involve the provision in service areas for an adequate number of skips or compactors arranged suitably with adequate circulation between them and the tenants' units, and/or subsidiary collection points. The container lorries will pick up from the final disposal points, so adequate width, turning circles and headroom must be allowed for.

Large skips may require 17–18 ft headroom for transfer to the container lorries and these may be operating at frequent intervals. As an example, one large food supermarket in a regional shopping centre requires a minimum of two removals a day at peak periods from this section of the shopping centre alone, incorporating both dry and wet waste. This, where a compactor is not used, perhaps illustrates the advantage of the compaction system. One proviso regarding refuse disposal is that loose waste *must* not be allowed to accumulate, either at the rear of shops, in service areas and routes, or at basement level adjoining disposal units. This is a potential serious fire and health risk and these areas will also need to be sprinklered.

Whatever the disposal method, arrangements will be needed (as we have already seen) for transfer from individual units to the main disposal points. These may either be the responsibility of the tenant or of the centre management. In any event provision must be made for trolley access via horizontal service corridors, to service areas, lifts or chutes, from the individual unit to the disposal point. Where this service is provided by the management, more likely in multi-level large schemes, the tenants will be responsible up to suitable service points arranged adjacent to service lifts from whence the centre management will trolley the waste from the subsidiary collection points.

Standard refuse trolleys may be provided by the centre for the use of tenants. If refuse chutes are incorporated into the refuse disposal system they will need to be incombustible, compartmented, smoke vented, sprinklered and monitored.

Centre management's own refuse disposal also needs careful attention. Litter bins must be conveniently and frequently sited throughout malls and courts. Particularly this needs to be related to the siting of the take-away and restaurant food facilities. It is highly important to the attractiveness and good housekeeping of the centre that the frequent and convenient emptying and removal to service points of all litter is achievable.

Litter bins must be not only attractive, easily seen and inviting for the disposal of litter but also easily and conveniently designed for quick emptying and removal by trolley to service points. It is an odd reflection on our times that this periodic and frequent emptying is not only related to the size of the litter bin but to the need for keeping it empty as a precaution against bomb 'scares' and other terrorist activity.

Administration and staff provision

Offices will be needed for the manager of the centre and his staff – secretarial and executive – with probably a meeting space for the tenants' association. An enquiry point may be needed in the main mall accessible to the public. There must be adequate provision for plant rooms, storage, staff toilet facilities, rest rooms etc., and perhaps a staff canteen for management as well as security staff.

A security centre will be needed housing the warning equipment controlled with 24-hour operation and connected to every part of the centre. This includes sprinklers, fire alarm, burglar and other alarm systems, and closed circuit television. A rest room and toilet facilities to statutory or recommended standards for the number of security and other staff employed will also be needed.

General provision for customers

The shopping centre has to tempt shoppers to dally – providing points for rest and refreshment and varying degrees of entertainment, in addition to the primary aim of buying. It must have a very special appeal to women shoppers, who may represent up to 80% of the shopping population.

An essential to long-stay shopping is adequate and pleasant lavatory accommodation (now universally re-styled 'toilet facilities'). This must be adequate for both sexes and must be conveniently situated and easily identified, remembering the large proportion of women and also children. Many earlier centres have under-estimated the women's lavatory accommodation needed for a large centre. This must be generous and if possible, duplicated, so that should there be a drain blockage, it does not put the whole facility out of action. This occurrence is more likely than one may think. Pilfering results in empty wallets and handbags being disposed of in WCs. Possibly the provision of 6 in dia. drains rather than 4 in dia. may reduce the problem.

The more stark the appointments, the greater the degree of vandalism. Adequate supervision is the only positive way to combat this and to ensure agreeable use of these facilities by shoppers. Attendance on a permanent basis and accommodation for the attendant should be made in planning the facilities, which must also include toilets for the handicapped, the extent and siting of these being dependent on the size and location of the centre. A very high standard of maintenance is demanded and finishes must be sturdy and attractive, but of a good quality. Adequate washing facilities, hot water and soap dispensers, towels (paper or other), or hot air driers (these are not favoured by the public) and mirrors (full length please!) should be available. It is markedly evident that where due thought and care has been given to the design, this has been respected and vandalism remains at a minimum.

Locker rooms for storage of customers coats and parcels were provided in many early transatlantic one-stop centres, but bomb scares and terrorist activities have ruled out this facility. Banks of telephones must also be accommodated. Hoods rather than kiosks or booths will reduce risk of vandalism. They

A delightful solution to the telephone kiosk. City-2, Brussels (Photo: Nigel Woolner)

should be sited well within the centre to discourage outside use, and well-lit.

Another possible facility in the 'one-stop' centre is the package pick-up station, as sometimes offered by department stores and supermarkets. Purchases are accumulated at one discharge point – adjacent to the car park, where the customer drives up, collects and loads. This encourages leisurely shopping without the limitation imposed by weight and bulk of purchases. On the other hand it may involve a complete system of carefully treated spiral package chutes, converging conveyor belts, etc.

A large centre will probably need a first-aid room, and possibly a rest room and provision for nursing mothers. These may conveniently be attached to women's toilet facilities.

A supervised play centre for younger children is a popular and useful adjunct, though it involves the

employment of staff and consequent financial outlay which will probably be reflected in service charges. Its size will of course depend on estimated demand. It will need to be accessible but not necessarily visible to the malls, well lit, supplied with toys and other equipment, and if not adjacent to women's toilet accommodation, will need its own.

Pause points for shoppers to rest, review their programmes and re-arrange their purchases etc., also need planning with care. Seating, while offering a convenient stopping point, must not be too luxurious or comfortable. Shoppers must move on and allow re-occupation of seating and the danger of attracting the 'down and outs' of various categories must also be avoided. Seating must be sturdy and permanent and need only minimum maintenance.

Sunken areas are attractive, but must be designed with care, and with no danger of tripping over steps or curbs – remembering that shoppers tend to be looking at the shops, not the floor!

Special promotions, such as Christmas decorations, local authority celebrations and trade promotions will

Package pick-up station at Yorkdale, Toronto

North concourse, Eldon Square, Newcastle, showing sunken area and coffee shop (Photo: Brecht-Einzig)

Example of a play feature

Victoria Centre, Nottingham, the Emmett Clock (Photo: John Rose and John Dyble)

Fountain at Staines, Middlesex (Photo: Nicholas Halton)

be a feature of any centre and need to be planned for, both spatially and with adequate servicing. Provision should be made for temporary lighting, public address systems, adequate floor loading and access, and with regard to fire precautions, plastics and flammable material generally being ruled out.

Play features in open play areas for children are not only a great help to harassed mothers, but if conveniently sited, are a delight to the elderly and unoccupied, who, it is found, like to watch them while pausing between purchases. The play features must be expertly designed, and should be safe and indestructible besides being amusing and interesting to the children.

Major features of general interest, such as the Emmett Clock at Nottingham's Victoria Centre, if successful add much to the centre, both in promotion appeal and as a local attraction. They do however need consideration in terms of access for maintenance, durability and running costs, which are inevitable, if such features are to be integral elements of attraction. Nothing has so far taken the place of water features – water is alive, variable and refreshing. Fountains, waterfalls, water sculptures are an excellent element where used imaginatively. They are also, (though this has to be tolerated!) a constant headache to the centre manager – requiring cleaning, emptying and supervising; they must not constitute a hazard to children, or adults – or a temptation to be used as litter bins. Again the higher the quality of finish, maintenance and supervision, the less the tendency to vandalism. From observation it seems worth comment that 'still' water invites trouble more than active movement of fountains or 'waterfalls' These when provided should preferably play throughout all opening hours of the centre.

Routine cleaning and maintenance

Reference has already been made to maintenance, and instead of considering it at the end of the book I have included it in this early chapter as a vital design ingredient.

The importance of maintenance seems regrettably underestimated at the stage where it should have its own priority heading in the brief. A shopping centre has extremely complex maintenance problems as a management function and ease and economy of maintenance needs to be built into the project at the start.

Many criticisms of shopping centre design by management can be traced to maintenance difficulties and perhaps there is no building type which relies more on efficient day to day servicing and maintenance techniques for successful operation. A shopping centre showing signs of vandalism, or rubbish not cleared away, of untidiness, dirt, staining and deterioration of materials, is a shopping centre in decline and the worse it gets the more difficult the remedy. So the architect must appreciate and understand not only its significance but also its technicalities.

It will be of great assistance to the architect if centre management is involved in the preparation of the Brief. An experienced centre manager, if involved at an early stage, can outline essential requirements and operational methods and identify traps which may otherwise catch the unwary designer.

The subject affects so many of the design elements and decisions, from planning to detailing that it is not easy to isolate these in terms of maintenance. It comprises attention to the building in terms of three very different types of operation.

1 Daily and periodic cleaning and servicing;
2 Repair and long term restoration and redecoration;
3 Adequate physical provision for cleaning staff and materials.

It is necessary to recognise that every material and every item of equipment and finish will require maintenace of some kind or other. An axiom of good maintenance is 'immediate reaction'; litter must be removed as it accumulates, repairs carried out as damage occurs, and vandalism instantly wiped out. The centre must be designed to make all this possible; so how is it to be done?

Planning for maintenance
One consideration is likely to be provision of adequate space for the maintenance operation. There will be maintenance staff, comprising both cleaners and service maintenance engineers and technicians. In a big centre they will be operating throughout the day as well as when the centre is closed. They will need canteen, toilet facilities, changing room, lockers etc.

Cleaning by hand, whether of large areas or in small pockets is quite impractical in the shopping centre, due to the scale of the cleaning operation, time available for its execution, and the economic restraints on the amount of labour required. So the idea of an army of Mrs Mopps with buckets and brooms is just a fantasy!

The whole operation will have to be mechanised and space and facilities must be provided to house tools and equipment. For instance cleaning machines in a big centre will be very sophisticated; they may, when filled, weigh up to a ton. They will need hot and cold water supply, special sump drainage for emptying and cleaning, and plug-in facilities for battery charging if battery operated.

The Clarke-a-Matic TB32A, a combined scrubbing and drying machine, which is battery operated. The Clarke-a-Matic will operate for eight hours on six batteries and requires a 12 hour recharging cycle (Photo: Sloman and Pettitt)

Maintenance area in a closed centre

For electrically mains-operated machines, conveniently situated socket-outlets must be available for cleaning all parts of the centre. It may be that both machine types will be accommodated. Battery-operated machines are needed during opening hours, when trailing flexes are inadmissible, and also for emergencies e.g. power failures. Electrically mains-operated machines are lighter to manoeuvre and do not rely on recharging for immediate use.

There will be buffing machines, litter clearing and plant watering trolleys, instant cleaning and other equipment, all requiring a considerable amount of storage space and power and servicing facilities.

Secure arrangements for storage of cleaning materials and replacement equipment are essential. These may be both valuable and potentially dangerous and lock-up areas with convenient racking arrangments will be needed. Cleaning and polishing machines as well as trolleys will need to be wheeled around the malls, courts and service areas, so ramps will be needed at changes of level along the routes where curbs and steps are not navigable. Service lifts must be of dimensions and loading to take the cleaning and servicing equipment and must be conveniently available to the storage areas.

External maintenance

Maintenance to the external areas of the centre must not be forgotten. Exposed roads, ramps and roofs forming part of the vehicular service routes and unprotected pedestrian and vehicular shoppers' routes, entrances and car parks, will need particular attention in winter if subject to ice or snow. If these areas are not taken over by the local authority and remain under the control of the centre management (which is highly desirable), facilities for tackling this will involve salt and grit stores of adequate supply together with garage space for snow plough, tractor and road clearing machines. As has already been mentioned allowance must be made for a lack of expert driving skill on the part of the shopper, and in a 'one-stop' or 'edge of town' location it is a great asset to have ice and snow-free conditions in the car parks and the approaches to the centre.

Maintenance policy

Of course all this will need research, probably the best solution being investigation of centres and methods already operating as there is surprisingly little specialist advice available. The architect will need to agree the maintenance brief with the developer. This will include the number and type of staff. If a contract cleaning firm is likely to be involved consultation is needed at this stage; and information from manufacturers of cleaning equipment should also be obtained.

The provision for maintenance must be as elastic as possible to allow for later changes in policy and methods.

Difficulties in arriving at appropriate solutions are of course increased if the centre is not going to be operated by the developer after completion. Here I will again dare to sound a note of warning; local authorities are not usually equipped, by reason of their experience in very different fields, to appreciate or operate the highly skilled specialised and top quality maintenance operation needed in a shopping centre. Therefore, if local authorities are to be involved in the centre operation they will need considerable direction and advice as to the maintenance standard to be provided for.

Access and cleaning methods related to materials

One main design consideration is access for cleaning, repair and replacement. For instance, how will lamps, tubes and fuses be replaced, light fittings and special features cleaned and serviced, water features drained,

Maintenance of soft landscaping – one solution at Milton Keynes

A maintenance problem?

etc? Fountains and pools will need daily surface clearance and cleaning with draining probably fortnightly. The introduction of swimming pool techniques, e.g. filtration plant, would simplify this process though of course at increased capital cost.

Paving will need repair, surface water and soil drains need cleaning. As far as possible such operations should not take place during opening hours except in emergencies and a method of dealing with such emergencies with minimum disturbance to customers should be established.

The architect should also consider the following questions. Can crawlways or gangways be provided within the false ceiling area to avoid the need for servicing towers? Can cleaning machines reach all appropriate areas? How about glazing?

Glass is a special problem as it is the one material that can only be satisfactorily cleaned by hand – even squeegees need an operator at the other end of the pole! Glass also needs more frequent attention than any other material and is more liable to breakage. It also has two faces both needing cleaning. Careful thought is needed in devising cleaning methods for large areas of glazing and, in particular, of roof glazing. It is also necessary to consider facilities for unit shops as should they have glazed shop fronts they will need to clean their windows very frequently.

Servicing of mechanical and electrical plant, and ducts will need gangways/gantrys for convenient access, remembering also facilities required for meter reading of tenant's meters, whether or not housed in service areas.

Next we come to the question of selection of materials. This is dealt with generally in a separate chapter. Looking at the problem from a maintenance angle, the main factors are wearing quality, relating to function as well as appearance, and vulnerability to

vandalism, again related to accessibility. Vandalism must, sadly, be accepted as inevitable so finishes accessible to vandals must be of kinds which are durable, can be cleaned chemically or otherwise from graffiti, and which are not temptingly easily damaged. Curiously the long-term traditional building materials such as brick and stone are difficult to protect and maintain in this context.

Another main consideration is of course the type and method of cleaning and its periodicity; floors will need at least daily cleaning and vertical surfaces must not be ignored. Those within human reach will be rubbed and soiled more quickly than vertical surfaces beyond reach, which will however be affected by long-term deposit; this also applies to ceilings and soffits. Air conditioning affects the situation as filtered and recirculated air will maintain relatively clean conditions.

It is my personal anxiety that insufficient research has so far been applied to examination of the possible effects of air conditioning on physical health, in particular, as it is affected by maintenance of the system. It seems to me that there is need for s sophisticated maintenace routine to keep an air conditioning system clean, sterile, free of bacteria and dust throughout; including pipework ducts, fans, filters, renewal of water used in condensers, etc. I hope this may in future become a demanded item in the maintenance schedule.

All vertical surfaces will need cleaning and/or redecoration at intervals, and the question as to when and how must be answered and costed at the time of selection. Conjunction of materials requiring different types of cleaning must be carefully handled. For instance a vertical skirting matching floor finish cannot be cleaned by floor cleaning machines so it is advisable to keep the upstand to a minimum to avoid hand cleaning. Careful detailing is necessary throughout; such things as junctions between escalators, lifts, staircases and floors must not provide dirt pockets which again can only be hand-cleaned.

Decorative features, balustrades, design of mall furniture, litter bins, etc. also need careful examination. Litter bins must have interior linings light enough for easy emptying, but big enough to take litter between emptying (which will be many times a day). Litter, particularly in fast food areas, is a major problem as most of the items used will be disposable – i.e. paper cups, spoons, plates – one set for each sale! Dark floors show up litter much more than light ones. Whether this is an advantage or disadvantage may depend on the effectiveness of the maintenance arrangements!

A further maintenance consideration is fire prevention. Fires are easily started in typical shop rubbish –

i.e. cardboard boxes, textiles, plastics, loosely piled – particularly if these are allowed to accumulate near such heat sources as powerful lamps, electric motors, or parts of a heating system. No loose waste storage should be allowed but this implies adequate provision for satisfactory storage as a design requirement. A further seasonal risk is the insertion of Christmas decorations. Good, efficient and continuous maintenance and supervision is essential throughout the complex if fire dangers of this kind are to be avoided.

In selecting materials, it must be remembered that day-to-day cleaning will be wet or dry depending on finish, i.e. vacuum cleaning, polishing, swabbing, washing and dusting, while periodic attention will include either cleaning or redecoration and servicing. Dry and wet cleaning areas should not be contiguous. A surface water system will be needed to drain impervious floor areas, with floors laid to slight falls, and gullies at suitable intervals. This system should also handle excess water from sprinkler operation or fire fighting.

It is of the utmost importance to consult with the mechanical services engineers in considering the question of maintenance of engineering services. Convenient access for servicing, and consideration of equipment in its relation to long life, access for easy renewal (large items must not be overlooked), orderly and concise routing of services, positioning of access panels and clear maintenance directions, all must be insisted on.

Where vital equipment is involved, duplication or standby extras may be necessary. Such things as lifts out of action, shut down of central heating or electrical installation in large areas for repair or adjustment, too many light fittings on one switch, all represent unnecessary problems for the shopping centre.

The planning of tenant mix will affect the maintenance problems of the centre. These will be considerably eased if restaurants and snack bars, food shops and fast food areas, which are likely to generate unacceptable waste and smells and excessive litter are kept together and segregated from the high fashion element of the centre.

The maintenance of soft landscaping is touched on in Chapter 8. This includes adequate provision for water, drainage, repainting, removal of waste and maintenance of correct temperatures.

When all is said and done, design for easy and efficient maintenance is largely a matter of common sense allied to experience. It is a contribution the architect can and must make to the efficient running of the centre in maintenance terms.

Chapter 6

The unit

The retailer

To produce a successful centre it goes without saying that units offered to retailers must meet their conditions for efficient trading. These vary amongst specialist trades which means that compromise decisions are often necessary, since occupation of all units will not be decided at design stage. All the more the architect must understand and respect the basic needs of the specialist retailer in designing the centre and the unit shop.

In the case of the large space user, as we have seen, sites may be agreed early and their premises are likely to be the subject of individual negotiation and briefing, possibly even the shell being designed by their own architect under overall control by the centre architect.

As for individual units it may seem surprising that strong criticism, certainly in the UK, is levelled by shopping centre tenants at the basic design of the shell and also of controls which they claim are over-restrictive and cause difficulties, in fitting out and in their effect on efficient trading. This suggests a need for detailed knowledge, examination and understanding of the problems of the individual retailer by the centre architect and in some cases the developer.

There is no doubt that compromises will be necessary. Different traders will ideally want conditions which are either irreconcilable or will appear too late in the project to be accommodated. This is all the more reason for the developer and the architect to appreciate the implications of design decisions concerning individual shop units. It helps to have experience of individual shop design. Both general and particular trading problems must be studied in order to provide satisfactory trading units. I used to persuade design staff concerned with shop design actually to serve in a shop to see for themselves the conditions and restraints of retailing in practice – a rewarding experience.

So let us examine some tenant requirements which should be designed into the overall shopping centre concept.

General considerations applying to all units

Regulations and approvals

Regulatory requirements need to be cleared by the centre architect with the various authorities involved, on the basis of occupation. Due regard should be paid to vital outstanding requirements unknown until premises are let and taking into account that units are often not let before construction or may change at a later date. Foresight is needed in negotiation.

In the UK, clearance will be needed at least under Planning Acts, Building Regulations, Means of Escape, Health and Safety at Work Act, Fire Precautions, the Petroleum Acts as well as many other Acts and Regulations as appropriate (See Appendix).

Requirements of Insurers must also be ascertained at the earliest possible moment as they may be more onerous in certain respects than statutory regulations.

All known conditions, approvals, waivers, insurance conditions, must be clearly communicated to prospective tenants, preferably as part of the letting brochure.

Bearing in mind the variety and compass of controls involved, clearance of the 'shell' without anticipation of the needs of prospective tenants may well lead to unforeseen expense to the retailer in constructional alterations and difficulty in efficient trading.

Service access

On the grounds of both amenity and fire safety no unit should become a 'dead end concrete box' but should always allow secondary access and some form of extract ventilation at the rear.

Each unit has to be individually fitted out probably more than once in its life. Unobstructed access is needed for plant machinery and materials to all individual units. Access must be available at the time of shop fitting, whether before or after the opening of the centre and so arranged as to cause minimum disturbance to trading units and malls in use.

Permanent and routine trading access has already been dealt with in the previous chapter. Where not directly at ground level, alternative emergency access needs to be offered to avoid isolating the shop should normal access routes be blocked.

Electric, gas, water and Post Office mains supply must be available to every tenant at a point of entry. Position of tenants' meters will depend on the requirements of the appropriate supply authority, who may require concentration of meters in service areas for easy meter reading, or alternatively, accept metering in each unit.

It is obviously important to establish these requirements early. They may be onerous and affect design. Limits on the length of mains entry, or access demanded to service mains at every joint are examples.

Constructional requirements
Maximum flexibility is of course an unachievable ideal, within the constraints of economic viability, fire precautions, thermal and acoustic controls and site limitations. Moreover the construction system will have to suit differing sets of conditions – at least the unit shop, the large store and the mall.

Provision must be made for accommodation of specialist services to be provided at fitting-out stage; these include heating, cooling, ventilation, lighting, refrigeration and sprinklering, depending on tenant use. Staircases, lifts, hoists, and in larger units perhaps escalators, should also be considered.

The need for flexibility must be acknowledged in deciding on construction systems for shop units. Whatever system is adopted, provision will need to be made for future trimming of new openings in multi-storey developments with clear indications given before letting as to constructional limitations. Unless a flexible system is adopted such extensive methods of trimming as the costly thermal lance (which has its own disadvantages) may be necessary where tenants have to be provided with additional wells, holes, etc. to avoid disturbance, noise and dust to trading units.

The Fire Authority may require staircases in two level units to be in particular positions, e.g. customer stairs discharging directly adjoining the mall – in which case in order to obtain clearance, staircase wells may have to be agreed, in standard positions, at construction stage in advance of letting. This requirement must be clearly indicated in letting plans etc. and decided in sympathy with the retailer's likely requirements. In multi-level shops successful retailing

is likely to be closely linked to staircase/lift/escalator/service positions which will vary between types of retailer, trading policy, frontage, department allocation, shape of retailing area etc. Rule of thumb decisions by the centre architect regarding vertical access positions are not conducive to tenant satisfaction.

To enlarge on vertical circulation problems, customers have to be enticed onto other levels, by stairs strategically placed to attract, (not obstruct), – offering interest during and at the end of their 'run'. 'Blind' stairs without sight of the target area, perhaps enclosed and/or in long boring single flights, without display or interest, are a major deterrent to successful trading. On the other hand service stairs need to be convenient to staff, and need minimum effort (easy rise and go) – therefore of minimum height. Hence one explanation of the resistance of the smaller retailer to unnecessary floor to floor heights.

Storey height is a critical factor and needs careful investigation related to the disposal and height of units, as while large users require maximum headroom for service voids and deep structural supports, small shops, as we have seen, do not want unnecessary height which will result in unnecessary capital and annual costs for heating, cooling, fitting out – maintaining a larger cube than they need for trading merely to suit the larger user. Should retailers wish to reduce ceiling height by a closed false ceiling they may be faced with a need for double sprinklers to protect the void together with adequate smoke reservoirs below the ceiling incorporating grilles or slits though open ceilings, such as slatted louvres which may meet these requirements.

While large units can usually accommodate columns in their layout if dimensions can be agreed to suit aisle widths, etc., small units need areas free of obstructions. Columns and service ducts, either horizontal or vertical, should not encroach on sales areas or shop frontages, if possible, but in any event only to an extent clearly indicated in detailed dimension in letting plans. The tenant must be fully aware of any limitations to be integrated into his shop fitting and layout when taking the shop. Therefore minimizing size and positioning of columns, as well as the grid dimensions must be taken into account when determining the type of construction.

Limitations regarding the selection of finishes and other materials to comply with Fire Safety and other Regulations should be cleared at approval stage for the tenants' information.

Provision must be considered in constructional detailing for interior fixings such as those for suspended ceilings, partitions, mechanical and electrical installations, light fittings, sprinkler installation, wall and floor finishes (carpets on screed?), with adequate tolerances between structural and finished floor levels. The shop front will be considered later in another chapter.

Staff facilities

All shops require staff accommodation, the minimum being lavatory accommodation, usually needed for both sexes and in accordance with Regulations. In the UK this was specified in the Shops, Offices and Railway Premises Act (now taken over by the Health and Safety at Work Act) and requires separate lavatory accommodation for each sex in the case of more than five staff, with drinking water and washing facilities, hot water supply and stipulated numbers of lavatory basins, WCs and urinals as may be appropriate related to numbers of staff. Provision of domestic hot water is usually left to the tenant.

Lockers and provision for wet and dry outdoor clothes, including drying facilities, and a rest room and/or galley or kitchen accommodation are other minima.

Adequate plumbing and drainage connections are essential. Cold water storage tanks may be local to the shop or from general supply. If the former, adequate 'head of water' must be maintained with mains supply available for drinking water and careful planning of water supply and drainage routes is needed to avoid interference with the areas allotted to individual units.

Some centres have offered communal staff lavatory accommodation in lieu of provision for each individual unit. This is not always welcome, as there is a security risk involved in allowing uncontrolled staff movement outside the retailers' own premises – particularly in the case of valuable 'small item' trades such as jewellery. There is also an element of maintenance, supervision and protection against vandalism involving management costs and service charges needing to be balanced against capital cost of providing individual facilities.

Mechanical and electrical services

Mechanical and electrical services are dealt with in Chapter 8.

The volume of trade, number of staff and high levels of display lighting may result in the necessary removal of excessive heat as a major ingredient of service planning, space heating being a comparatively short term activity, seasonally and diurnally and depending on geographic location. This generated heat may cause problems if allowed to discharge into the malls, while a slight pressure towards the malls from the shop unit will prevent 'stealing' of cooling or heating from the mall by the shop unit. This is unlikely to be acceptable in the UK due to Smoke Control Regulations. Reverse

pressure may slightly inflate running costs of the centre to the benefit of the shop tenant and may upset the calculated balance of the system unless designed for but may be advisable to meet smoke control requirements.

Similarly the likely lighting levels within the units relative to that of the malls is an important factor and only an adequate level of display lighting to shop fronts will give the necessary impact to the mall frontages and continuity of display. However the malls will need sufficient lighting to attract shoppers in from outside and to give a feeling of interest and participation – the balance must be right.

Types of trading unit

We now need to examine more closely the likely mix of trades and services called for in the centre with resultant implications for the designer, the centre manager, the retailer. Table 1 overleaf lists main trading categories, divided into 'food' and 'non-food' shops.

The table shows the immense variety available in shopping centre trading, which can offer the shopping public the widest possible selection in 'one-stop' conditions.

Trading developments

It is of interest to follow developments in specialist shop trading and their influence on shop design, whether operated by individual traders or by 'multiples' – a chain of shops. A major revolution in UK trading has been the rise of the multiple. Although some multiples are comparatively modest in number of outlets, locally or regionally based, the national and powerful chains of outlets wield considerable influence through their competitive prices, standardised goods ranges, their familiarity to the public (with consequent popularity) and public appeal, as well as their ability and expertise in site selection and negotiating power.

The dominance of the multiples has resulted in a shopping pattern specific to the UK. This in itself is a limitation to their field of competition, and has given the specialist 'boutique' or individual speciality trader the alternative attraction of scarcity, individuality, specialist buying of unusual and perhaps luxury merchandise, as well as spontaneous reaction to fashion, climate, local conditions, not available to the centrally controlled multiple.

It is of great advantage to the centre to entice the local and individual trader into the centre. Possibly this may mean offering temporary accommodation to units displaced by redevelopment sometimes in association with the local authority.

Another development affecting design is the rise of the shop equipment 'system' – stimulated by the growth of self service. This consists of a 'meccano set' of parts which can be assembled into display and selling components. These include not only shelving, counters, gondolas, self-service racking, cabinets, but partitions, wall panels, lighting pelmets, with signing and ticketing etc. Thus shop equipment 'systems' make possible flexible planning and virtually free-standing internal shop-fitting within the shell, needing only floor and ceiling finishes, (with perhaps frieze finish above units) as permanent finishes.

Table 1   Main trading categories

Non-food

Antiques	Leather and fancy goods
Art gallery and craft shop (Commercial)	Mail order showroom
	Menswear
Bank	Miscellaneous repairers
Betting shop	Moped, cycle and motor accessories
Bookseller	
Building Society	Motor trade
Cameras and photographic equipment	Needlework goods
	Newsagent
Chemist	Off-licence
D.I.Y.	Optician
Dry cleaner; Launderette	Perfumery and cosmetics
Electrical goods	Pet shop
Estate agents	Philatelist/Numismatist
Florist, garden shop	Post Office
Funeral director	Radio, music, records, hi-fi, video
Furniture, home and office and soft furnishing	
	Shoe repairs
Gas and electricity showrooms	Shoe shop
Haberdasher	Sports equipment, toys and games
Hairdresser – Womens, Mens	
Hardware, ironmongery, decorating	Stationer, printer
	Sweets, tobacco
Hearing aid centre	Travel agent
Household goods	Womens and childrens wear
Jeweller	Wool shop

Department stores will cover most of the above.

Traditional food

Main categories of food shops and their produce are:

Greengrocer	Fresh vegetables, fruit, flowers, frozen vegetables.
Fishmonger	Fresh and frozen fish, cured fish, shell fish, poultry and game.
Butcher	Fresh and frozen meat, meat products, poultry and game, fats.
Grocer	Bacon, eggs, cheese, fat, packaged frozen and tinned foods, cereals, biscuits, beverages, dried fruits and preserves, sauces, spices, dry goods, soaps, detergents, cleaning materials, pet foods, paper products, chemists sundries, toilet and hygiene requisites.
Dairy	Milk, eggs, cream, butter, cheeses.
Baker	Bread, cakes, biscuits, flour, pies.
Confectioner	Chocolates, sweets, cigarettes, cigars, tobacco, newspapers.

Most of the above categories, food and non-food, are now combined into compound shops, comprising several trades, supermarkets and hypermarkets will serve all the food categories and frequently non-food items as well.

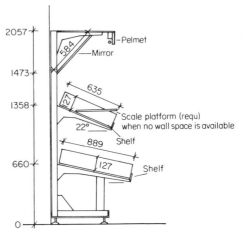

Section of typical wall shelving (food sales)

The main differences in the type of system concern the bracket design and method, fixing and shape of standard. The fixing may be into slotted standards or by sliding clips – the standards may be tee, channel, rectangular, or tubular.

There is a significant industry concerned with the manufacture of these systems. Many manufacturers have their own 'in-house' designers prepared to undertake layout design, which has a considerable influence on the shop unit – both large and small.

The development of trading expertise amongst the manufacturers and suppliers of the equipment, and the availability of their advice to the trader means that the standard of design and planning advice within these firms influences the final product of the less sophisticated traders who, if without their own consultants, may rely on supplier's guidance in design and layout. There is obviously a danger of repetitive and monotonous treatment unless imaginatively used, but there is also the advantage of flexibility and reduction of the need for permanent finishes.

Other interesting developments concern money transfer and cash systems. The increase of violent crime, the need to increase speed at check-out points at self-service stores, the increasing volume of trading in individual large units, together with the technical advances of the computer and micro-circuitry are influencing cash systems and leading to the introduction of new methods.

The traditional method of till emptying from checkout or at cash tills by security trolleys has many disadvantages. The trolleys need to be weighted in order to be manoeuvrable. They should not use lifts due to problems of security and handling and they create readily mobile cash and are therefore subject to theft. Trolleys are labour intensive as they need escorts, which (it must be faced) give only lip service to security as they will be little help in case of smash and grab raids. It is estimated that in a large store, 500–700 man hours a week may be allocated to cash collection! In considering all matters of security it has to be remembered that though insurance may cover the financial cost, the confusion where theft has taken place leads inevitably to a drop in takings and damage to the image of the centre and loss of trade.

There are now emerging alternative cash transfer systems. One is the pneumatic one-way process; this consists of a cash aid box, probably built into the till fixing and connected to a cash office the travel time of such a system being, say, 6 metres a second. The tubes require a minimum radius at change of direction. As this is a mechanical system, constructional design allowance must be made for its introduction with fire check precautions where penetrating fire barriers.

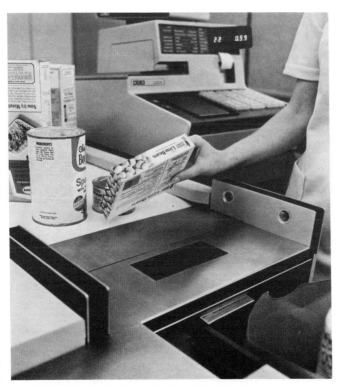

Special 'scanner' till. (Photo: National Cash Register)

One possible development of this system which has been suggested in a shopping centre is the provision of a pneumatic ring main between the units and a bank sited in the centre; this could be by means of, say, a 10 in diameter carrier that could deal with 120 customers per hour per station. It would obviate the security problems of banking cash manually but has an evident disadvantage; presumably all tenants would have to accept the use of the same bank! It is nevertheless a potential development worth notice.

As regards purchase of goods, and the taking of cash from customers, there has been a revolution in till design with the advent of the computer till and the laser scanner. This system has been popular for some years in Germany and the United States and has been introduced into certain British stores. Basically, every item is labelled with its bar code. To operate the system special tills are linked to a 'behind the scenes' computer which memorises price details of every item on a 'price file'. The bar code labels on the item are passed over a scanner built into the till or checkout, the code number is transmitted to the computer which identifies the item and prints its description and price on the till receipt, details being shown on a display in front of the customer. The computer also monitors the need to replace stock, provides sales movement data item by item and produces recommended orders for suppliers.

The advantages of this system are obvious. It increases the throughput of customers by, it is estimated, 20–30% at any one check-out and consequently check-out points may be reduced in number or at least kept static in large units with increase in customers. An up-to-date stock record is provided and because of the speed of reporting, a reduced stock turn. It has been estimated that for instance a supermarket stock turn of 3½ weeks can be reduced by this system to 2 weeks, thus a 40% stock turn saving.

The explanation of the 3½ week stock turn is interesting; it has to be remembered that retail stores do not manufacture but they rely on wholesalers and manufacturers for stock replacement. It is the speed of this communication routine that affects the stock turn and thus the speed at which the goods can be sold and the volume of trade.

This system may not require a full computer room but at least computer cabinets or micro-processors have to be housed either in or adjoining the cash office, with computer telephones to the main headquarters computer centre. The system as described is applicable mainly to the multiple large trader with central buying systems. Wide adoption will depend on a bar code labelling system at present in its infancy in the UK. So far, the Article Labelling Society is dealing only with food and supermarket goods but ultimately it is proposed that every article in common use on the shelves of shops handling convenience shopping will be bar coded by the Article Labelling Society. It is anticipated that by the end of 1982 80% of grocery items will have 13 digit bar coded labels marked at source by manufacturers. With this method specially designed 'guns' can be used by staff to apply an 8 digit bar code to items before they go on display. Price shelf labels which are computer-produced (and automatically reproduced at each price change) indicate prices to customers. So it is possible for a retailer to have his own bar coding machine and to introduce the system in advance of a national scheme.

A further development is the possibility of payment by specially designed 'credit' cards shown to the scanner and linked to the computer. Will this obviate, or at least minimise, the problems associated with cash transfer and the till?

The shop front

The shop front facing into the mall through which the interior is first viewed fuses the design of the mall and the design of the unit into the shopping centre. The result of this fusion, under overall control of the centre architect, is as we have already noted, the major design draw of the centre. To do this with skill, an understanding of merchandising, display policies and display methods is needed.

The imposition of over-regimented shop front control is a contradiction in terms. The entry to the shop as presented to the customer is the trader's self-expression. Each trader relies on exerting an individual and specific emphasis in order to draw in the public, consequently demanding maximum display frontage related to shop width. The diagrams illustrate the various components of the traditional shop front, with some typical shop front plans.

It is easy to trace the evolution from the early High Street shop when the owner of a house wishing to trade knocked out the ground floor and put a beam or 'bressumer' across the front to support the upper floors. The owner then set up his 'stall' (hence, the term stall riser and stall board) and opened the shop; closing it by 'putting up the shutters' at night. Technical developments such as plate glass and artificial lighting led gradually to the sophisticated standard 'High Street' shop front of today. Traditionally, materials for holding the shop front glazing were, first, timber, and later bronze or stainless steel drawn on a wood core. Today extruded metal sections are used, in particular aluminium which can be finished in a number of varying colours.

Many traders who are used to the traditional street shop front are not aware of the advantages and altered conditions offered by the covered mall – or even the open mall designed and managed centre. It is obvious that many of the features of a High Street shop front are not essential, particularly in a covered centre and the ultimate solution is to have no shop front at all and walk straight through an opening the full width of the frontage, into the shop. This treatment suits, in particular, the larger store and those stores with checkout points and self-service trading. Other types of retailer, including the smaller trader, may also be stimulated to reorganize shop interior ideas in such a way as to display merchandise without requiring a shop front. However certain traders will continue to require shop front display and it is as well to understand why such traders find this necessary.

Some multiple traders, such as shoe shops, as a policy, display every 'line' in their shop windows, and some may even have standard seasonal displays designed for use throughout their outlets. These obviously, therefore, need certain minimum and maximum standardised window arrangements and require shop window display, whether open-fronted or enclosed.

At the other extreme, the luxury fashion or jewellery shop may utilise 'shock tactics' in display, with dramatic effect (say one diamond on a velvet cushion or the magnificent fur coat!) The more this variety of treatment can be accepted and catered for the more exciting and attractive the centre, provided that it sets the scene for this scale of retailing operation.

Again, certain types of goods which rely on shine and sparkle for display need protection from dust; these include shoes and leather goods, china, glassware, silver and of course jewellery, which in addition needs, together with silver, furs, and other valuable items, special security protection. This necessitates not only enclosure in a show case but burglar alarms of various kinds.

So how is the traditional shop front affected by being in an enclosed centre? Firstly, of course, materials need no longer to be weather-resistant nor is the careful weatherproof detailing of the standard shop front required. There will be no need to consider the problem of condensation on the shop windows and with full air-conditioning both in the mall and in the unit the problem of dust can be considerably reduced; there will be no need for shop blinds and, in fact, no need for a fascia. But here we come to the question of overall control. Each shop must, of course, be allowed to identify itself in its own way, but why is there so much emphasis by controllers, whether planners or centre architects, on the provision of a standard horizontal definition by fascia? This component I suggest is an anachronistic vestigial relic of the con-

TYPES OF SHOP FRONT

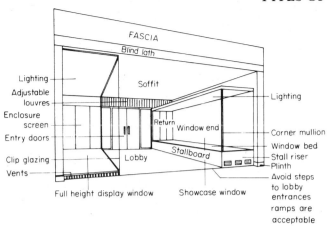

Perspective showing components of typical shop front

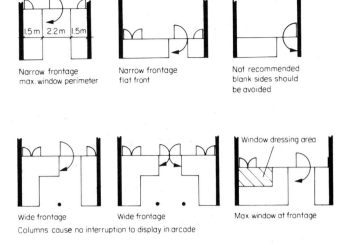

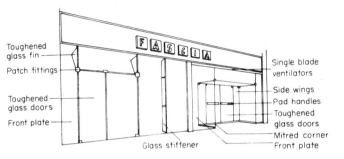

All-glass construction to shop front

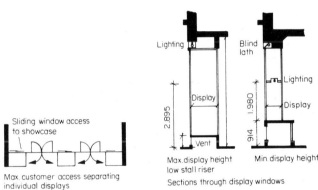

verted High Street house into a shop! There may be an argument in the High Street for defining the horizontal extent of the shop in order to preserve an existing street-scape but there are cases even in the existing open street where vertical division between units can be more attractive and certainly more logical than a horizontal one.

The definition of the shop unit within a shopping centre will be in the control of the shopping centre architect. There may in the UK, however, be a requirement under Fire Regulations in a closed mall centre of a minimum fascia depth between the shop and mall, to provide a smoke barrier, though a false ceiling with 25% perforation is allowed at a lesser depth. Moreover, 'fascia' panels of Class 3 flame spread material are only allowed for $2\,m^2$ maximum area, with $1\,m^2$ Class 0 separation from that adjoining.

Whatever the control over the 'fascia' design it should be possible, I suggest, to allow for the larger unit to express its full frontage without having a standard 'fascia' restricted in bay width by vertical divisions to that of the smaller unit. This can result in

a confusing and unnecessary repetition of name over several bays and a 'camouflage' of the true trading pattern.

Control by the centre architect is a perplexing business. The centre architect should accept that as retailers point out, it is not conducive to successful retailing or pleasant shopping to impose over-restrictive controls in type of display, window design, signing, or other characteristic trading features, in order to present a 'unified' total concept in which the individual shopping expression is subordinated to a standard overall pattern. Is it wise or even justifiable to impose one designer's definition of 'good design' on all members of a total shopping complex? A certain degree of licence is inherent in successful operation of an industry dependent by its nature on the vagaries of fashion, and variety of treatment will give interest to the malls.

Having said this, control 'upwards' to ensure quality of materials, durability, high maintenance standards – both routine and long-term – with sufficient discipline of design to contain units adequately within

Brunel Centre, Swindon (is this the road to Mandalay?)

Fairview, Montreal. Restrained treatment of the disciplined mall

Milton Keynes.
The two illustrations above show examples of fascia width restricted by vertical divisions

Fairview, Montreal. Each shop has freedom of design within its area

Milton Keynes. One retailer's reaction to the above. Setting back behind the free-standing columns has allowed a full-length fascia treatment

City 2, Brussels. No standard fascia definition. (Photo: Nigel Woolner)

the centre framework is essential so as to maintain the agreed design character of the centre.

How are shop fronts designed and by whom? In the UK there are many consultant designers and architects who specialise in this field. A number of multiples have their own 'in house' design teams; some shop-fitters also employ qualified designers – though unfortunately by no means all – and many smaller traders rely on shop-fitter's designs. It has to be acknowledged that the general standard of shop front design in the UK is not as imaginative and enterprising as one might wish, and is below the standards of inventiveness set elsewhere in Europe and the USA.

Dissatisfaction with traders' proposals has driven some developers to produce a list of approved designers and/or a design guide indicating certain solutions to shop front, shop sign and fascia which would meet with approval. This, though understandable, can lead to just the blueprint one wants to avoid. Moreover, any highly successful designer, if employed by too many units may impose his own handwriting heavily on the centre. Perhaps an alternative solution might be to demand a designer qualified under one of the professions e.g. RIBA, SIAD, with examples of work to be submitted. Thus new and adventurous design ideas might be brought forward.

In any event the skill of the centre architect, focused on the possibilities of the tenant mix, will be extended to the full to produce the variety, sparkle and centre atmosphere envisaged, by exerting just enough control to ensure the necessary quality and intent of design. This should be achieved without going over the top and imposing the centre designer's image at the expense of shopping interest, in favour of uniformity of expression. The stimulus and variety needed to supplement the draw of the large anchor unit *must* be provided by the smaller retailer.

The small shop (or specialist unit)

Let us now examine the smaller unit, which provides stimulus and variety needed as an extra attraction to the large unit.

What is a small shop? It may deal in any single, or a number of the table's categories. In the UK the London Building Act, Building Regulations and the Means of Escape provisions all deal separately with shops of sales area less than 280 m² (3000 ft²), and not more than three storeys (one of which may be a basement storey). These are defined in the British Standard Code of Practice, Chapter IV (Means of Escape in case of Fire) as 'small shops'. A Fire Certificate under the Fire Precautions Act is not required for shops employing fewer than 20 people, or 10 above the ground floor. So many specialist units in a shopping centre will come into this category, which is a useful definition of the small shop.

Accepted preferred dimensions for the small shop are:

Frontage of between 5.5 m (18 ft) and 7.3 m (20 ft) with a depth of main sales floor, depending upon trade type, number of trading levels and potential of 13.1 m (40 ft) to 39.37 m (120 ft).

The Quadrant Centre, Swansea, (Photo: Henk Snoek) and Fairview, Montreal. Two contrasting treatments of the elevational design of the frontage of a major anchor unit at the focal end of a mall

In these units maximum ground floor (or entrance floor) sales area is demanded, – a single sales floor being preferred if adequate in area. Additional sales area, if required, is preferred on a floor lower than entrance level, better than 1st floor trading and giving easier passage for customers and less obstruction of floor area by the staircase. In a shopping centre it may be possible to enter both floors direct from the mall but this will require two 'shop front' or 'shop entrance' treatments probably reducing actual sales area and involving extra fitting-out expense.

The floor area needed for ancillary use – stock and staff rooms, preparation, receiving and unpacking areas, manager's office, etc. – must be related to depth of main floor, number of staff and stock holding. This will depend on system and frequency of delivery – stock turn, mark up, sales potential, catchment area – and of course type of trade. Multiples have standardised requirements; individual traders will have their own ideas, and the availability and location of space, number of storeys within the malls, etc. will help to determine allocation, ideally in consultation with prospective tenants.

These differing characteristics are expressed in shop design and display and have transformed the appearance and character of traditional shopping areas. (Some typical layouts of small unit non-food shops are shown in the illustrations.)

Many non-food shops, such as chemists shops, shoe stores, women's fashions, have gone over to self-selection or self-service, requiring open entrances, with full view of interior, maximum circulation space for customers, maximum display and accommodation of stock on the sales floor, and sometimes check-out points. This naturally produces a very different design expression from customer service shops, and attracts a certain type of shopper with quick turn round, maximum intake and recognisable price ranges.

A few examples are given below as guidance to requirements of some shop types. Each trade or service will have different specialist requirements for space and service installations, which should be 'researched' by the centre architect to ensure ease of satisfactory fitting-out and equipment.

Women's and men's fashion shops
These may vary in size from the specialist unit selling one type of merchandise only to the larger (400 m² selling space or over) fashion store selling a number of related items.

Windows and all display will need flexibility to take provisional seasonal display, size and design depending on character which must be identifiable by the 'shop front' (or its substitute in an open mall) together with the interior design and finish. The ideal interior is a flexible plan with movable equipment. While self-selection merchandise is displayed on free standing wall racks with wide circulation routes, personal service will probably involve protected counters and cabinets with specialised displays at prominent points. This creates a totally different atmosphere from the 'walk round' now familiar self-selection routine.

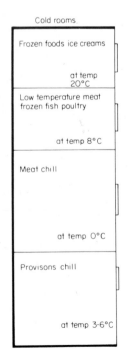

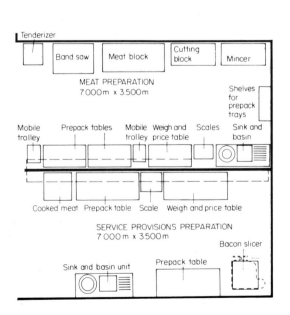

Typical layout for meat and service provisions;
preparation rooms
Cold room storage related to temperature
higher temperature: smaller area
lower temperature: larger area

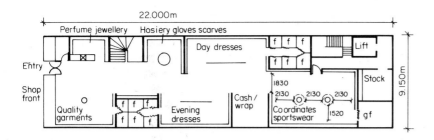

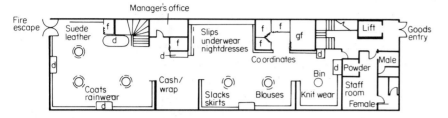

Typical layout for women's fashion store
  f. fitting room, min. size 1200 × 900 mm (with staff assistance
  1200 × 1200 mm)
  g.f. group fitting room
  d. display

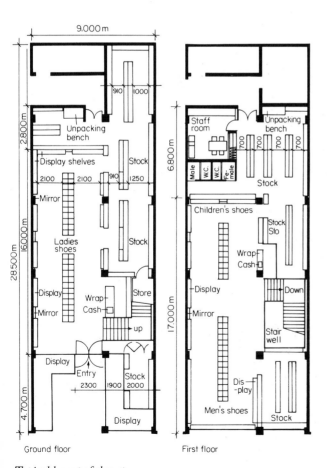

Typical layout of shoe store

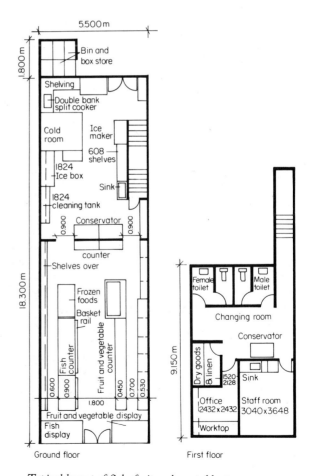

Typical layout of fish, fruit and vegetable store

51

There may be centralised service desks with cash tills or registers and wrapping counters – this going also for self-selection. Fitting rooms may also be a requirement. Display lighting will need mobility and variety.

Shoe shops
Correct planning of stock areas is the essential key to successful trading, as the necessary merchandise in all sizes must be readily available related to lines on display. The layout of stock areas will control the time taken to serve a customer or to replace stock taken from self-service bays. In customer service shops the chair layout is a controlling factor.

Jewellery shops
The articles on display are small and valuable. They need to be viewed from short range, lit to emphasise their 'allure', while needing special security measures, e.g. window grilles, protected cabinets, burglar alarm systems, safes for night storage, and special display techniques. Service is personal, generally from behind enclosed glass-fronted display counters.

Hairdressing
This may be a very desirable 'draw' for a shopping centre – particularly with the tendency to 'unisex' hairdressing. The 'shop front' and signing will identify the type of service. The interior will comprise three basic service positions:
Dressing table, for cutting, styling, setting, 'blow-drying'.
Shampoo basins.
Driers.
There will also be a reception area, cash desk and cloakroom. There may also be beauty rooms, and galley kitchen for customers' snacks. Adequate provision (with sufficient water pressure) to provide for constant and reliable hot and cold water service to basins, as well as ventilation (due to use of hot air driers) requires special attention.

Other trades
Other specialist trades worth noting are:

Dry cleaners and launderettes which will also require special services, e.g. electrical, plumbing, ventilation and extract.

Furniture Display areas suitable for large displays, and perhaps 'room settings' etc. will be needed.

Hardware, stationery, bookshops These will require heavy floor loading.

Chemist shops Require security provisions for drug storage and facilities for making-up prescriptions.

Small specialist trades
There is also a demand for small specialised trades and service outlets needing narrow frontages and minimum storage (even from, say 6 ft frontage 12 ft depth upward!). These units should, with effect, and sometimes conveniently, be offered to attract the local 'speciality' small retailer who cannot by reason of his restricted turnover afford the rent and size of a standard unit, but offers a particular inducement to shoppers who might not otherwise be attracted to the centre. Classic examples are the repairer (shoes, watches) the second-hand bookshop, the philatelist or numismatist, the craft shop and the key-cutter.

Specialist food shops
These may trade in one or several of the food categories listed in Table 1. Their internal layout and requirements will be generally as those of the self-service food store, though their display methods will vary. Their insertion into the centre needs careful handling in relation to maintenance, amenity and general suitability, and they are better sited as a group rather than interspersed amongst, for instance, fashion shops.

Banks
A bank is a necessary facility in the one-stop centre, though an urban centre may be able to rely on availability of banking facilities on the perimeter, – outside the centre.

Sometimes a cash point service conveniently situated will be an acceptable substitute for full banking facilities. This is best sited somewhere off the main circulation routes of the mall, and separated from shops units.

Banks have two disadvantages within the centre. First, unless very carefully sited they disturb the shopping sequence and secondly, their opening hours will not coincide with those of the centre. Their requirements are specialised and will include construction of a specially protected strong room, probably computer facilities and special security measures, including structural integrity and secure cash transfer arrangements.

The large unit
General requirements
We have seen how the disposition, number and character of the large units influence the centre. They include the department store, variety store, supermarket, hypermarket. In order to design them into the centre it is necessary to assess their trading methods, requirements characteristics and certain basic differences from the smaller retailer which apply to all large space users.

Large units will pay a reduced rental per square foot as compared with the smaller unit, so the taking of maximum internal space related to frontage will be an advantage to the developer. The large unit does not rely greatly on window display, and overlong frontages can be wasteful in fitting-out and use of display resources without much affecting turnover. As nothing is more detrimental to the shopping potential of the centre than 'dead' or blanked-off frontages along the mall, a 'T' or 'L' plan, allowing small units to be tucked in along the frontages, is one useful solution.

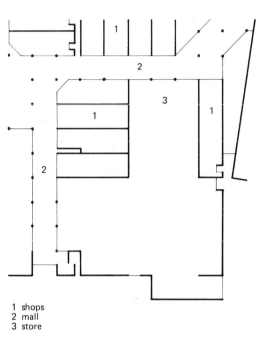

1 shops
2 mall
3 store

Quadrant Centre, Swansea. T or L Plan showing small units along the frontage of large store

The large units will however want wide entrances, perhaps with open fronts, with strong views into the store at all levels.

The large space users will want maximum uninterrupted sales area for flexibility in layout, and the preferred grid is not likely to suit the standard unit width.

The ideal solution is to accept the differing requirements of small and large units and vary both horizontal and vertical grids as between them in the basic design. Where this is not possible one solution is a multiple of the standard unit, say 11 m (36 ft), on the frontage which will give various permutations of standard unit and suit the large user. The depth of beam required for large spans will of course stretch the vertical dimensions, and this may be expensive as well as unacceptable to the small unit, remembering the

increased cost of extending external walls, stairs, lifts, escalators and pipes and service ducts. Where not serving the small unit also, a grid of 7.3 m to 9 m (23–29 ft) on the frontage, by 9.15 m (30 ft) deep may be a useful guide.

Height from floor to underside of structural slab should not be excessive, and may be approximately 4 m (13 ft) with 5 m (16 ft) absolute maximum. This should allow for adequate duct space and smoke reservoirs with an acceptable ceiling height, say 3.66 m (12 ft) beam depths in framed construction must be taken into consideration as limiting the free space available. Where a key trader demands extensive storage of greater height than 5 m a specially designed unit will be the best answer, if justifiable and agreed early enough.

In multi-level units it is important to ensure that perimeter walls follow the same lines vertically from floor to floor without horizontal projections to facilitate vertical circulation planning of lifts, escalators and staircases.

Large space users are likely to prefer to provide and control their own mechanical and electrical services, including heating, ventilating, air conditioning, refrigeration and perhaps security (though this is likely to be connected into the centre security system also). Adequate and convenient plant room area may need to be allowed for.

Means of escape, structural fire precautions, compartmentation sprinklering, smoke control and smoke venting will need to be negotiated individually in respect of each large unit, and this should be undertaken as early as possible in the planning of the project. Under UK provision, a large unit, over 1500 m^2 floor area per floor, will need its own smoke control system to contain smoky gases within the store. It will also need fire shutters or incombustible window entrances onto the mall. Shutter openings of maximum size 4.5 m height 8.5 m long are permitted.

We have already considered servicing the large unit. With increasing fuel and transport costs the routine use of the maximum size vehicle must be accepted, i.e. 15 m (50 ft) length with 4.9 m (16 ft 6 in) height clearance, and with related turning and parking space. Loading bays with platforms, where required, must be planned into the scheme to serve all large units from commencement. Many large space users will insist on delivery positions within their own control as part of their own leased area.

The department store
The department store is the most complex and sophisticated shop type. It will encompass most of the trades and services enumerated in Table 1, brought together into one trading and financial control.

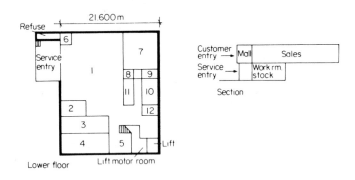

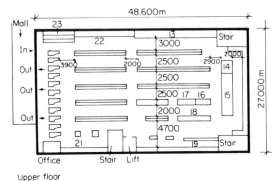

Typical layout of supermarket: 1. Grocery store room; 2. Frozen foods store; 3. Service provisions store; 4. Meat preparation; 5. Fruit/vegetable preparation; 6. Security cage; 7. Toilet/cloakrooms; 8. Manager's office; 9. Kitchen; 10. Staff room; 11. Wine store; 12. General office; 13. Cooked meats/dairy; 14. Frozen meat; 15. Poultry; 16. Fish; 17. Home freezer; 18. Ice cream; 19. Serviced provisions; 20. Fruit/vegetables; 21. Self service wine/spirits; 22. Promotions; 23. Trolleys

It is axiomatic that site allocation should precede detail planning, design and construction of the centre, and it is unprofitable to consider erection of a department store shell without consultation with the department store management. But certain requirements will have to be determined at planning stage.

A department store will require a minimum sales area of 10 000 m², more likely to be 20 000 m², and therefore by definition will need to be multi-storey. An irregularly-shaped site may not be a disadvantage bearing in mind the large number of varied uses to be incorporated into the store.

Entrances from the malls must be distinctive and inviting, with strong incisive signing indicating the extent and dominance of the store.

The store is likely to provide its own design brief, and perhaps even its own design and construction team, but it must nevertheless be integrated into the centre, under overall control of the centre architect. Some major requirements therefore need to be understood.

Circulation of goods will be from point of service entry, through receiving, unpacking, stock-rooms, to display and selling points, and possibly also back through packing dispatch, or return, at point of service exit if not taken out by the customer. Allocation of departments will follow a trading policy, affected by unit selling time. Small items and 'impulse sales' goods being on entrance floors and 'demand' goods on upper and lower levels, the relation of entrances from the various malls is of prime importance.

A large staff (up to, say, 300) will require separate staff entry for signing in and checking out, with adequate staff locker rooms space, lavatory and rest room accommodation, staff canteen, first aid or medical centre, besides lecture rooms and other training facilities. Display teams will require studio and workshops.

Administration may include offices for finance (including access for account customers and possibly a computer room) personnel, advertising and management, besides office and interview space for buyers. Waste disposal will be needed for each floor. Confidential information may require a baler or shredder and a baling room (say 3 m × 3 m).

Workrooms for repairs and servicing of electrical goods, making up of curtains and carpets, etc. may be needed, and a café, restaurant and customer toilets are almost certain to be required.

The whole concept will revolve around the sales areas on various floors as connected by lifts, staircases and escalators to customer entrances and exits on the one hand, and staff and services on the other (see illustrations).

A major complication will be fire protection regulations, particularly 'compartmentation' to contain spread of fire. Under the UK Building Regulations the maximum permissible compartment is 4000 m² with sprinkler protection; 2000 m² without. Smoke reservoirs and smoke extraction will also be needed.

If a food hall is incorporated into the store, requirements will be much as for supermarkets and/or individual food shops, with adequate space for refrigeration, food preparation, specialised waste disposal and drainage, hygiene and stock provision.

The variety store, supermarket, super store, hypermarket
These units are becoming increasingly difficult to define as they constantly expand in size and choice of merchandise.

The variety store sells a variety of goods and ranges in size from, say, 200 m² to 15 000 m² sales area, offering a wide range of merchandise mainly by self-selection. The sales area will be fully open, with self-selection goods displayed on racks and counters, and visual identification of departments limited to display and signing. It may embrace a food section, but although this is likely to be fully self-service with check-out points, it may not encompass the same full range of household convenience goods as the supermarket.

Different types of variety store will have different sales emphasis (Marks and Spencer, British Home Stores, Littlewoods, Boots are obvious British examples of the 'variety' of trading). Other large units are mainly food stores, comprising the supermarket, super store and hypermarket.

The supermarket is generally understood to be a self-service food shop of an area between $400\,m^2$ and $2000\,m^2$ sales area and usually devoted almost exclusively to food retailing.

The super store with a sales area greater than $2500\,m^2$, though based primarily on food, also stocks non-food lines.

The hypermarket is an extension of the super store, mainly in size, and consequently in range of goods offered both food and non-food. The accepted idea of the hypermarket is that of the one-stop out of town project for the car-motivated shopper to whom it appeals on grounds of convenience. It differs from the greenfield shopping centre in being operated by one trader on a strictly utility basis. However, there are successful examples of the introduction of hypermarket principles into the urban shopping centre. An example is Tesco in the Victoria Centre Nottingham which is to all intents and purposes a hypermarket within a centre. It is interesting to note that this unit started as a department store and was only later transferred to Tesco.

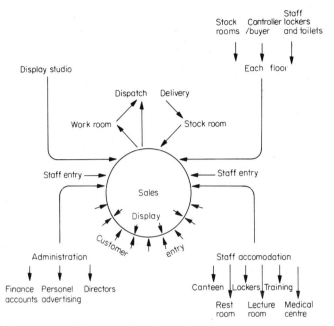

Disposition of elements and analysis of circulation in a department store

The food store

The mainly food store differs in some major respects from non-food retailing and needs separate examination when considered in relation to the shopping centre. It has to be accepted that profit on food sales is comparatively low and the big firms need non-food lines and corresponding increased sales area to boost their profits while needing a high proportion of food sales to maintain a regular flow.

Between 1961 and 1978 the proportion of consumer spending on food (UK figures*) fell from 24.5% to 18.8%. The traditional 'food only' supermarket seems on the decline, giving way to the 'mini-market' corner shop or small limited range discount store at one end of the market and the big over $25\,000\,m^2$ superstore, with plenty of space for more profitable non-food sales at the other. The gross profit margin in a superstore could be, say, 15%, with food items at 12% and non-food items 20%. Fresh food needs a bigger gross margin than groceries to account for wastage, labour and preparation. Obviously the more intensive the use, the lower the % of turnover goes on overheads except for variable cost such as wages.

Some analysts believe that the UK can only take another hundred or so superstores; this would pre-

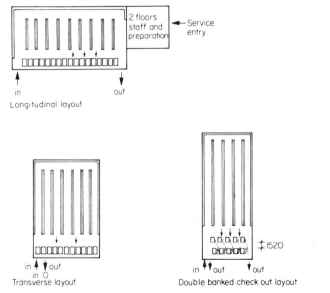

Three methods of layouts for check-out points layouts are determined by size and shape of site. Generally, double banked check-outs are used for very narrow frontages to allow for a faster customer throughput. A bar runs centrally between check-outs in outer lane to determine direction of thoroughfare

* These figures are from an article by Patience Wheatsheaf *Sunday Times*, February 3rd 1980

sumably result in fierce competition for prime sites, and the shopping centre, offering good transport facilities and other benefits, will presumably increasingly attract and welcome the presence of the superstore/hypermarket unit.

The earlier centres have shown a reluctance in accepting the self-service food store, either excluding it or siting it on the perimeter. There is an argument that food shopping takes place frequently, thus serving a limited catchment area, and once trolleys or baskets are filled and heavy, the shopper tends to leave the centre to go home ignoring comparison shopping. Nevertheless the super store has certainly found its way into the British centre, sometimes as a major component of the complex.

Its success as a major attraction will depend to a considerable degree on facilities for easy trolley access to car parks and general encouragement to return to the centre after loading. Immediate access to public transport, such as bus stations, is also necessary for the non-car-owning population. Maybe promotion is needed to emphasise sales priorities, i.e. comparison and leisure shopping first, convenience shopping at end of visit.

Specialist requirements for self-service food stores governing various types of food sales will be those also applying to specialist food shops. The main food categories have been given in Table 1. They separate into 'dry foods' and 'wet foods'.

The main layout for dry goods will be island and wall racking related to check-out points. Customer and counter service will be needed for delicatessen and certain provisions ('wet foods') adjoining preparation areas. Chilled and deep freeze cabinets, both for counter selling and self-service will be sited in permanent positions, needing drainage connections as well as refrigeration services. The off-licence will need special security measures and approvals. Preparation areas with cooking, baking and pre-packing facilities must conform to hygiene standards with adequate sink, waste disposal and washing facilities.

The proportion of perishable to non-perishable goods will affect the layout of storage, cold storage and preparation areas, where perishable goods, e.g. meat, fish, cheese, bacon, will be prepared and pre-packed.

A major consideration will be the method of servicing and restocking sales shelves. This may be by fork-lift truck, and the type of container will relate to floor to ceiling height, type of storage container and customer access. The storage requirements of a large store, particularly if a mainly food store, must be ascertained as early as possible, as they will affect elevational design, servicing, fire safety and construction. Some companies work on a storage racking height of more than 4 m.

A very serious consideration is that of mechanical, and electrical services, in particular of refrigeration and its accompanying problems.

A major reason for the success of the self-service food store of all sizes and grades is refrigeration. The refrigerated unit, the cold store, and at the receiving end and from the shoppers viewpoint, the domestic deep-freeze, all affect the selling process, and have by no means been finally resolved. One result of the success of the domestic deep-freeze has been the emergence of sales units successfully offering food produce only for transfer to the domestic deep-freeze (which requires urgency of transport between point of sale and domestic transfer). Skill in siting of food emphasis shopping is therefore a major consideration – surely better on the way *back* to car parking and exit, than on the way in to the centre.

The layout arrangement of racked-out departments must be planned in relation to the check-out points through which every customer must pass, and where congestion will occur. This is a good argument for direct access from check-out points for customers with their trolleys to car park without traversing the mall where trolleys are not usually allowed.

The food retailing industry has a very special and important influence on social, environmental and economic natural life. A considerable amount of analysis and reasearch is continuing, and its results should be studied by the architect and all those concerned with the general and particular problems of providing the framework in which food retailing is to operate.

Supermarket layout. Use of space on irregular site: 1. Basket stackers;.2. Trolleys; 3. Cigarette kiosk; 4. Dairy; 5. Cooked meat; 6. Fresh meat; 7. Poultry; 8. Bakery; 9. Delicatessen; 10. Home freezer packs; 11. Ice cream; 12. Frozen foods; 13. Fish; 14. Sugar and eggs

The market

It may be that in assembling the site for a shopping centre in an urban area the local authority may impose as a condition the accommodation of a market. This need not be a disadvantage; in fact it may be a considerable asset to the centre. But it is important to appreciate the difference between market trading and that of a shopping centre.

The main characteristic of the market is that it is a public area, open or covered, provided with stalls where a trader may sell his wares on recognised market days subject to paying a statutory charge. The UK legal definition is 'the franchise right of having a concourse of buyers and sellers to dispose of commodities in respect of which the franchise is given'. The holder of the franchise has the sole and exclusive right of holding a market within 6⅔ miles of his own market. This however does not interfere with the provision of a shopping concourse where a trader has no *right* to space for displaying or selling of his wares

as he has in a franchise market on recognised market days. There will be a market authority responsible for control, which in a market attached to a shopping centre is likely to also be the local authority.

As an adjunct of the shopping centre the market has proved itself a draw but it needs to be correctly designed and sited. It must have direct access from the street, car park or public transport system and also connect into the centre to generate pedestrian flow.

In design it must offer a complete contrast to the remainder of the shopping centre. The building, basic amenities and stalls will probably be designed by the centre architect although the market may be managed perhaps not by the centre management but by the market authority. It must be remembered that the attraction of the market is low overheads and bargain prices, and the contrast between the sophisticated amenities of the main shopping centre and the simplicity of the market stalls is part of its essential character and the market traders' overheads must not escalate.

'The Market'. The new market is an extension of the existing Grainger market. It is designed around a double-height volume through which escalators rise to connect to the mall system. A 4 m unit for smaller traders suits the standard grid (Photo: Brecht-Einzig)

Brunel Centre, Swindon. The market. (Photo: Martin Charles)

Where a market is replacing an existing one it is as well to examine the conditions and facilities previously available; they must not be increased to the extent that they jeopardize the economic advantage of the market. We are surely familiar with instances where long established markets functioning in unplanned locations have been moved to new purpose-built accommodation with disastrous results. Too often the ambience disappears under a new architectural framework which with the best intentions, while providing much needed hygiene and complying with all current regulations, loses the essential market character.

The construction should preferably be wide span warehouse type, probably utilising daylight in order to minimise running costs. If two-level, the upper level is likely to have balcony access to perimeter stalls connected to the lower level by escalators, the roof being visible from the ground floor level. In this case, access to the shopping centre proper should be available at both levels.

The full degree of sophisticated environmental services needed for a shopping centre are unlikely to be either economic or beneficial in a market though adequate ventilation is essential and careful attention is needed to servicing. There must be ease of access for the delivery and storage or goods and the removal of waste and rubbish. Permanent finishes must be easily cleaned and durable, allowing for 'muck-down' and floor cleaning facilities with adequate drainage. Sanitary accommodation i.e. lavatories and washbasins will need to be provided bearing in mind the statutory requirements for sale and preparation of food.

Storage areas may be grouped perhaps at the rear of perimeter stalls; possibly in wired-off sections accessible to individual traders.

Consideration must be given to the mix of permanent and non-permanent stalls. Perimeter stalls will attract higher rents and must be provided with a service corridor at the rear for easy stocking. But many small traders only exist by means of a stall on a daily basis e.g. flower sellers. This type of trade will contribute considerably to the overall atmosphere for the market and should be encouraged.

Specialist food traders, such as fishmongers, should be located together allowing ease of comparison shopping, and enabling more sophisticated services for ventilation and washing down with removal of waste provided in one part of the market rather than spread throughout the whole area.

The design of the market stalls must be considered carefully in relation to the traditional market concept. A stall will be a simply contained framework providing selling space in terms of display, storage and service area with a fascia or a means of displaying a 'logo' or with possibly, in the case of permanent stalls some provision for lock-up storage.

Variety is a major factor in giving life to markets. Standard fascia and type faces for stall holders are a ridiculous denial of the whole market idea. Probably stalls will have open ceilings and very basic artificial lighting; a certain vulgarity should be encouraged, not resisted. The 'cheap and cheerful' image is an essential characteristic of the market stall-holders selling potential.

Stalls therefore must be designed as a simple element of incombustible material capable of withstanding rough treatment. The art of designing new market accommodation generally must lie in providing a flexible infrastructure allowing the tenant maximum control over his own selling area.

Chapter 7
The architect's role

Consultation

The point is now reached for consideration of the architect's specific role in the implementation of the sketch design of the centre into production information, erection and commissioning, and the particular characteristics of specialised procedures which will be required.

The local authority is bound to play a key part in the creation of any shopping centre. Often it is involved financially to some degree, but anyway controlling planning, building and fire regulations and being responsible for supply of many essential services. It is more than possible that the aims of the developer and the local authority may not always coincide and it is advisable for the architect to get to know and understand the departments concerned and to be able to negotiate with them on a day to day basis.

The consultant team will have been assembled and involved in consultations throughout the early stages. They will, it is hoped, have included the structural, mechanical and electrical, landscaping and graphics consultants. Also consulted will have been the escalator and lift, sprinklers and ventilation and refrigeration equipment specialists, the local authority and/or private contractors concerned with waste disposal, as well as the Statutory Authorities for electricity, gas, water and drainage and the insurance broker to the developers. There will have been others as well.

As we have seen, leasing will start at an early stage, in advance of construction. Therefore leasing documents will be required in advance of production drawings. They should comprise, as a minimum, a brochure giving the following information:

1. dimensional floor plans, showing location of anchor stores and occupancy types,
2. specification giving extent of provision of finishes to shell,
3. a description of services,

4. extent of design constraints on tenants,
5. indications of finishes, materials, character of communal spaces, and malls; community facilities offered to customers and tenants,
6. details of approvals and waivers given and required.

This is a basic service from the architect and must be comprehensive, clear, accurate and fully descriptive for the use of the retailer.

Models of the centre, both general and possibly in some detail, will be helpful. Adjustments are likely, both at this stage and later as production documents progress, to suit tenant demand, in particular for the major users who may be employing their own architect for erection of their own building within the general complex.

There will also be 'participation' exercises with the local community who will need, both individually and through local societies, to be informed and persuaded of the desirability of the scheme.

Approvals

Simultaneously consultation must take place with consulting authorities, concerning, in the UK, the Health and Safety at Work Act, Building Regulations, Fire Precautions, Smoke Control, Means of Escape, Access for Fire Fighting, the Police (concerning security), Environmental Health Requirements, Insurance clearance and all other controlling Acts and Regulations needed to implement proposals into approvals.

It is not enough to deal with the shell only. The completed units must be envisaged, considering finishes, staff and stock provisions, vertical and horizontal circulation, so that all possible likely restrictions can be planned for in advance, and waivers considered and obtained, or tenants forewarned, as necessary.

59

In the UK existing Building Regulations are not appropriate to the closed shopping centre (see Chapter 9). Waivers will be required, needing consultation and negotiation with local authorities and probably directly with the Deparment of the Environment. The Fire Authority will also need to be consulted and sufficient preparation time for consultation before finalising of plans must be built into the programme as this may be a lengthy process, involving many facets of the design.

In ascertaining and meeting these requirements the developer's Insurance Co. will also have to be satisfied, in line with the requirements of the Fire Offices Committee rules as appropriate and a balance drawn up comparing capital cost with requirements of the insurance company for various premium rates, before decisions are finalised. Plans showing sprinkler and other fire safety proposals, with specific information about water supply and standby 'power' supply will have to be submitted to the insurers for approval.

Contract and production information

Due to the length of time taken in assembling the site, settling finance, obtaining Planning, Building Regulations, Means of Escape and other principal approvals etc., pressure will be on the architect and the contractor for minimum time to elapse between establishment of final brief and completion of contract. The type of contract will affect the time, scale and content of production information.

Competitive tenders may be required, or alternatively the contract may be negotiated by the developer with a contractor (or the contractor may even be the developer). The contractual method will affect the phasing and type of production information as it may not be possible within a telescoped programme to provide all production information (i.e. drawings, specifications and bills of quantities) before commencement, and the contractor must be fully aware of the conditions.

In the case of a negotiated contract the contractor may be brought into the discussion covering construction. This can be productive in terms of time, cost and programming but it must be remembered that the contractor's responsibility ends virtually at completion of the contract, and decisions made in order to facilitate quicker and perhaps more economical construction do not necessarily result in the best long term economically successful solutions in terms, for example, of flexibility, durability and quality. These matters need very careful analysis before decisions are taken.

Two absolutely vital elements in the successful execution of the contract are maintenance of agreed programme and budgetary control. It must be appreciated that retailing is seasonal, – to miss a scheduled peak trading period can involve serious loss of return. These peak periods such as those coinciding with national holidays – Christmas being a major example – need a lead-in period of perhaps several weeks to take full advantage of the potential. So disturbance of programmed opening dates, however far ahead, will be a serious matter for the developer and the retailers, and every effort has to be made to maintain completion dates to suit desired peak trading. The progress charts and overall contract programme should be formulated with this in mind. Phased completion needs to be considered in the context of the calender and its likely effect on the various units, the letting agent and/or developer being involved in the programming as well as those retailers who are already committed.

The need for close immediate and reliable knowledge of running costs of the centre throughout the contract is absolute. In an exercise where the delicate balance between capital expenditure and income controls success or failure, contract costs cannot be allowed to escalate unnoticed or unreported. On the other hand there is no venture where variations are more likely to appear, due to site conditions, late requirements of tenants, etc. and of course the likely length of the contract. So a carefully disciplined and continuous cost check must be part of the supervision procedure – this of course covering all sub-contract and consulting work – and regular, say, monthly intervals reported back to the developer so that wherever possible steps can be taken to compensate. The microprocessor and the computer may increasingly play a part in arriving at quick solutions based on comparisons of alternative courses of action and their effect on the contract and the centre.

When the contract is programmed for phased take-over, this will be affected by availability of services which will have to be specially designed to suit the phasing programme as they may have serious repercussions on the working of the centre. For instance, draining down of the sprinkler installation might even involve closing that part of the centre already trading, where cut-off valves in sprinkler installations to occupied shops are not permitted under the F.O.C. Code. As an alternative, freezing of sprinkler mains may be necessary, though this is expensive.

The contract will inevitably have to be so phased and arranged that retailers at the time of taking over their units, whether in advance of completion or at any later time (say for changeover of tenant, or revised shopfitting schemes), can rely on adequate arrangements for direct supply to shop of building materials, plant, power, etc. to equip their units, while Means of Escape, Structural Fire Precautions and other requirements are maintained for units trading during building or shop-fitting works. Retailers will need assurances that they will not be disrupted by later modifications.

In a large complex the contract will need to take special strict fire precautions, particularly at fitting-out stage when combustible materials are stored on site in bulk, and final facilities and warning systems are not complete. Dry risers, access routes and other fire fighting facilities need to be programmed to be available at this stage and throughout the contract and liaison with the Fire Authority must be established at commencement. Completed shells and other areas not in use and not yet sprinklered should be protected by hoardings or otherwise to avoid their use for dumping of goods or waste which may become a fire hazard.

But whatever the programme, certain main elements of production information peculiar to the shopping centre must be resolved, developed and included in the main contract, remembering all the time the division between processes carried out under developer's contract and those left to the retailer.

Chapter 8
Technology

Construction

I need not here embark on a technical dissertation on comparative structural systems applying to all large building types. It is, however, necessary to refer to the specialist difficulties encountered in determining the best constructional method for an individual shopping centre – each one of which will have its own special problems.

A major specific of the shopping centre is the likely difference between requirements for shop units and those for the malls and courts, as well as ancillary functions. The shapes, dimensions, mechanical and electrical requirements and services will be different. Moreover, the shop units will probably be handed over to tenants as shells for fitting out, while the malls and common parts of the centre will be designed and controlled by the centre architect down to the last detail.

The construction may need to support a multi-storey superstructure, of say offices or housing, or have basement or roof car parks or have designed into it various ancillary uses. Many of these considerations may determine or affect the structural system or systems. But basically certain rules apply.

Shop unit construction needs to be as flexible as possible from two aspects, unit size and use within the unit. Flexibility of the constructional system is needed because of the varying needs of retailers. Particularly in multi-level units each will have their own preferences for staircase, escalator/lift, hoist and duct positions. (There is also a Means of Escape problem, referred to in other chapters). Moreover, tenancies – and even size of unit tenancy – may change during the operation of the centre, and consequently new openings may need to be formed, existing ones filled in and unit dimensions altered.

A framed beam column system whether R.C. or steel, is more flexible than flat slab and column, though the latter may be quicker and more economical to erect and, with shallower construction, result in

lower overall height. *In situ* R.C. – e.g. flat slab, waffle, etc. – may also be more practical in erection and is probably the system favoured by contractors as being within their control. This system is more likely to be acceptable in mall or court construction where design decisions once made will be a permanent feature of the centre, though depending for its economy on regular spans this may not always be relevant. Precast or infill beam construction may also be easier to adapt rather than *in situ* systems of main beam and column grid, with cross beams. Infill precast planks and structural topping of approx 8 ft span, for example, offer maximum opportunity for forming new stair-wells and other openings, though there is an argument against precast slab construction under vehicle load.

Steel frame is an economical, flexible and easily erected system if it does not require fire protection by means of solid cover. Generally, in the UK, in single storey buildings where the roof is a true roof and not a vehicular or service deck, unprotected steel is permissible. Otherwise the fire resistance rating is likely to be a minimum of 2 hours requiring adequate cover. This applies to malls also. With concrete casing, steel immediately suffers from the disadvantages of reinforced concrete, wet trades, shuttering, setting time resulting in as large or larger members as R.C. Dry casing may be an alternative solution for beams, though columns will need solid casing as protection for durability.

Thus, for various reasons, steel is not at present likely to be the preferred solution for multi-level shop unit construction. However, things may be changing; an interesting recent development is fire protection of structural steel which could influence future choice. An increasing range of lightweight non-asbestos materials for fire cover is becoming available. Developments in boards, sprays and intumescent paints are also likely to change the present situation in the 1980s. It is even possible that some fabricators will be able to supply to site steel treated with a combined fire and corrosion protection system. Another potential area of development is the production of steel with high temperature properties enabling structural engineers to design steel frames able to withstand fire.

If conditions and Regulations allow exposed steel, the cost of corrosion protection of steel used externally and exposed must be considered. New improved 'weathering' steels are being developed which will not need corrosion protection. The new weathering steel has been shown to stabilize in the UK after about two years to a shade of brown or purple and is easy to weld. But care in detailing to avoid continually wet surfaces and staining of the materials is needed and the steel should be 'blast cleaned' after fabrication.

Whatever system is adopted Fire Protection must be incorporated into the shell construction as shops may not all be shop-fitted before trading commences and empty units must have full structural protection. In the UK all construction of a covered shopping centre must be incombustible and horizontal compartmentation between levels, even within small individual units, must be 2 hours minimum fire resistant, – or 4 hours under basement conditions.

Dimensions

We will now look at dimensions. Grid size must be related to standard unit. Dimensions giving a shop frontage centre line to centre of between 5 m (16 ft) and 6 m (19 ft 4 in) is usually found to give a workable shop unit, but a grid width as large as possible will give variety of unit letting. An 11 m (36 ft) grid for instance will allow a permutation of frontages between 3.7 m (12 ft) 5.5 m (18 ft) and 7.3 m (24 ft) but the longer the span the deeper the beam, and consequently the greater the required floor to floor height.

The demanded front to back depth of unit may vary between 12 m (40 ft) and 36 m (120 ft) which will help determine the grid depth while allowing variation of unit plan shape. As far as possible, too, the grid dimensions should be constant throughout the units as variation will result in variation also in beam size and consequent 'stretching' of the vertical dimension and overall height.

Large units may request an enlarged grid, perhaps to suit their modular planning and this can probably be conceded when letting is agreed at inception. The determination of a suitable grid is complicated where basement car parking is incorporated, as an economical car park grid of 16 m × 19 m (52 ft × 62 ft) is not compatible with shop dimensions. Altering the grid at any level involves complicated construction, wasteful in construction time, beam depths and cost, although pressure to do this may be brought on the developer by key tenants.

Where offices, flats or other different use buildings are superimposed on the centre it may be inevitable,

involving a constructional transfer system with its attendant complications.

In designing the structural frame, beams supporting party walls between units should not be wider than the walls they support, as where hoists, lifts, staircases or escalators are required by tenants they are likely to be sited against the party walls and will want flush vertical surfaces to maximise use of shop width, (see diagram).

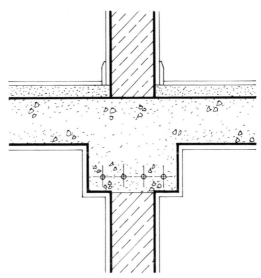

Unacceptable section through party wall between units

Load bearing division walls between units are to be avoided, as precluding redeployment of units to suit the larger or smaller retailer. So a column and beam or slab system whether reinforced concrete or steel is almost certain to be the solution. Beam depths should be kept to a minimum to allow service voids and smoke reservoirs to be of economical vertical height; mushroom construction also suffers from this disadvantage as well as being inflexible.

The position of columns between mall and shops is important as already indicated. Columns do not necessarily have to be situated on the main shop front line, as they tend to restrict shop front design and the use of individual scale to express the larger unit. Columns can play a subsidiary role to the shop front in order to allow variety of treatment and emphasise the individual retailers.

There are many examples of the column grid being kept clear of shop front lines by being sited forward into the malls, or behind the shop front. If it is necessary to place them on the shop front line they should really be so positioned that shop fronts to small units are not unduly restricted and in a multiple-unit shop front the 'fascia' and other tenant's design members can run past and in front of them. This will avoid the somewhat absurd device – a 'stammering' repetition of shop name or logo on adjoining divided bays in one occupation already alluded to. It should be accepted that retailers may like to express the size of their unit, and this is also of interest to shoppers. A rigid vertical emphasis offers the danger of a monotony of treatment and a distorted scale.

Floor to floor height also poses a problem. Large space users will want, say, 3.66 m clear height with adequate depth (say 1.2 m) between ceiling and structural slab for ducting. The type of false ceiling will also influence floor to structural slab height as an open or slatted ceiling will obviate the need for double sprinklering regardless of depth of void, and also enable the void to be used as a smoke reservoir. In the case of a solid false ceiling this will need to be considered as within the floor to false ceiling height, or provided by grilles or slots in a solid false ceiling. The depth of the smoke reservoir will be calculated from the soffit of the deepest beam.

Smaller units may prefer limited height, say, 3 m max. floor to floor, to avoid excessive costs in heating/cooling, ventilation, and in multi-level units to avoid unnecessary effort by staff or customers in vertical circulation.

In single level trading it may be possible, by providing a height of 4 m (14 ft) floor to underside of slab, to offer smaller units the facility of mezzanine or balcony level storage or sales, if they also have the option of a lower false ceiling.

Normal loadings for shopping centres would be in the following order:

Malls: (a) 100 lb/ft² Public pedestrian access only
         5 kN/m²
     (b) 200 lb/ft² Pedestrian plus light fire
         10 kN/m² tender access only.
                  (i.e. Land Rover or similar).
     (c) 300 lb/ft² Access for all fire brigade
         15 kN/m² units.

Large shop units including stores: 10 kN/m² (200 lb/ft²)

(Also needed for storage of books, groceries, stationery.)

Small shop units including stores: 7½ kN/m² (150 lb/ft²)

Note: Generally storage loadings are determined on basis of height of storage at a rate of 2.4 kN/m² per m/height.

If the roof and other intermediate levels are to be used for servicing, fire fighting, landscaped areas, car parking, plant rooms, play centre etc., the slab and finish will have to be designed accordingly.

If servicing is at roof level, goods vehicle loading in the UK must be to MoT standard (the maximum permitted *wheel* load is 7.5 tonnes). Passenger car

Brunel Centre, Swindon. Roof servicing area

parking only requires 3.83 kN/m² (80 lb/ft²). Landscaping for lawn – say topsoil and drainage – will be within this limit but trees in concrete 'boxes', for instance, may impose point loads of 53.65 kN/m² (½ ton/ft²).

The construction of the roof ramps, and canopies and their finish is critical, as damage or water penetration requiring internal repair may involve heavy claims by retailers for loss of profit. The position of insulation and the type of jointing are major danger points. A maximum length between joints should be 150 m (500 ft).

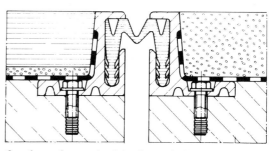

One form of expansion joint for roof taking vehicular traffic

It may even be necessary to design to 'fail-safe' standards involving gutters and evaporation trays under joints. (Not everybody appreciates that long term shrinkage in concrete construction is an even bigger problem than expansion – it can amount to 1/10 in in 20 ft – requiring rejointing as often as every 5 years and this must be considered in the maintenance budget. Another factor is that too shallow a slab, even if structurally justifiable, may produce vibration in the mall, if subjected to heavy traffic. The human body can detect 1 micron (i.e. 1/1000 mm) as has been found in practice (see BRS Digests Nos. 117 and 118).

The main design decision determining the construction of the mall will, of course be the sectional profile related to width. Is it to be glazed or part glazed to allow daylight to be incorporated? Is the construction to be expressed such as by exposed steel trusses, lattice beams (even perhaps where regulations permit, laminated timber trusses) or will there be a decorative suspended ceiling – open, closed, translucent, panelled, coffered? What shape? Will there be clear-storey lighting, domes or lantern features at focal points? The options are endless and the construction will follow them.

Similar principles to those for the units will govern decisions regarding type of construction but the solution may be different.

Floor decks on upper floors may become cantilevered or edge-supported balconies possibly in a long open mall connected by bridges. Upstand balconies or edge beams may contribute to smoke control. Air conditioning, sprinkler systems, service ducts, intake and extract grilles, must be integrated, with smoke control outlets.

The relationship between height of shop front and ceiling height of mall may be governed by smoke control (UK Regulations). If solid mall ceilings are envisaged they may need to be a minimum of 1 m higher than shop front opening to provide smoke reservoirs.

Roof design will relate to daylight provision – open, fully glazed, with or without translucent intermediate ceiling – clear storey, or solid with artificial lighting only. Whatever the solution, smoke venting must be allowed for and the roof construction kept as flexible as possible to allow for correct distribution of ventilation outlets, whether natural or powered, as well as for smoke vents. Exposed steel is permissible under UK regulations for roof construction; steel trusses, lattice beams where permissible even laminated timber, as well as R.C. beams, portal frame or other arched construction are all available options – as well as many others. Of course mall span, column positioning and spacing will be prime factors – and relationship to unit grid, as well as to the aesthetic concept of the centre.

Floor loading may need to take special vehicles – including the fire tender – 200 lb/ft^2 is usual except where special small vehicles are available for use in pedestrian malls. Where there is no vehicle load, and pedestrian only, 100 lb/ft^2 may be adequate. The floor construction generally must be sufficiently rigid and with deflection so designed as not to affect finishes. Cracked finishes present serious difficulties in repair without affecting trade, and where neglected will lead to a deterioration in the attractiveness of the centre.

Gulleys and surface water drainage systems will be necessary to deal with sprinkler discharge, and cleaning processes, roof leakage or flooding. All floors will need to be waterproofed.

The mechanical services systems will need to be integrated into the structural design. Condensation as a major enemy must be faced and designed for, in accordance with best practice.

Illustrated examples in chapter 10 indicate the wide variety of choice available in mall construction. Mall spans may vary, as we have seen, from say 4.5 m for subsidiary arcades to 12 m or more for major malls – so centre courts may require wide span construction up to 21 m with suitable support. External walls may be infill panel or load bearing, where this does not inhibit flexibility or future expansion. Height will depend on number of storeys to units, together with design decisions. Mall and court height will vary according to choice as we have seen.

Change of floor level with steps at shop entrances is not acceptable. Gradual ramps are possible, but one or two steps form a dangerous hazard and a deterrent to shoppers, so changes in mall level where unavoidable need very careful handling – designed into the constructional scheme from the start.

Finishes

Selection of external finishes to the centre will be part of the aesthetics and of the developer's policy. To what extent will the large space users be allowed their own individual expression? Is the centre a 'one-stop' isolated concept with consequent options in elevational design, or must it blend into and/or contribute to an existing, or newly conceived, urban scene in selection and use of materials?

In the UK this is likely to be a matter for negotiation and agreement with the Planning Authority. Lightweight cladding systems may be acceptable in greenfield sites but less likely in established urban communities. Whatever the conditions, external facing materials must be durable and maintenance-free – and present an image of permanence and quality. Climatic conditions and weathering properties must be taken into account in selection, as well as maintenance, and appropriate provision made for surface cleaning. Where natural lighting is to be introduced particular attention will be needed in selecting transparent or translucent material – glass or its substitute. Factors which must be taken into account are quality of light, penetration, degree of protection against solar gain, fire resistance and accessibility for regular cleaning.

An attractive and striking appearance of the centre is to be aimed at. It must announce its existence, on approach and from a distance, but not be offensive to the surrounding landscape or townscape.

Adequate allocation of cost for high quality construction and elevational design, as justified on the grounds of low maintenance and of publicity and attraction to the shopper, must be accepted as an article of faith in the design of the centre. Where the individual large space user is permitted some latitude, this must be subordinated to the cohesive appearance, quality and 'image'.

The extent to which finishes are provided for retailers will be determined at briefing stage. The 'turnkey' concept is not popular in the UK where the multiples at one end of the spectrum, with their sophisticated and standardized requirements, and the fashion boutique at the other, relying for success on individual design image, want freedom of design and layout within their own unit. So generally tenants are provided with a shell, rental allowances being made for fitting out. Malls, consequently, are the major coordinating design feature of the centre, and require utmost skill and care in development, design and finish. They will be totally in the control of the developer and his architect, though financed by service charges from the retailers, and completely maintained and serviced by the centre management.

Fire precautions determining 'spread of flame' flammability, and smoke hazards, will be restricting and finishing materials in the UK will have to meet Class 0 Classified rating for 'spread of flame'.

A high degree of expertise in reconciling all these constraints while providing within acceptable limits an attractive and practical design – to suit all the multifarious likely uses for the malls – will be *de rigeur* for the designer. Exactly the same restraints will govern choice of the retailers' finishes for the various units and will have to be approved by the architect on behalf of the developer.

A shopping centre endures intensive use with very fast and intensive throughput of user. Selection of materials to provide minimum maintenance, durability, and certainly high quality standards are essential in public areas, – malls, car parks, etc. In no circumstances must any part of the centre, internal or external, be allowed to look shabby, so adequate provision for maintenance by staff with adequate equipment must be made at design stage, with routine and long-term maintenance schedules and processes considered at time of selection of materials.

Energy conservation is becoming a major issue in construction, and thermal insulation to required standards will be needed. On the other hand, overheating is a constant problem in shop design, due to high lighting levels and density of occupation, which may be intensified by solar gain. Malls, if naturally lit, must be carefully designed with orientation, height, cross ventilation, baffles, and colour schemes and finishes, co-ordinated to avoid discomfort from direct sun glare and heat.

Finishes also need to be considered in regard to other qualities, as well as durability and replacement. The acoustic effect of all finishes taken together must be carefully assessed; a certain modicum of background noise is a necessary adjunct to a shopping centre in order to give a feeling of 'busyness' and activity and to screen individual conversation and movement. But excessive noise or echo caused by interaction of reflective surfaces is distracting and there is a need for clarity and audibility of public address systems and background music. Individual retailers systems must be carefully monitored to avoid nuisance.

Floors will suffer an inordinate amount of wear and are better in pattern and limited module size to facilitate replacement and avoid expansion cracking. Terrazzo, marble or clay tiles have been proved satisfactory finishes (though marble is expensive in repair and replacement) and there are some interesting recent examples of reconstructed marble laid monolithic in bays. Cost of replacement and future availability of matching materials must be faced. Colour is important; dark colours will absorb light and show up litter. Pattern and colour can be used interestingly to identify circulation routes and other functions and generally the design and selection of flooring materials will be a major exercise related also to landscaping. Although some centres have used small areas of carpet in rest areas effectively this must be considered in relation to cleaning and wear.

Walls must be 'graffiti'-deterrent at least for a height of 2.4 to 3 m (8–10 ft). To provide WC and other service doors in veneered or painted surfaces for instance is asking for trouble. Hard, easy-clean, durable surface finishes such as melamine, terrazzo, tile etc. are recommended.

Ceiling finishes for public areas will need to be chosen in relation to many factors – both aesthetic and practical. The first decision will be whether open or sealed? This will be affected by arrangement of service ducting and intake and extract grilles, – and access for their maintenance. But the main practical constraint will be that of fire protection. Sprinklers will need to be duplicated if voids above solid false ceilings are too deep, say more than 1.2 m and smoke reservoirs, the extent of which is likely to be determined by calculation, will need to be provided below solid false ceilings, but can be above suspended ceilings with a certain free area (in the UK 60%).

The method and type of lighting will also affect ceiling design, of which it is a part. In the case of natural as well as artificial lighting, open ceilings can often incorporate services which (though visible) are acceptable. The reflective properties as well as colour of any ceiling or soffit will contribute positively to overall appearance and character.

In short, the selection of materials and finishes is one of the architect's main contributions to the establishment of an individual and successful project.

Mechanical and electrical services

The extent, quality, method and system of providing environmental control to the shopping centre is of prime importance, and vital in determining the long-term success of the venture. It involves consideration both of the public areas, and of the facilities to be provided to retail units, and how to combine them. Not claiming to be a technical paper on mechanical services, this chapter will merely outline those factors that must be taken into account by the architect in making these decision.

The provisions and siting of gas, water and Post Office services to individual tenants must be established early on in the design process. Likewise the position of the tenants' meters as the authorities may require concentration of meters in service areas for easy meter reading. These requirements may be onerous and affect design. Limiting the length of mains entry, and access to supply services at every joint and the need for gas mains to be directly vented to the open air, are examples.

One restriction to be avoided in the design is the 'concrete box' totally enclosed on three sides. On the grounds of amenity and fire safety all units should allow for extract ventilation and secondary access at the rear.

Shop interiors present specialised problems of ventilation and lighting. They usually have minimum external wall surfaces while being long in relation to their width; this means mechanical ventilation is needed, adequate to expel heat generated by a high level of artificial lighting and heavy occupation at peak periods and to provide an acceptable number of air changes per hour. In an enclosed centre the problem is intensified by the need to provide comfort conditions in the malls, while there is no intake for natural ventilation from the malls into the shops as there is in the open centre or 'High Street'.

A measure of control of the mall environment is a necessary ingredient of the closed centre; the question is one of degree and allied to this is the extent to which heating, cooling, ventilating and other mechanical services are to be offered to the tenant, what system is to be adopted and how services to tenants are to be paid for.

Firstly, a comment on the term 'air conditioning'. This is often loosely used to describe a system of introducing and extracting, under controlled conditions, filtered air, warmed or cooled, with full or partial recirculation – at least this is my interpretation – and it is of course incorrect. True 'air-conditioning' includes control of humidity. Although this is not normally included in a shopping centre installation, I may continue to use the term 'air-conditioning' for the sake of simplicity, where relevant. A more accurate description is 'tempered air' or 'climatic control'.

The malls
There are a whole host of differing opinions on the extent of climatic control to be provided in the public areas of the enclosed shopping centre. The system will be influenced by the developer's past experience, geographical climate, local customs, regulations governing health, escape and other fire precautions and energy conservation. It will also be related to type of lighting and the extent of control over the services used in the retail units.

Siam Centre, Bangkok. Recessed windows giving daylight to malls

67

There has been a recent tendency to react to pressure for energy conservation and revert to designing of malls for mechanical ventilation only, without temperature control, with major use also of natural lighting. The argument may be that shopping conditions will be climatically similar to those operating in the 'High Street' but with greater protection and amenity. This calls for careful analysis.

Natural lighting in itself presents problems which have to be solved, relevant to decisions on the 'air-conditioning' package as it can more safely surprisingly be successful when backed up by full climatic control. There are few, if any, climates where solar gain through glazed areas, at least in summer, can be ignored, even with the use of tinted glass which is, in itself, an additional cost element. Adequate measures are needed for dispersal, together with careful design devices, to protect glazed areas from direct sun and not to project direct sunlight and glare into vulnerable shopping areas.

There are obviously many physical ways of achieving this, for example, the use of diffusers under roof lights in the form of translucent suspended ceiling features, lay-lights, the recessing of mall windows under deep canopies protecting them from direct sunlight, clear storey glazing, the design profile of the roof, the height of malls and also, of course, orientation. In the northern hemisphere unless restricted to North or East aspect it is likely to be necessary to design natural or powered roof vents to extract the heated air before it reaches the malls. In winter conditions, the opposite problem – double-glazing – does not provide fully effective insulation against heat loss in low temperature conditions.

The effect of condensation must be allowed for, and easy access to glazed areas for cleaning and repair, as although careful detailing may ensure virtual self-cleansing of external glazing, internal surfaces will need periodic attention.

All this is a significant cost item in the capital and maintenance budgets and calculations must ensure that the saving in artificial lighting is not offset by the extra cost of providing a comfortable environment and steady temperatures in all weathers.

I have dwelt here on natural lighting because of its effect on environmental conditions. Of course there have always been successful closed shopping centres relying to a greater or lesser degree on natural lighting in the malls by skillfully solving these problems, but many of them are combined with 'air-conditioning'.

To omit temperature control and rely only on mechanical ventilation does appear to present a risk of missing out on one unique attraction of the closed centre – offering a comfortable environment as a contrast to extreme heat or extreme cold outside, and therefore a considerable extra inducement to shopping. Without temperature control there will be many periods when the mall conditions will be less than comfortable. The temperature may be of insufficient contrast to uncomfortable conditions outside and the air-movement needed to achieve adequate (perhaps six) air-changes per hour in warm conditions, may not be acceptable.

Unless natural ventilation can be achieved, large extract and intake fans may, in capital running costs, overtake the apparent saving in not providing temperature control. It has in any case to be recognised that without cooling, the mall temperature is bound to be higher than the ambient temperature outside which although an asset in winter conditions, is a serious disadvantage in hot weather. These considerations have to be weighed against capital and maintenance costs and the need for energy conservation, but a wrong decision will have a major effect on the future success of the centre.

It is of course possible to provide winter heating without summer cooling by means of unit air handlers. At Milton Keynes for instance the shopping arcades are heated by gas-fired warm air heaters, roof mounted. They are plenum units modulated to full fresh air in hot weather in response to temperature detectors in the ducts. Warm air curtains protected the entrances; however, this system has now been modified by the provision of entrance doors but still without cooling (see Chapter 10). The ducts have been selected so that duct expansion, cooling coils and integrated condensing units can be added if necessary, the cooling capacity being about half the heating capacity. It will be interesting to see if this facility is added and how the centre appeals without cooling.

Evaluation of the various alternatives is becoming more predictable with the advent of computer-aided design in calculations and comparisons of heating and cooling loads for varying conditions of design and decisions can already be made with more assurance than was previously possible. (This technique has been used, for example, in deciding on the system to be used in the regional centre at Peterborough, for the Peterborough Development Corporation.)

If a mechanical intake/extract system is adopted it must be designed to suit the centre, either a 'tailored to measure one-off' system of fans, ducting, louvres, etc., or unit ventilators mounted at high level. The system will almost certainly need automatic control by temperature detectors and smoke detectors.

Smoke ventilation will have to be designed into the ventilation scheme and perhaps incorporated with a mechanical extract system, the design of which will be consequently affected by the fire safety requirements. There are on the market unit ventilators automatically controlled by thermostat, and aerodynamically designed for natural air extract. They will also incorporate smoke ventilation, controlled by smoke detectors and fusible link. The preferable operation is electro-pneumatic, which is more easily controlled than the alternative – electro-magnetic. A compressed air supply and pump will be needed which can be situated in a plant room, or accommodated in a space specially planned.

The secret of successful natural ventilation is to provide enough volume rather than to increase the speed of flow. If this cannot be achieved, powered extract is the alternative. The area of ventilation required for day to day natural ventilation where air conditioning is not provided is likely to be less than that demanded for smoke ventilation. There must also be adequate air intake at suitable levels to provide required air change (perhaps minimum 2 per hour in winter to 6 per hour in summer) so designed as to avoid draughts, be unaffected by wind pressure, and perhaps contribute to the design of the smoke control system.

Whatever type of mechanical ventilation, or climatic control is adopted, a sophisticated monitoring system will connect it to the central control security centre, referred to in a later chapter.

One problem of ventilation (and smoke control) must be faced. Large units with considerable storage areas will themselves have to provide specialised ventilation (both natural and smoke venting) and this may substantially affect external elevational treatment, particularly if storage is not single level with available roof space and roof access. The problem is sharpened if storage areas are at basement level.

This leads to the other major consideration; the extent of provision of services to tenants. Retailers are becoming increasingly worried over service charges in shopping centres (which may even equal the rent!) and it is fair to say that on the whole they prefer to provide their own environmental systems, with or without the benefit of optional heating and chilling facilities, or condenser mains. It is likely that such facilities will be paid for by apportioning the capital cost, to be incorporated into the rental together with the service charges for operating costs.

If it is intended to provide chilled and heated water to tenants it is as well to recognise their differing requirements. The large user, the department store, the chain store, the supermarkets or super-store, will need an extensive plant, and food stores will also need specialised refrigeration; so almost certainly the large users will wish to provide and control their own service even if provided with heaters and chillers.

The small unit on the other hand may well be satisfied with a lower performance level if allied to a lower service charge; in many cases requiring ventilation only, without cooling. Heating may be obligatory in order to maintain temperatures to statutory levels (in the UK this is 60.8°F within one hour of opening) for the benefit of staff. It seems odd to the writer that while minimum heating requirements are laid down by statute there is no such restriction on the upper limit! There is need for a balanced system, as, depending on the climate, heating may be required in the winter as against cooling in the summer, there being a theoretical moment at which neither is needed.

The process of cooling is the more sophisticated in that it is a technique of removing heat rather than providing it and that the equipment designed to chill water will in itself generate heat. One service offered to tenants may be a condenser main supplying water at a stated temperature for use in tenant's own air-handling units, which discharge the water back into the main to be returned to the central cooling towers and recirculated.

A further specialised problem of the enclosed shopping centre is that of the open shop front. Leakage of the air conditioning of the mall into the shop will cause excessive landlord's operating costs if the shops are providing their own systems. One solution to this is for the tenants' ventilation systems to operate at an air pressure slightly higher than that in the malls. This however will be affected by smoke control regulations where these operate. We will see later the effect on design of smoke control. Certainly, in the UK, unless satisfactory safeguards can be devised, systems using higher pressures in the shops than in the malls are unpopular with Fire Officers. In current UK practice the preference is for a balanced pressure air-conditioning system for the malls with a separate balanced system for the units.

Elsewhere there are examples where acceptance of a full air conditioning system in the shops, provided by the developer, is a condition of letting, with extract into the malls, which are thus air conditioned while acting as recirculation and extract ducts. This system forces the air conditioning costs directly onto the retailer, both as regards capital cost and service charges. Such a system relies on sprinklers and pressurised escape routes for fire protection together with automatic 'cut-off' or reverse flow in the event of fire-warning.

In the UK the opposite system is more acceptable. In this case air will be extracted from the malls, drawn through the shops to the rear, perhaps with some direct intake behind the shop frontage; this allows a slight pressure into the unit from the mall. Variable pressure and variable volume control may be built into the system.

*Hempstead Valley. Roofscape showing package air-handling units.
(Photo: A. M. Pope)*

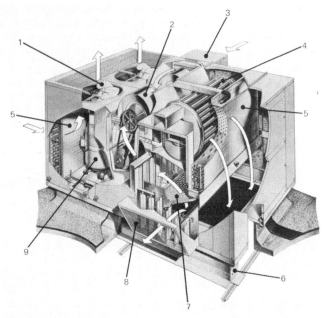

1 Condenser fans.

2 Dual centrifugal belt-drive circulation fans.

3 Power Saver system.

4 Gas fired heating section with options of direct electric, low pressure hot water coils, oil fired heating.

5 Condenser and evaporator coils.

6 Roof Mounting Frame.

7 Washable polyurethane air filter.

8 Power Saver exhaust hood.

9 Compressors.

An air-handling unit (Photo: Lennox)

Whatever method of environmental control is adopted to provided tempered air, the types of system available may also range between two extremes:

1. A central plant servicing the public areas and supplying such services as chilled water, chilled air, hot water and/or compressed air or even steam, to all the tenants through a flow and return ducted system with provision for return water cooling etc. Perhaps extending this to full air conditioning of retail units as appropriate.

2. Self-contained package units suitably dispersed, to service the malls with provision for package units to each store to be installed by the retailer, perhaps also with the facility for return water cooling. These are available, of considerable capacity. They can be located, preferably on the roof, to serve the public parts of the centre as well as individual units. Roof loading must be adequate to support the units, and provision must be made for the necessary pipework and ducting together with visual masking of the equipment where necessary to provide attractive elevations and roofscape. Roof surfaces must be designed to allow for maintenance and replacement without danger of leaks.

A central plant is likely to be either gas fired or oil fired; package units may be supplied by gas or electricity. These units incorporate cooling while a central plant will require water cooling equipment at high level on the roof.

Both systems and their permutations have specific advantages. Decisions as to which to be used must be made early enough for necessary provision to be incorporated into the planning.

A central plant location might be in the basement, on the roof or even at surface level, or may be divided into smaller zoned plant rooms, with or without a central energy core. Plant rooms need considerable

Roof at Brunel Centre, Swindon, showing natural lighting combined with louvred ventilation

Linked package services on a roof. (Photo: Lennox)

floor area and height – 'underground' plant rooms will themselves need mechanical ventilation – oil storage must meet special conditions and comply with statutory requirements.

Package units will need adequate siting space, almost certainly at roof level. They may need screening for aesthetic reasons, and must have adequate access for servicing. There may be a network of mains services to be accommodated on the roof. A large centre will need a considerable number of units but installation is comparatively simple as they are delivered as complete units (sometimes onto an existing roof by helicopter!) They can be installed in stages, to serve successive phases of construction and individual shops as these come into operation. This can be done more easily than with a central plant, which needs to be fully operational as part of a first phase.

Though summer cooling presents the more acute problem, winter heating must not be forgotten. The required temperatures in the malls should be constant during shopping hours, within a small range – say 18°–24°C (65°–75°F) in winter to 21°–24°C (70°–75°F) in summer. In considering operating controls, indoor planting demands a minimum temperature of 12°C (52°F) for survival of tropical plants.

The comfort of staff working in the centre out of hours must also be catered for and temperatures will have to be maintained outside shopping hours accordingly. In a multi-use centre it may be desirable to unify heating and/or air-conditioning of the differing uses, other than shopping, into one system or to provide, even though separately, for the various uses within the area of the shopping centre structure.

Particularly this applies if the whole complex is under unified management. This will of course affect the choice of system and economies of operation.

To summarise various options; first the two extremes of providing tempered air to the malls:
1. Shops to provide full temperature control to an agreed standard, extracting into the mall which benefits from using the extract system of the shops (not favoured in the UK due to Fire Safety provisions. Such systems would need 'fail safe' reverse flow in emergencies).
2. Malls and public areas treated, extracting from malls through the shops, which may obtain some benefit from the extraction system. There is the alternative of providing a complete system of treatment of malls and public areas with facilities offered to shop units, ranging from chilled and heated water to a condenser circuit, or facilities for siting of their own air-handling units.

Whatever method of climatic control is adopted will materially influence the planning and profile of the centre, in routing and integration of vertical and horizontal services and the consequent duct work, position and design of intake and extract to malls and units, fans and siting of major items of equipment. The system will also need a sophisticated system of monitoring by connection into the control centre, as will be referred to in a later chapter. It is also likely to constitute a major element of capital (and maintenance) cost.

Luton Centre. Interior showing outlets with grilles (Photo: Lennox)

Lighting

The problems of lighting a shopping centre are highly technical and the equipment available is constantly changing. One main design problem will be to maintain the correct balance of illumination between the shops and the malls; to provide in the malls and courts an adequate overall lighting level adding interest and a further dimension, with variety of lighting to highlight planting features, special areas and so on but not to the detriment of the shops or shop fronts. All this must be at an acceptable running cost.

Artificial lighting levels in shops are extremely high as they cannot rely on daylight owing to their configuration and the need for high intensity to attract customers and display merchandise. It should be assumed in calculating overall electrical demand that the lighting load may be between 40 and $50\,\text{W/m}^2$ overall in shop units; these of course will provide their own electrical installation but a measure of control will need to be imposed by the centre. For instance, all shops should be lit when the centre is open, particularly the shop fronts.

A minimum lighting level should be demanded as the centre will rely very largely for its impact and attraction on shop front lighting which needs to be brighter than that of the mall, say 600–700 lux, at the entrance though this may fall to 300 lux within the shop; certainly a minimum lighting level at shop entrances can reasonably be demanded. In the open centre where shop fronts are glazed, a high lighting level is necessary in any event within the shop front to compete with daylight and to avoid reflection.

The problem of lighting to the malls in the open centre will be similar to that of any street, though scale and design of suitable lamp standards or canopy lighting must be sympathetic to the character of the centre; a modicum of flood lighting should be introduced to identify features, sculpture, planting and provide interest. When the artificial lighting goes on at dusk the whole character of the centre will alter. This also applies to closed centres relying on daylight for major lighting of the mall, though the problems are intensified and there are many additional ones.

As already indicated, malls in a closed centre will be lit to an overall acceptable level by a system of general lighting supplemented by feature lighting avoiding monotony and blandness. There is a considerable diversity of opinion about mall lighting levels and their relationship to shop front lighting. Although it is generally accepted that shop front lighting should be a dominant feature and will therefore contribute to the lighting of the mall, desirable mall lighting levels may vary between 80 and 150 lux. The contrast between 80 lux and a shop front lighting of 600 would appear to be too great; too low a mall lighting level can have a depressing effect. The feeling generated in the malls must surely be one of sparkle and interest. Lighting will be accentuated by the colour and materials used in finishes, particularly those of ceilings and floors as is evidenced in the design of some British shopping centres with dark ceilings and dark floors which absorb rather than reflect light.

The entrances to malls should be sufficiently brightly lit to form a focus looking in from the outside, in contrast with the surrounding external scene, particularly in a developed area where a positive message of invitation and excitement is needed. This is a major constituent of the entrance design, others being dimensions, type of signing and so on as we have already seen.

Now to some practical considerations. Lighting design will in the main be a matter of choosing the type of lamp, type of fitting, situation and distribution to give the required illumination, direction and character of light required.

There are many options open in the design of general lighting to malls and courts, with the introduction of high-pressure mercury and high-pressure sodium discharge lamps (as an alternative to the familiar fluorescent tube).

These newer lamps have considerable advantages; they give more light for the same heat; as an example, at the rate of 250 W the mercury lamps will give 7–8 times more light for the same heat than fluorescent lighting. Moreover the estimated life of a mercury lamp is quoted as 10 000 hours, and that of the sodium 20 000 hours (or put another way indefinite!) This is in itself is a considerable advantage as accessibility for lamp changing is always a problem in high malls and courts. These high pressure discharge lamps have special features; they nearly always have remote control gear. The gear might be say $8 \times 4 \times 2$ in per lamp and must be in ventilated positions as it generates heat. Fittings can be chosen which have the accompanying gear enclosed in steel casing.

There are as yet no high pressure sodium discharge low wattage lamps; the mercury lamp which has been in use for a considerable time already is available in an 80–125 W lowest rating and 50 W has now been introduced. Both sodium and mercury lamps have suffered from the disadvantage of poor colour rendering, the mercury being in the blue range while the sodium till recently gave too yellow a light to be used in any situation where natural effects were needed. We have all experienced the shock of seeing ordinary human beings under the effects of the low pressure sodium street lamps turn into ghostly faces from another world. However in the newest high pressure sodium lamps the colour is improving, getting whiter

Specialised fitting for plant lighting (Photo: Philips)

and the solution is to combine these with mercury lamps. In the New York City Corporation Building Speciality Centre, the lamps are grouped in threes, one sodium to two mercury-vapour, each rated at 1000 W. The efficiency and spread of these lamps would give for example at a height of 4 m from the ground, 125 lux with spread of 3 m centres in both directions. From this it can be seen that there are great advantages in their use, with fewer light sources and economy of installation and maintenance.

However general lighting is not sufficient and a display lighting dimension must also be available. For floodlighting the tungsten halogen, quartz iodine filament lamp is in general use but for individual highlighting of display features the various available types of spot light fitting using tungsten filament silvered lamps of various types one still probably the best available choice. It must be remembered that these are uneconomic in comparison. Not only are tungsten filament lamps more prone to failure but they are of a considerably lower efficiency, see Table 2.

Table 2

	lumen/W
GLS lamp	10–12
Tungsten halogen	18–20
Fluorescent	40–70
MBA (high-pressure mercury)	60–80
MB1 (high-pressure sodium)	80–100

Figures taken from the Illuminating Engineer's Society Code of Interior Lighting, February, 1977

Discharge lamps have simple circuits and little to fail but they take ten minutes to run up to full operation. Again it must be emphasised they are for general lighting and need to be supplemented by 'architectural' light to pick out features and give 3-dimensional depth and variety.

Where daylight is introduced into the malls problems of colour are encountered. Variations are exaggerated in daylight and there is an immediate awareness of the contrast with the artificial lighting which may be discordant. The other choice is whether to bring on the artificial light suddenly or gradually. It is not possible to dim high pressure discharge lamps as with tungsten and fluorescent lamps. Switch control will probably be by time switch and can be solar controlled as for street lighting. This can be arranged to camouflage the change-over by gradually increasing the artificial lighting as daylight fails.

Further developments are experiments into small high pressure discharge lamps of good colour to take the place of tungsten and with the advent of microcircuitry a built-in control gear within the lamp holder may become possible. It has been said that within a few years these lamps may revolutionise the domestic lighting industry, but this has yet to be seen!

Service and warehouse areas must not be forgotten in considering lighting. Lighting installations in racked out areas will have to be kept high and clear of fork-lift or other distribution systems. The lamps will be industrial fittings; lighting levels are likely to be, say, 150 lux and where racking extends almost to the ceiling overall general lighting may not be possible, each racking row having to be independently lit to avoid shadow, probably in this case by fluorescent fittings.

One cardinal principle in design of 'landlords' lighting, both in public and in service areas is that in order to reduce vandalism and the risk of crime there should be no 'dark spaces'.

Emergency lighting
The whole centre will have to be provided with an emergency lighting installation not only in case of fire but to cater for possible power failures. The interpolation of the typical emergency lighting fitting can be an irritation to the designer. A requirement will be instant operation, i.e. within 30 sec of failure.

The emergency lighting system in all communal areas will be designed into the landlord's lighting scheme with control also over that in the large units. The fittings will be either self-contained (fed by trickle charge in normal running) or fed from a central system, operated by a standby generator automatically started, or by central battery storage. If there are two alternative town supplies available, one being what is known as 'a firm supply' from the Supply Authority to provide a 'standby system', this may be preferable though it also has a disadvantage in that a power strike or power failure would inhibit the supply.

The disadvantage of central battery storage is the considerable accommodation space and ventilation needed, with disciplined regular maintenance. There may also be a noticeable voltage drop between the central point and the furthest emergency light position.

The disadvantage of the self-contained fitting is its visual interruption of the designed ceiling pattern – already confused by ceiling grilles, light fittings, sprinklers etc.

The location of the standby generator is important, with particular respect to its cooling and aspiration. It should preferably not be internal as it needs a well-ventilated area with calculated intake and exhaust and be of a size related to starting currents and the motors served. Generators may be diesel or gas fed; dependent on circumstances. For diesel, oil storage must be provided.

A standby generator will anyway be needed to serve emergency equipment such as warning system, smoke venting, sprinkler pumps, fire lifts and passenger conveyor where these latter are acceptable as Means of Escape.

Vertical circulation

Vertical circulation is a primary consideration in multi-level centres and even in a one-level centre it is likely that there will be some variation in levels between the different entry and exit points. In multi-level centres we have already seen that the character and positioning of vertical access will be vital factors in the success of the upper levels.

Certain factors must be borne in mind throughout while determining the type, position and arrangement of the various forms of access. In particular steps and staircases must not form the only method of movement from one level to another. All kinds of wheeled objects will be used in the centre: for the shopper – pushchairs, shopping trolleys, prams and wheelchairs; – for the management and for the retailer – cleaning, litter and refuse trolleys, trucking for stock, mobile scaffolds for maintenance etc. A further point is that retailers object strongly to steps at shop entrances. Slight changes in level may be solved by ramping the malls, as at Eldon Square, Newcastle. It needs careful handling; decreased mall height at the upper end of the ramp must be adequate to avoid a feeling of constriction while shop floor levels must be so arranged as not to inhibit the position of the

Hempstead Valley. Treatment of ramped access. (Photo: Colt International)

entrance to the shop or require flights of steps. It is useful to have ramped walkways between the malls and toilets or car parks at differing levels, in addition to mechanical means where space permits.

For major movement of shoppers between storey levels, escalators and/or lifts are essential. Any large shopping centre will require escalators as lifts will have insufficient capacity although these will be required for movement of wheeled objects as already described and for the handicapped. In planning vertical circulation, any large centre should have duplication of lifts and at least of the 'up' escalators to allow for servicing and breakdown. Escalators and/or passenger conveyors will need to be carefully situated to give the minimum of visual obstruction and to attract the customers from one level and discharge them at another along the required flow routes. Under UK fire regulations, escalators and passenger conveyors will need fusible link shutters at the *upper* level where they pass through a compartment floor. Fire escape requirements will also require a minimum number of staircases as a means of escape.

Escalators and passenger conveyors
The provision of escalators for shopping centres has its own problems. It is as well to review the options and limitations.

Escalators come at two inclinations at 30° and 35°. The 35° angle escalator is the preferred type; the 30° angle is wasteful in space being only necessary for high speed heavy traffic, e.g. low supervision escalators carrying the public in heavy volume in public transport conditions. The 35° angle escalator is the obvious choice for a shopping centre. Its maximum travel is 6 m vertical height with a limit of speed of approximately 0.5 m per second (100 ft per minute). Escalators are available in three widths – 600 mm, 800 mm, 1000 mm. The capacity of a 1000 mm width 35° escalator at a speed of 0.5 m per sec is theoretically 9000 people per hour assuming an average of 1½ people per step. This would only be achieved at peak periods in a situation such as a London underground station and is far higher than would ever be necessary or achievable in a shopping centre.

However from a practical point of view 1000 mm width is really necessary in shopping malls to allow shoppers with packages and or children, or two people together, to mount or descend the escalator. Moreover the difference in price between a 600 and 1000 mm escalator is only about 20°.

The smaller escalators are useful more for individual units and shorter travel. An escalator with a travel of, say, 5 m can be supported at each end without intermediate supports. The machinery will be housed underneath the escalator at both the top and bottom, the necessary depth being, say, 1200 mm deep.

There are two main escalator systems as regards construction, either the lattice girder type or the welded box type. There are also two systems of providing motive power, either a distribution of smaller motors or one big one; but the maximum load as a guide may be taken as 12½ kW per 6 m travel unit. A minimum horizontal travel distance from the point of incline to the end of the frame would be 2.6 m. From the design point of view some manufacturers can produce matching level ends for the down and the up section, if they join, though the alternative is to have a longer travel at the top than at the bottom of the escalator. This is where the flow from floor to floor is arranged as continuous, but pedestrian flow past the largest number of shops will be encouraged if up and down escalators are entered at opposite ends.

Modern design of escalators has greatly diminished the possibility of accidents. New European standards for control of design and operation of escalators are being drawn up and the UK British Standard is lining up with these. Nevertheless it is worth considering closed-circuit television for controlling escalators. Any failure or stoppage of the escalator needs to be dealt with as soon as possible and consequently escalators must be wired into the control system to be dealt with

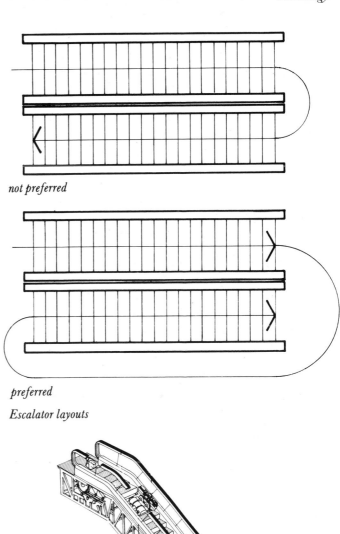

not preferred

preferred

Escalator layouts

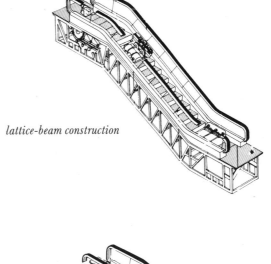

lattice-beam construction

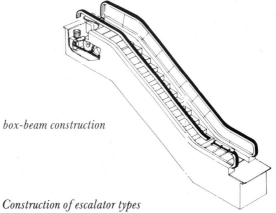

box-beam construction

Construction of escalator types

at security headquarters. Moreover there should always be more than one escalator, to allow for breakdown, maintenance and repair.

Escalators by their nature form a visual barrier but this can be minimised by the use of a glazed balustrade to the upper half of the escalator, normally in armoured glass. Unfortunately it is not possible to fully glaze an escalator as although there is an attraction in the idea of seeing the moving parts, these run in oil which makes this impracticable. Alternatively, they can be aggressively designed to indicate access routes, say, by siting them across instead of along the circulation route and using the balustrade as a directional indication to encourage vertical movement. The escalator must be well lit; fluorescent lighting may be incorporated into the handrail as a design feature.

External escalators have additional requirements. All equipment must be water-resistant, so that where not visible it will be galvanised and where visible must be in stainless steel, aluminium or other equally weather resistant finish. Water will penetrate the escalator within the truss so catchment areas and drainage gullies must be provided at the foot of the run, the internal soffit being constructed as a flat surface forming a water drain from top to bottom. The gully must be designed to separate oil and water; the oil will be removed as part of the servicing routine, the gully being accessible from the access panel.

To cope with snow and ice, thermostatic heating will be required in the form of tubular heaters supplied as part of the package by the escalator manufacturer. Glass balustrading is not suitable for external escalators owing to the difficulty of weather-resistant detailing.

Escalators have certain disadvantages, in particular the difficulty of providing for wheeled traffic such as prams, pushchairs and trolleys. An alternative is the 'passenger conveyor' which is a moving ramp. The passenger conveyor is a ramped escalator with a steady incline instead of steps which enables passengers to transport wheeled carriers of various kinds without difficulty. It is also safer and easier for the disabled or handicapped and for children. Its disadvantage is the length required as the maximum angle to which it will work satisfactorily is 12%; also it needs to be supported vertically at every 15 metres of its length. However where space allows it is an excellent solution from the point of view of the convenience of the shopper.

Whether a down conveyor is needed as well as an up is questionable as a 10% fixed ramp is quite practical for shoppers with wheel trolleys and prams and wheelchairs in a down direction and would take up the same approximate length as the adjoining up ramp with its flat areas at either end. Comments on the special requirements of external escalators, of course, also apply to passenger conveyors.

Siam Centre, Bangkok. Directional graphics on an escalator to lead shoppers to centre

Brunel Centre, Swindon. Passenger conveyor.
(Photo: Henk Snoek)

A further development suitable to serve supermarket shoppers might be the combined passenger and trolley escalator. This is not a very satisfactory affair by reason of its width, and a recent innovation is the trolley conveyor. The latter is designed for installation adjacent to a escalator (or staircase). It requires no pit, and is claimed to occupy only ⅕th of the space required by a combined passenger and trolley escalator.

Lifts

Lifts will be required in all multi-level centres which cannot rely exclusively on escalators. Small lifts are no use in shopping centres; it is better to have a few adequate capacity lifts rather than a large number of small ones (though never only one, in case of servicing or breakdown). A twenty-person lift is a recommended size and wherever possible these should be single entry.

Adequate circulation space is needed adjoining all lift entrances. A minimum speed is suggested as 0.5 m/s for a 3-floor lift; doubling the speed even over 5 floors increases the capacity only by 10% and increases the cost by 25–50%! It is interesting that the oil hydraulic lift is returning as a preferable alternative to the electrically-operated lift. It is cleaner, and an attractive variation in considering the possibility of the visible lift. The conventional bank of lifts with enclosed shaft is a difficult design feature to make inviting, and as a visible interference, is therefore likely to be sited in a subordinate position from the circulation routes.

The transparent lift in a glass cage can be an interesting feature and the oil hydraulic lift may run on one polished ram. A ram alongside the car, connected at the top to a telescopic ramp facilitates the use of this feature. The freestanding visible lift or 'wall climber lift' with a visible mechanism is likely to cost at least twice that of the conventional type.

The design of the conventional lift cage is important; nothing is more depressing and claustrophobic than to enter a typical car park lift. An attempt should be made to introduce the customer to the centre by attractive design of lift entrances and lift interiors.

Goods lifts are essential to the multi-level centre. Here the pattern changes and sturdy construction is the priority. The cost of the lift is to some extent relative to the degree of self-levelling. That for a passenger lift, or one to accommodate small wheels, may need to be within half an inch; this distance can be considerably increased in the case of goods lifts. These may be 1, 1½ or 2 ton capacity; recommended sizes are given in BS 2655 and 5655.

In a multi-storey centre it is likely that the Fire Brigade will request that a goods lift be availble for fire-fighting. It will need to be of adequate capacity

City 2, Brussels. Wall-climber lift. (Photo: Nigel Woolner)

Lucky Plaza, Singapore. Wall-climber lift

and carrying load, with manual over-ride control, off a stand-by generator, and telephone communication with the control centre.

In matters concerned with escalators, passenger conveyors and lifts the insurance company concerned with insurance of the centre should be consulted at an early stage as their requirements must be met and will affect the premium.

All forms of vertical access are integral with the design and planning of the centre and the specialist manufacturer and consultants concerned with its provision should be consulted at briefing stage. All too often the complaint is made that as a result of failure to achieve this consultation difficulties are encountered when it is too late to do other than effect a not totally satisfactory compromise.

Hard landscaping

There are two major types of hard and soft landscaping in shoppng centres – that which is outside in the open air and that which is within the closed mall centre.

External landscaping will normally be a major feature of the one-stop centre as well as of the open mall or composite open and closed mall type of edge of town or urban centre.

Hard landscaping concerns paving, roads, retaining walls, fencing, banks, steps, changes of level, ramps and the integration of escalators or passenger conveyors, gently into the floorscape. It must also incorporate design of guard rails, balustrades, fencing, temporary or permanent, railings etc. and the siting and design of street furniture, kiosks, lamp standards, litter bins and signs. It will include the selection of suitable paving materials which may need to identify without abrupt change those areas suitable for wheel load, and those suitable for pedestrian traffic only.

All materials used must, of course, be durable and weather-resistant with provision for easy washdown cleaning, as pedestrian circulation routes must in no event be allowed to become muddy or dirt collecting. Here, as in all other parts of the centre, first class routine and long term maintenance is essential. Materials must be selected with this in mind so that in any case of failure or damage repairs can be made easily and quickly. One thing to avoid is the use of specialist pavings which are not easily repeatable or may go out of production.

Hard landscaping can be used very effectively to assist the functions of the centre. It will also form the setting for features of aesthetic interest, such as fountains, pools, play features, sculptures and soft landscaping. Trolley parks, pedestrian walkways from car parks, main circulation routes can all by marked out clearly by use of materials, which will break up the monotony of the 'floor-scape'.

Safety is a major factor; materials must be non-slip, vehicle routes must be easily seen, with, provision for prevention of formation of ice and clearance of snow in climates where these are a possibility. Changes of level must be clearly defined and handrails provided where necessary. The handicapped must not be forgotten and wheelchair circulation routes must be incorporated.

Soft landscaping

Open mall
In the open centre, soft landscaping should be a dominant element. Some American centres such as Oak Brook, Chicago, set the shopping in what is in fact a most agreeable park or ornamental garden where shoppers appear to stroll amongst the shops. Certainly there are immense opportunities for landscaping and planning in any open centre.

Soft landscaping in the open shopping centre will have to take into account specific constraints. Trees and shrubs must not obscure shop frontages, vistas, signing or other features, and need to be designed into the scheme – like everything else – from the start with due regard to their total mature height and spread.

Deciduous trees, and shrubs present a maintenance problem; due to the autumn leaf-fall leaves can be dangerous on wet paved areas and will clog gutters and drains. Flower beds will need maintenance thoughout the season and must be designed to suit the capacity and skill levels of the maintenance staff available.

Selection must take account of site conditions. Vandalism can be minimised by group planting, avoiding the planting of saplings but including some thorned species, with proper staking and tree guards where appropriate. 'Air drainage' around planting will reduce frost pockets. Wind-hardy plants must be chosen for draughty positions and north-east draughts avoided. Raised beds may be needed in water-logged areas.

Enclosed mall
When we come to the closed mall centre, most of the foregoing conditions still apply (other than those concerning the weather) but there are additional considerations.

The materials used, although they will not need to be weather-proof, will still need to be waterproof and easily maintained and cleaned. They will very probably be of a different character, suitable to the interior

EXAMPLES OF OPEN MALL LANDSCAPING

Oakbrook, Chicago

Oakbrook, Chicago

Paramus Park, New Jersey (Photo: Nigel Woolner)

Brunel Centre, Swindon

scale and condition. Soft landscaping will be of the utmost value in any closed centre and may make all the difference between a bleak utility 'discount store' image and one of luxury and invitation. Again the landscape architect or designer must be brought in at the beginning not the end of the project if success is to be achieved.

We have already seen that there is a point load problem where trees are to be provided on suspended floors or roofs. All areas of concentrated soft landscaping, shrubs, flower beds etc. will need designing into the structure in regard to load. Siting of soft landscaping must be considered as part of the overall plan and again height and spread must be in scale and must not obstruct or confuse the overall visual effect of the centre.

Enclosed mall landscaping has other technical problems; deciduous trees and shrubs are out, as a concentrated leaf-fall cannot be accommodated. It appears that no deciduous trees natural to our climate will survive under the artificial conditions of the closed mall as they require seasonal changes to stimulate their growth. But tropical and subtropical plants are suitable because they accept an equable temperature and these include some deciduous trees and shrubs such as members of the Eucalyptus, Jacaranda, Yucca and Ficus families. These do not shed their leaves in the autumn but the leaves erupt like teeth, the old leaf falling when the new leaf takes its place. As this process is continuous through the year it is easier to absorb as a maintenance item.

These remarks are a general guide only, as useful in briefing the landscape specialist or contractor who will be contributing his own planting plan for consideration.

The temperature cannot fall below 52°F without danger of damage to plants and this will affect the design of the heating and ventilating scheme; some control of humidity may be necessary. Draughts are another problem and will also have to be carefully sited to avoid damage.

Where the main light source is daylight, this must be controlled to avoid excessive or distorted growth which will be dependent on light values at floor levels. Fluorescent lighting can be advantageous and will actually stimulate growth if near enough to the plants, but tungsten or high-pressure discharge lamps if too near the plants or too strong, can cause scorching.

Grassed lawns at upper levels such as to form a roof garden, must be used with discretion, as mowing and getting rid of the mowings, may pose a problem. An alternative may be the flat growing 'heaths' as ground cover, (as proposed at the Friary Centre, Guildford).

Other technical considerations must be observed. Planting will need to be in sterilised compost, and planters will need liners, (unless they have drainage provision). Plants left in their production containers camouflaged by mulch make for ease of change where necessary.

Irrigation in a large scheme may be by automatic spray on a 'ring main' system, time clock operated in large planted areas, or watering points will have to be provided in suitable positions. Water softeners may be advisable in hard water areas. Pesticide control will be needed, operated by sprayer (during closing hours); foliage will need spray cleaning after application.

All soft landscaping will need careful and specialised attention during the establishment period and continual watering, replacement, disease and pest

Milton Keynes. Mall

Milton Keynes. Mall

THESE THREE ILLUSTRATIONS SHOW SOME EXAMPLES OF SOFT LANDSCAPING IN COVERED MALLS

Hempstead Valley, Gillingham Kent. (Photo: Colt International)

control, pruning and replanting as part of the general maintenance routine. Unless qualified staff are available, this may have to be let on a contract basis.

One final word of warning to those who may be tempted to the use of artificial flowers and plants. These can be a fire hazard and may be so regarded by the Fire Authority!

Signing and graphics

Although this subject is dealt with at this stage in the book this does not indicate that it need only be considered late in the project! On the contrary, signing and graphics are an integral part of the design and really need consideration from the word 'go'. Thus, it is beneficial if the graphics designer can be appointed at the same time as the other consultants and brought in to the early consultations.

It is necessary for the architect, as well as every one else involved in the project including the planning authority, to appreciate the essential function of graphics and signing. For a centre to make itself felt it must communicate with the shopping public in advance of entry, and establish the language of the directions and identifications which they will meet. This will also extend to promotional activities both within the centre and elsewhere. Thus the function of the giant sign advertising the presence of the shopping centre in the USA. Some of these signs are extremely interesting and striking designs and should not be dismissed as a vulgarity.

The centre must be signalled to the public from outside with an identity, and a language established by which the public will recognise all the activities of the centre and appreciate the visual significance of the directions. It is sad that so many Planning Authorities in the UK have rigid prejudices which make for unnecessary difficulties at the outset for the shopping

Ghirardelli Square, San Francisco. A successful example of arresting but well mannered signing

public and for the developer. It would be better to admit that graphic identification need not be an eyesore – in fact it can be an embellishment.

The design of a centre symbol, if to be adopted, is extremely important. Not only must it be striking, recognisable, and different from any other but it must be an agreeable design, easily applicable to all forms of signing from the illuminated sign down to the letter heading, which presents certain technical problems. The use of the 'logo' can expand well outside the actual centre; for instance, in one example waste disposal skips being handled by a private contractor bear the centre symbol. There are plenty more opportunities for exploitation!

Once inside the centre, clarity and character are equally essential in order to inform and direct the shopper. There is an interesting example of an apparent misfire as reported at Les Halles in Paris. Here, because of the nature of the project, the centre, although a covered multi-level complex, was signposted in accordance with Parisian street signing to give the impression that the public was still in the street atmosphere. The public is said not to have at first appreciated that in this different type of street concept there was vertical as well as a horizontal dimension and to have ignored the vertical signing with consequent detrimental effect on the multi-level trading.

There are, of course, many ways of explaining the centre; one obvious solution is to offer illuminated plans clearly showing all functions and units on their various levels and the circulation routes. These, to be successful, must be prominently displayed and in easily examined positions clearly legible and related to the actual physical circulation routes and units. If adequately framed and protected and lit by a standby source, this can assist the Fire Services when called to an incident. Surely the test of success in graphics and signing will be the lack of confusion amongst the shoppers, the lack of complaint or enquiry. It is almost certain that an information kiosk of some kind will need to be located at a key point in the malls and no doubt feed-back from this will establish the rate of success of the directional design!

The character of the graphics is of course a matter for the designer but it is very important that all the visual indications in the centre including symbols and logos should be in character and easily related and distinguishable. Therefore it is as well to avoid standard lettering of the type likely to be seen in adjoining locations such as motorways, public transport system, etc., although it must not be so individual as to be difficult to read. Individual symbols should be made use of where appropriate as it is to be hoped that not only the indigenous population will use the centre!

Where the centre forms part of a multi-use complex consultation with other users will be necessary in order to identify those areas where a joint design programme can be agreed, and those where individual and different signing types are preferable.

There are many facets of the graphic designer which can be utilised in the centre. The use of colour coding for instance, though this must be used with caution and it will need to be closely co-ordinated with the decorative colour schemes. Not everybody is quick to observe the significance of colour-related information and some shoppers are colour blind. It has been found self-defeating for instance in the case of car parking; individual numbering of car park spaces in large multi-storey car parks is almost mandatory if shoppers are not to get lost. However there are examples of excellent colour coding for instance in the London Transport underground system.

Another use of signing is to minimise the effect of blank spaces, and in particular as temporary relief of empty units, or hoardings masking shop fitting or other alterations. Quite a lot can be done to avoid the depressing effect of these dead areas by interesting graphics or murals. There may be opportunities of commissioning permanent murals or providing a framework for advertising, also offering a means of revenue. Certainly there should be no dismal blank tunnels forming circulation routes between parts of the Centre, or between car parks, public transport systems or the High Street and the centre. Every opportunity should be taken to make these routes bright and inviting.

This is not, I repeat, something to be considered in haste, at the end, as a cosmetic exercise. The visual effects of all surfaces and areas as well as the provision of adequate space for necessary signing, etc. should be taken into account from the very start of the planning of the project if it is to be totally successful.

As we have seen, individual shop signing must be allowed to be dominant and individual but must be carefully considered so as not to be confused with the centre directives. This makes it all the more necessary to have an easily identifiable language for the centre itself, all signs and directives being positioned where they are not confused with the signing of the shops. It is here we must consider for a moment the problem of the individual shop sign. Some control will inevitably be required, but not such that the shop loses its individuality or that shop signing as a whole loses its dominance.

We have already examined the problem of the fascia and there needs to be some control over dimensional prominence of signs if one shop is not to 'shout' at the expense of the next. Some form of control over the illumination will also be necessary; the major focus of the mall must be, as we have seen, the shop. As the eye must not be distracted from the merchandise by the signing, the lettering illumination must not be stronger than the illumination within the shop. By contrast, a dead length of frontage without illuminated signing may break the shopping interest, so a general policy of illumination is essential, controlled by the centre's design team. Projecting signs are a problem; they may form part of an overall concept and can be very attractive, besides being a help to the shopper and to the trader. However, it is not wise to allow the odd projecting sign except where the shop is so sited, perhaps in an irregular position, that it becomes important to signal the shop presence to the shopping public.

Identification of addresses is important and while during construction a 'production drawing' type of reference is likely, at completion there must be a change-over to an address system more allied to the conventional one. In a large centre the malls and courts will need names, whether 'East Mall' or 'Mid-summer Boulevard', for example, will depend on developer's policy; but whatever system is adopted it must be consistent, clearly marked from all entries, and notified with plans to the Fire Brigade, Post Office and retailers. The system must also be co-ordinated with the control panels in the central security station to avoid confusion.

Clear marking of fire exits, Fire Brigade entry points, hydrants, service entries and exits, through routes for vehicles, escape routes for pedestrians, etc. must all form part of the graphics package as will temporary signing for emergency or repair works, temporary closures and diversion. There should be no room – or excuse for – afterthought or temporary signing put up by management or tenants, not co-ordinated with the graphics image.

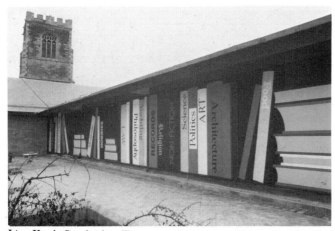

Lion Yard, Cambridge. Treatment of hoardings. (Photo: P. Murdoch)

Chapter 9
Legislation

Of all subjects affecting shopping centre design perhaps the most difficult to write about is legislation. It varies tremendously between countries and in its interpretation even between districts – or even in the same district – and its impact on the design of the shopping centre is total.

The main factors controlled by legislation may be said to be those of planning, construction and all aspects of fire safety. A further constraint is related to provision for specialist uses of various kinds, and care and protection of staff.

It would be interesting to do a research project on the influence of building legislation on shopping centre design internationally and to analyse the effect of the various systems on the final result. I do not propose this here, but will try to highlight some aspects of UK legislation which most affect shopping centres. Assuming a general knowledge of national legislation by the applicant, a look at the UK system will suggest likely areas of control elsewhere. So this chapter deals with UK conditions only.

Planning

Throughout the earlier chapters in this book has been the theme that a shopping centre will be successful in direct ratio to the resolution of the various planning problems integral to its realisation.

There is bound to be a fundamental difference in attitude on the part of any planning authority towards a proposal to build a shopping centre on a greenfield site or one located in an urban area. The 'greenfield' site will be looked at in the context of its likely effect on 'downtown' shops and shopping, its reduction of land available for agricultural use, its effects on the rural landscape, traffic, utility supplies, etc.

The implications of providing a shopping centre on an urban site are different but no less serious. I will quote the words of Jean Lous Solal as published in a paper to the International Council of Shopping Centres 1978.

'To solve the problem of the downtown shopping centre there is a need for the joint efforts of all the disciplines of knowledge, architects, sociologists, engineers, economists, political scientists, the support of Government at all levels, along with the organisation and management skills which private developers alone can provide to give entrepreneurial drive, competence, dynamics and creditability to any project. Since our urban problems are a compound of physical, social, economic and political elements there is a need for an overall concept plan which will focus on the aspects of planned space use relationships, and accessibility. The private businessman or shopping centre developer cannot do this concept planning all by himself'.

The obtaining of UK planning approval for a shopping centre is likely to be a complicated and lengthy process involving negotiations with the appropriate local authority and perhaps central government, consultation with the local population – residents and traders – followed possibly by a public enquiry and planning policy towards shopping centres varies widely from place to place.

Apart from questions of aesthetics, suitability of treatment, conformity with the structure plan and scheduled use, there will be the whole question of desirability – how will the area be affected by the introduction of a new centre, both environmentally and commercially? In the UK a Department of the Environment circular has required local authorities to inform central government of applications for erection of 'Large new Stores' involving gross floor space of $10\,000\,m^2$ $(100\,000\,ft^2)$ or more, so that the application may be called in for decision by the minister if planning issues of more than local importance are involved. This indicates the importance in planning terms of the introduction of shopping centres, hypermarkets and discount stores, into the community and their likely effect on existing conditions.

The planning procedures may involve a considerable amount of research; provision of statistics on existing and forecasted shopping patterns, population trends, traffic flow and many other considerations, and quite probably special presentation of the scheme with models and drawings to show not only the Planning Authority but also local opinion what they will be getting.

An additional complication could be the straddling of local authority boundaries which would arbitrarily affect a new site; an urban site is not so likely to over-run County boundaries involving several authorities, though the catchment area served may well do so. I have commented previously that there is no British national policy for shopping though there have been some Government papers issued forecasting shopping patterns.

Planning Authorities may restrict the GSA of a project to keep a balance with other shopping centres or main shopping areas in the vicinity or they may insist on certain other uses being introduced. They may, and often do, have views, on the siting of service areas, the 'roof-scape' if visible from above, and indeed all aspects of the project. But the major hurdle may be the acceptance of the shopping centre idea in the first instance, and in negotiations it will be important to demonstrate the advantages it will offer to the locality. Certainly the strict planning controls of the UK system have provided less scope for the extremes of competition found in the USA following excessive retail development.

Additional approvals will be needed if the site is within a 'Conservation Area' where demolition of existing buildings cannot take place without permission or if any existing buildings on the site are 'listed'. In the latter case approvals will be required in respect not only of demolition, if proposed, but also for any proposed alterations, possibly even to interiors, and perhaps retention of certain buildings to be integrated into the scheme, for example Nelson Street at Eldon Square, Newcastle.

Should any alterations to existing road patterns be envisaged, these need special, sometimes lengthy procedures, while any developments near trunk (or classified) roads, and/or new access points will have to be referred to the Ministry of Transport, New 'cross overs' or entries from existing roads into the site will need the approval of the Local Authority. Trees in a Conservation Area cannot be felled without permission, nor can trees with a Preservation Order on them.

Availability of local authority services – water, sewers – will also affect the outcome as well as supplies from the Nationalised Boards – gas, electricity, telephones.

There may be a requirement to notify the local Archaeological Society of the proposals before commencement. The Community Land Act is in process

Retained facade at Eldon Square Shopping Centre, Newcastle. (Photo: Nigel Woolner)

of being repealed but the Development Land Tax will affect the application though due for reconsideration.

UK planning legislation generally is currently under review. Briefly at present there are two tiers of planning authority – the District and the County – with referral to the Secretary of State for the Environment on appeal. He may also call in a project for consideration. There are time limits on the Local Authority for decision on applications, which are deemed to be refused if no decision is given within the time limit, unless the applicant accepts postponement. On refusal there is a right of appeal to the Minister.

There is no doubt that an understanding of the functions and requirements of shopping, both of retailer and shopper, by the officers of the Local Planning Authority can contribute immensely to the quick resolution and viability of a shopping centre scheme, while reinforcing the architect's skill and enthusiasm in providing for his client a successful solution which is at the same time appropriate and sympathetic to the particular site and environmental surroundings.

Legislation generally

There are many elements of the shopping centre controlled or affected by legislation other than the obvious and major factors of planning, construction and fire safety. A reference to the Appendix will indicate, at least to those operating in the UK, some likely areas for enquiry and resolution where appropriate.

There are particular factors in UK legislation that need mention. The Health & Safety at Work Act, Parts 1 and 2, and the Fire Precautions Act make no provision for approval prior to completion so no matter how much early consultation takes place there is always the danger that due to changes in personnel or policy additional demands may be imposed requiring alterations, disturbance and additional cost, at 'handover' stage of the finished job. This is an unsatisfactory state of affairs Moreover, these two Acts imply 'continuing control' during the life of the building(s) concerned and covering any later alterations with continuing certification as complying.

The Health and Safety at Work Act, and Fire Safety legislation also impose requirements during erection concerning safety of operatives and fire control. Dry risers for instance are likely to be demanded, to be maintained throughout construction.

Building controls

In the UK building standards are governed by building regulations which in Scotland differ from those of England and Wales, while London has a different system of building control under the London Building Acts.

A reform of the system has been promised but the Building Regulations which came into force on January 1977 are likely to remain operative for some time. Two amendments have already appeared and no doubt more will follow! The regulations are complex and not wholly consistent; in some cases they govern the minutiae of design of detailed components by mandatory regulation, in others they specify requirements generally, giving 'deemed to satisfy' examples which will meet them or quoting British Standards or British Standards Codes of Practice as complying.

Certain features of Shopping Centre design will require special attention in achieving compliance with Building Regulations, in particular, the first amendment previously referred to. This requires 'a building or part of a building to be so designed and constructed that the enclosing structure provides adequate resistance to the passage of heat' together with 'provisions specifying alternative but not exhaustive measures which if adopted will be deemed to satisfy the mandatory requirement'. In other words buildings must have adequate thermal insulation to satisfy the standards of this amendment; previously the building regulations only set down standards for dwellings.

The restrictions imposed by this amendment may well affect the design of closed malls and courts in covered centres and many already erected will not comply. It is unlikely that future relaxations will be forthcoming, as the intention of the amendment is the conservation of fuel and power.

A major consideration in complying with the building regulations in a shopping centre will be that of intermittent completions, as units will tend to be occupied in series, and not all at the same time. As we have seen, the occupations and tenancies may change during the life of the centre. It is very necessary for the centre, including all units and all aspects of it, to be designed in such a way that when completed it can comply and comply continuously. Tenants must be given adequate information concerning approvals already given or stipulations in order that the fitting out of their units may be carried out accordingly and all regulations safeguarded during fitting out or refitting.

However there is, in fact, one major area where a shopping centre differs materially from any other building type and this is fire safety.

Fire safety

It is significant that I have not been able to find in any book on shopping centres published in 1973 or earlier, the subject of 'Fire safety' or 'Smoke control' in the index. Today no shopping centre could be responsibly designed or executed without special regard to design for fire safety in all its aspects; treated from the outset as a major factor. Whatever the degree of control by local Regulations the architect has a responsibility to the developer, the retailer and the shopping public to design for fire safety and to understand its governing principles and their implications.

The need for fire precautions and fire warning is paramount, but elaborate warning and control systems can be so much in evidence as to be daunting to the staff, particularly in smaller units. In my opinion these need to be offered and accepted naturally as part of the administrative system and the staff need to be confident of the system rather than threatened by it.

Fire safety involves two considerations – safety to life and protection of property. Methods of protection of property are mainly specified by the Insurance Companies and their advisory bodies. Safety to life is the subject of legislation. This deals mainly with construction, spread of flame, means of escape and prevention of the spread of fire and facilities for fire fighting.

Structural fire precautions and means of escape are dealt with under part E of the present UK building regulations. Under these regulations buildings are divided into purpose groups and it has been ruled that a shopping precinct or shopping centre is a 'shop' under purpose group 5. However, in no way can a shopping centre comply with the conditions laid down for the construction of a 'shop' building of purpose group 5, so relaxation of the regulations will be essential if such a complex is to be erected. Though the local authority has power to relax or dispense with certain requirements of the regulations an exception has been made in the case of a shopping precinct, and negotiations for relaxation of the regulations in these cases are negotiated with the Department of the Environment direct. It should be said that in Scotland and Inner London the procedures and regulations vary, the technical requirements being generally similar.

It should be explained that the above remarks apply mainly to covered shopping centres. Open shopping centres are as a general rule able to be considered as individual unit buildings, each to comply. The architect designing an open centre as one complex must ensure that each unit complies with the relevant provisions as regards periods of fire resistance, means of escape, flame spread, separation between shop fronts, etc. and must arrange for such conditions to be laid down in respect of tenancies to ensure that all tenants are aware of the restrictions and requirements as previously indicated.

Particular requirements of building regulations in regard to the construction of an open shopping centre which need to be drawn to the attention of the architect are those concerning compartmentation and unprotected areas. These in effect will control the width of open malls, or conversely may require solid window backs and glazed shop fronts to provide necessary fire resistance between opposing buildings. As we have already seen, canopy heights, road construction and widths, turning circles and so on must be adequate for entry of fire fighting vehicles; where applicable hydrants etc. must be available and clearly identified.

But it is when we come to the enclosed shopping centre that specialist problems arise. They may be summarised as follows:

(a) The means of escape from large and often complex buildings; an enclosed shopping centre is considered as one building with a high potential risk occupancy.

(b) The large size of the 'building', which is in fact a series of smaller uses of different sizes and fire risks all joined together and producing an usually high potential fire risk.

(c) The provision of adequate primary systems for dealing with an outbreak of fire, and in particular the handling of the inevitably large amounts of smoke which will be quickly produced and prejudice the safe evacuation of the building.

In 1972 the Home Office produced a Fire Prevention Guide (*Fire precautions in Town Centre redevelopment*) which, although some of its recommendations are gradually being superseded as a result of further research, still structures the required fire safety conditions of an enclosed centre, as a relaxation of ordinary Building Regulations.

A major reason why it is not possible for an enclosed centre to conform to normal relevant building regulations is that the volume of the malls with all the shops opening on to them is likely to exceed the maximum compartment size allowable as the shops will be divided from the malls either only by glass shop fronts or, with open fronts, not at all. In obtaining relaxation from this requirement, whatever criteria are applied to the means of escape and smoke control, a first priority will be that of sprinklering.

All shopping units, together with their storage areas and general storage areas, will need to be sprinklered. This is generally recognised internationally (and by the insurance companies) as a fundamental precaution, not only under the UK building regulations. There is however a difference of opinion about sprinklering of malls. The main aim of smoke control is to maintain a height of at least 2 m clear of smoke throughout the 'means of escape' routes through the malls for long enough to ensure safe exit, and there is a school of thought which suggests this can be interfered with by mall sprinklering which may cool the smoke and drive it down into the escape route. Alternative opinions suggest that this can be resolved by setting sprinkler controls in malls at a higher temperature than those in shop units to give additional time for escape.

Here a comment on the understanding of the main features of a shopping centre is necessary. The suggestion that sprinklers should be omitted from the malls depends on the definition of a mall as a circulation area only; directly it is used for any other purpose it becomes a fire risk like any other part of the centre and has to be sprinklered. This seems to me to highlight the British misunderstanding of the primary difference between an enclosed shopping centre and a shopping street, which is that the malls and courts should be areas for concourse, for relaxation, and for pause and interest, and most certainly not purely circulation routes between the shops. The provision of cafés, restaurants, fast food areas, play spaces, exhibitions and promotional activities in the malls and courts is becoming a feature of shopping centres in the UK as elsewhere and it appears to me essential to accept this basic function of the communal areas of the shopping centre; thus it would appear that sprinklers will increasingly become a necessity in the malls.

In order to reduce the risk of a fire spreading and engulfing the whole centre, large volumes, such as stores over 2000 m² (20 000 ft²) or areas of high risk, such as warehousing, or large units facing each other across the mall, must be compartmented. This can be done across the shop-front opening by provision of fire shutters. Alternatively, where appropriate and acceptable, solid window backs to the shop front display areas can provide the requisite fire resistance, though solid window backs only suit certain types of trading.

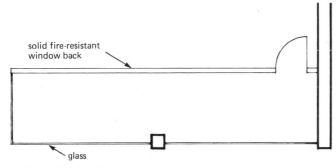

Solid window back

Fire shutters in themselves pose a problem. They are heavy and need substantial support, and although the permitted opening under UK conditions is 4.5 m high × 8.5 m wide, fire shutters of this size give rise to certain difficulties in operation. Also, wherever they are fitted to a unit an alternative means of escape must be provided for those inside. Single fire shutters do not provide acceptable heat insulation and double shutters may be needed. Sensing devices must be positioned each side of the shutters.

Where an existing shop or a series of units is to be incorporated into or joined to a new centre the compartmentation requirement will apply. The existing units involved may need to be brought up as near as possible to the standards applying to the new centre.

The compartmentation principles will also apply vertically between floors. Condition of relaxation will almost certainly be that in a multi-level centre the intermediate floors, even within a unit however small, must be of the appropriate fire resistance standard (say 2 hours, doubled for basements) and incombustible. Here I have discovered another anomaly, which is that the possibility of constructing a true multi-level centre does not appear to have credibility; the design of a shopping centre as an atrium type building several storeys high, now comparatively common in-

ternationally, seems to have no acceptance in this country, though as we will see, research into possible solutions is now under way. A gallery can be accepted within one storey if it is sprinklered.

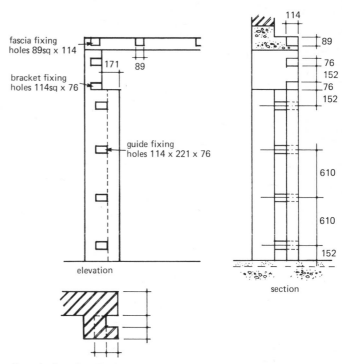

Detail of single rolling fire shutters

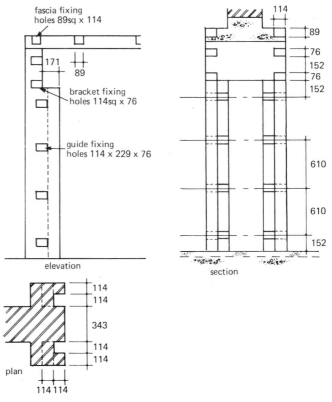

Detail of double rolling fire shutters

Means of escape

The principle of means of escape is the facility to reach a 'protected point', i.e. one protected from smoke and fire, within a given time. Means of escape provisions in enclosed centres must be of very high standard. Means of escape are at present administered under the Building Regulations and there is a BS Code of Practice describing the means of escape from individual shopping premises which, if complied with, is 'deemed to satisfy' these regulations in general terms. The Code deals with exit capacities, restrictions on distance from escape routes and alternative escapes, width of routes, escape from individual premises and is essential reading. But as a fire certificate is required for the complex as a whole, the Fire Precautions Act comes into play and the Fire Brigade will need to be satisfied concerning the proposals and moreover will not issue the certificate until completion.

Requirements will vary between authorities and it has to be remembered that the Fire Precautions Act is administered by the Home Office, a different Ministry from the Department of the Environment which administers the Building Regulations.

A major axiom is that escape should be possible in a direction away from the source of the fire. Thus there should be no 'dead end concrete boxes' within shop units, storage areas or passage ways.

A provision to be remembered is that secondary means of escape where provided from, for instance, the rear of shops, must be 2 m wide, kept clear of all rubbish, stores and so on and unlikely to be acceptable if routed through service areas unless safeguarded. Staircases between levels within small units (under 280 m^2 floor area) will need a ½ hr fire enclosure at one level with ½ hr fire-resisting self closing doors – increased to 1 hr in basement conditions. Basement areas, whatever their uses, attract specific fire-safety requirements as regards construction, means of escape, ventilation and smoke extract, which should be ascertained at design stage as they will affect space allocation decisions.

These examples indicate the intricacy of the conditions of compliance in the UK. Each case will be dealt with on its merits and the earliest and closest consultation with the appropriate Fire Authority will be needed. Staircases leading to the outside through a protected route are considered 'protected points' complying with certain conditions, one being that of smoke lobbies, i.e. two sets of doors opening outward onto the staircase. This is extravagant in terms of space and may be avoided by the use of the pressurised staircase (where accepted). Here a positive pressure must be ensured by the provision of very high velocity fans coming into operation, on a 'fail-safe'

principle, when activated by heat and smoke control devices. Calculations will be needed to account for possible leakage from 'free areas', such as around doors. There will be no automatic smoke vents, and delivery will be at each level through shunt ducts. Escape doors will open in the direction of escape onto the staircase, of course free of the escape route.

A carefully co-ordinated alarm system will be needed in a shopping centre. Alarms from various zones of the complex will be activated by smoke and heat detectors and sprinkler discharge, and also manually. These will be signalled to central control points where the security staff can take action. The Fire Brigade will also come in at this point, notified either by the staff or directly by the system. Besides automatic control of smoke vents, over-riding manual control must be available to the Fire Brigade at convenient points.

Perhaps the most specialised and difficult requirement to integrate is that of 'adequate smoke ventilation' as required by the building regulations.

Smoke control

Smoke control in a closed mall shopping centre has been, and is, the subject of much research and some differing opinions and will have a very definite effect on the design of the centre from the outset.

Smoke control with smoke ventilation is not a constituent of controlling or extinguishing a fire but is designed as a method of providing safe escape routes for the occupants on the one hand and clear access for fire fighting on the other. Basically it involves the dispersal of smoke from a fire breaking out within the complex to the outer air without interfering with the escape routes throughout their length until a protected point is reached. It involves the provision of smoke reservoirs and adequate smoke ventilation calculated to leave a theoretical 2 m vertical height clear of smoke throughout these escape routes for a sufficient period to empty the centre (or those parts affected by the fire) of its occupants.

Smoke travels at approximately 1 m/s faster than the exit speed of shoppers. It plumes as it expands on meeting cooler air and therefore, however it is extracted, it must be contained within limited lengths, to ensure vertical extract and prevent it cooling and dropping into the escape routes. Moreover, adequate fresh air intake must be provided for, with a greater volume than the calculated smoke extract.

This is an extremely limited summary of the factors involved in smoke control in shopping centres and those wishing to master the principles and understand the work of research now going on in order to apply them in designing shopping centres, are recommended to refer to the various papers and publications listed at the end of this chapter. It can be seen from these that the Fire Research Station has done and is doing a great deal of work on smoke control in covered shopping centres. Although it does not lay down regulations its advice will be taken by local authorities and the designs of future shopping centres will have to respond to this growing understanding of smoke control. Thus we come to some technical aspects of providing sprinklers and smoke venting in shopping centres.

Technical provisions – sprinklers and smoke venting

Apart from their use in controlling fire spread long enough to keep the escape routes clear for evacuation of the building, sprinklers are very largely a means of protecting property by confining the outbreak. So here we find a measure of outside control, other than statutory, concerned with Insurance.

There are two bodies concerned, the Fire Protection Association and the Fire Offices Committee. The Fire Protection Association is an advisory body concerned with the safety of life and property. The F.O.C. issues 'rules' which are adopted by the insurance companies in assessing premiums. Their rules for construction of buildings are a pretty blunt instrument to use in such a complex undertaking as an enclosed shopping centre and as far as construction is concerned architects are recommended to seek approval and advice from the insurers at planning stage as previously indicated. The F.O.C. however issues very technical and specific rules for installation of sprinkler systems in various types of building which must be followed.

Shopping centres as a whole are regarded as an ordinary hazard occupancy if complying with these rules which classify buildings according to risk with corresponding requirements. Covered malls and retail units need to be protected to the requirements of the '29th edition of *F.O.C. Rules Ordinary Hazard Group 111*'. A major consideration will be water supply; since for a sprinkler installation at least one hour's continuous supply will be required, the water authority must be consulted to see whether mains supply of adequate size and pressure will be available to comply with the F.O.C. rules.

In the UK, water authorities have a legal duty to provide water for domestic purposes, i.e. lavatories, kitchens, but no duty to provide a sprinkler service off their mains and they may insist on a break tank. The infill rate to serve the sprinkler system will vary, determined by flow and return tests related to the size

of the mains and the reliability of supply. For instance a 100 mm (4 in) mains supply to a sprinkler installation off a dead end feed is not acceptable and in any event must provide required flows and pressures at all times. (As the water authority has to provide fire brigade hydrants these offer a facility for mains testing and pressure tests can be taken between them). There are difficulties where new mains are required for greenfield sites; those needed for domestic purposes only may not meet F.O.C. rules requirements so the developer may be faced with a demand for meeting the cost of the difference. When mains pressure is insufficient, duplicated booster pumps will be necessary with or without a break tank.

So far I have dealt only with malls and retail units but storage poses a serious problem. Within the groups classified in F.O.C. rules the storage areas are considered separately as a worse hazard and extra high hazard protection will be demanded. Permissible storage heights to avoid additional requirements are set out for various categories and materials in the F.O.C. Tables. Category 1 is the least stringent within Group 111 comprising ordinary combustible materials

A typical warehouse stacking where 'flashover' fire spread could occur without venting. In multi-storey types it may be possible to provide ventilation vertically at a high level, (Photo: Colt International)

(and non-combustible materials in combustible wrappings) stored in bulk, in pallets or on racking; if stored to a height of more than 4 m, these will be an extra high hazard as a 'high piled storage risk'.

Some major units may demand a racking height of, say, 9 m so the Developer and his architect must face this possibility which significantly affects elevational treatment, planning of service areas and site area. Obviously determination of storage facilities of the major units should wherever possible be dealt with early in the design process, otherwise storage limitations may have to be imposed, deterring certain major magnets from taking space in the centre. Such devices as a mezzanine floor, dividing the racking into two vertical separate areas for sprinklering may help. Racking may involve siting of sprinkler heads within the racking, requiring a clear space of 150 mm between back-to-back racks to take sprinklers pipework.

Where high storage is required (and in other cases where pressure is inadequate) a reservoir will be demanded by the Fire Offices Committee rules, incorporating one tank and two pumps. As it is assumed that only one fire will take place at a time the tank will be sized for a maximum risk of a given size of fire (not the size of the centre); 100 000 gallons might be a normal tank size. This is quite a planning problem; it can be, with difficulty, provided underground needing suction lift. As the loading is likely to be a ton to 1½ tons per square foot it hardly seems likely that it could be practicable on the roof so it will be sited preferably at ground level.

In deciding the type and size of tank the lowest quote may not necessarily be the cheapest in terms of maintenance; the most maintenance-free type is likely to be the best, bearing in mind the problems concerned with shutting down the system while carrying out maintenance.

A pump house will also be required of, for example, 5 m by 4 m with a full pumping system served by at least two alternatively-operated pumps, probably one pump in National Grid network, with an alternative of either a diesel driver pump or a further electrical pump in the standby generator. A diesel standby will need to be run at least ½ hour a week, out of hours as it is noisy and diesel oil storage must be accommodated. The alternative of connection to the standby electrical generator may not be practicable as something like 100 h.p. will need to be the rating of the pump.

Where a reservoir has to be provided in order to meet the storage facilities of a unit, it may well be advantageous to utilise this for the sprinkler system to the whole centre, sizing it accordingly and agreeing apportionment of cost to the units concerned. Of course, the reservoir may significantly affect elevation-

al treatment and planning of the service areas and once more it is worth pointing out that the introduction of such an item late in the project can be next to disastrous and such matters need to be resolved as soon as possible at design stage.

To go back to the general requirements of the sprinkler installation. The simple type is charged with water at all times, discharged from the sprinkler head as soon as it reaches its activated temperature. Where pipework is exposed to frost damage a wet/dry system will be necessary; this will operate normally in summer months, but in winter water will be drained from the pipework which will be charged above the valve with compressed air from a small automatic compressor. On activation of the sprinkler head air pressure is

Examples of reservoir tank and pump house for sprinklers

reduced and the control valve automatically releases water through the head.

Pipe support methods must be to standards. In the UK these are set by the BSI supplemented by F.O.C. requirements.

The whole operation is related to the discharge per minute, with cover per sprinkler averaged over a given number of sprinklers in accordance with the general calculations of the F.O.C. rules. Voids and ducts will need sprinklering. Pipe sizes are set out in the F.O.C. tables.

There are certain areas in a shopping centre such as switchrooms, art galleries, and computer room where sprinklers would not be appropriate and where specialised warning systems and smoke extract must be considered.

A word on computer room design for fire safety. A computer room will need to be of 4 hour fire resistant construction, if not sprinklered. A computer is very vulnerable to smoke as well as to water and should be designed to prevent smoke entry. It may need a BTN gas system in lieu of sprinklers, though the Health and Safety Executive will require this to operate only when the area is unoccupied. There will be a fire hazard in stacked paper which should be in a service area beside, not within, the computer suite as data and paper stores are flammable. The gas system will operate all smoke detectors. In an automatic system (in an unmanned area) smoke detectors will normally operate on the 'double knock' principle, the first detection to give an audible fire warning, a second in another circuit to release the gas and operate dampers in the ducts.

However, computers are rapidly getting smaller while their potential work load is getting larger. It is possible that before long they may be accepted as a unit within a sprinklered area rather than isolated in a separate computer room.

Sprinklers within shop premises are normally activated at a temperature of 68°C but if the malls are to be sprinklered it is recommended that these should come into operation at a higher temperature, say 141°C, to avoid cooling of smoke interfering with the escape routes as previously explained. A larger unit may have a flow switch for its own system. Groups of standard shops may share a system, but not with the malls or other public or service areas.

The system will be zoned by valves each operated by pressure switches to give alarm to the control room as to which valve set is operating. Water flow alarm switches can be used to locate more precisely the main through which water is passed. Smoke detectors operating smoke vents are relevant to sprinkler planning. Where a sprinkler system is subject to frost a dry system may be necessary; as mentioned it will be

activated by compressed air and a compressed air chamber must be planned for.

Obviously it is important that the sprinkler installation should be integrated into the scheme at the start. Advice should be sought from the developer's insurance company, the specialist concerned with the installation, the water authority, the fire brigade, the local authority controlling building regulations, all of whom will have a hand in the design and construction.

So we come to smoke ventilation. It is not possible (even if space were available) to lay down at this present time definitive rules regarding smoke control. The Home Office Fire Prevention Guide in 1972 recommended that ventilation openings should be provided to release smoke and hot gases from pedestrian malls equal in total area to 30% of the mall floor area. Although this recommendation is still followed by some authorities, others require very precise and intricate calculations in accordance with BRSS publications, (these calculations being based on a maximum fire size of 5 MW which assumes a sprinkler controlled shop fire).

We have seen that extract vents must be at high level and related to compartmentation with smoke reservoirs, calculated of adequate size to extract smoke and gases. The calculations will relate not to the size of the area but to the assumed size of the fire! Ventilation may be natural or powered; if natural and so designed, it will need to be controllable, automatically operated by smoke detectors and fire-override fusible links as well as manual over-ride by Fire Brigade or security staff.

Ventilation may be built into the construction or provided as unit ventilators (see illustration of louvred type and smoke chimneys). These ventilators may also operate as natural ventilation in normal conditions. I have referred to the design implications of this in the earlier chapter on Mechanical Services. Calculations may show that confronted with high volume low temperature gases natural vents are not enough and powered extract may be necessary. This is most likely in two-storey malls, which will easily be disturbed by wind pressures due to low gas temperature. Fans will have to withstand high temperatures, say 300°C at ½ hour operation) and work on an emergency standby system; they are often provided in the form of unit extractors, designed for the purpose.

Certain design factors concerned with smoke reservoirs have already been touched on in earlier chapters such as the necessity for a down stand forming a smoke check between the shop and the mall. If an open ceiling is provided within the mall the smoke reservoir may be within the service area above; an alternative is a mall ceiling approximately a metre higher, say, than the shop units adjoining.

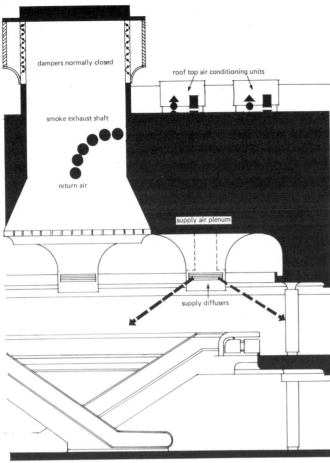

Labels within the diagram: dampers normally closed; roof top air conditioning units; smoke exhaust shaft; return air; supply air plenum; supply diffusers; supply and return in central area

Arndale Centre, Kirkgate, Bradford. Smoke chimney in Central Square. This acts by natural ventilation with pneumatically operated dampers arranged to fail in the open position. Note arrangement of louvres to allow for differing wind conditions. This is one of five in the malls

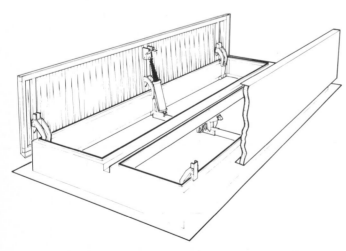

Louvred automatic fire ventilator. This unit can be mounted horizontally or vertically (Colt International)

A further problem arises in a multi-level mall; here the upper storeys must be protected from the smoke rising from the lower. This can be assisted by projecting balconies. There is also a limitation in length of reservoirs to approximately 60 m, to limit the distance escapers have to travel below smoke. It is evident that some form of screen is required to contain the reservior within acceptable dimensional limits and if this cannot be done by permanent physical features it may be possible to provide emergency screening activated by smoke detectors and fusible links. The size of individual smoke reservoirs should be limited to, say, $1000 \, m^2$ for natural or $1300 \, m^2$ for mechanical extraction.

Fresh air must enter the building to replace the extracted hot smoky gases; with a natural smoke ventilation system the area of inlets should be at least twice the area of vents in a single reservoir. With a mechanical system a lower area may be sufficient but the resistance of inlets must be taken into account when calculating the requirements of the fans. Positions should be selected to flush cold air throughout the malls below the ceiling reservoir and the speed of incoming air should slow down before contacting the smoke. Doors at the ends of malls may form suitable inlets if they are provided with automatic opening in the event of fire, and can be provided with smoke baffles sited a few metres along the mall, to check speed and reduce wind effects. It will be advantageous to provide a facility for manual and controlled operation of vents and smoke reservoirs remote from the fire so that they can function as fresh air inlets.

The diagrams illustrate these points. They are taken from *'Work by the Fire Research Station on the control of Smoke in Covered Shopping Centres'*, by P. L. Hinchley, published by the FRS. They illustrate the problem of smoke ventilation and some solutions.

Another technical point to be considered in designing for smoke venting is the effect of wind. The position of the vents must be considered in relation to any higher surrounding levels of the centre or of buildings which may result in down draught on outlets; also to avoid down-draught from different wind directions outlets may need to face more than one way. Aerodynamic design of vents, or even chimneys above roof level may be needed to counteract wind pressure.

Gases must not be allowed to cool before they reach the vents so the area must be related to the length of the extract route and, if on external walls, insulation may even be needed to ensure maintenance of temperature at least as high as in the space being vented. Of course, fresh air inlets also need to be considered in relation to possible wind effects.

In this chapter, I have only been able to touch lightly on the very complicated issue of providing satisfactory smoke ventilation in a shopping centre. I hope I have adequately stressed the importance of studying the problem and its implications concurrently with the design of the centre.

Other fire safety requirements

Hydrants, wet and dry risers
Water supply for fire fighting will be needed. Charged hydrants, with guaranteed adequate pressure and capacity, will be demanded at vehicle access levels at stated intervals, and within multi-level centres dry or wet rising mains.

The BS Code of Practice CP3 gives appropriate recommendations but the installations should be discussed at design stage with the Fire Brigade.

First aid fire fighting
It is not usually appropriate to provide equipment for fire fighting by untrained personnel or by the public.

Fire fighting equipment will be specified by the Fire Authority. Within retail units this will be the responsibility of the retailer. In malls and public and service areas, car parks, etc. it will be provided by the developer; the type and extent to be agreed with the appropriate Fire Authority, for use by trained security staff. It may include hose reels and fire extinguishers which must be protected from vandalism, and like all other items concerned with Fire Safety, must be regularly inspected, maintained and tested. Hose reels, if required, may need pumps depending on height related to water pressure.

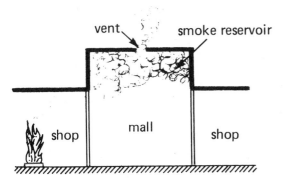

(top) Smoke reservoir in mall with ceiling height greater than that in shops
(bottom) Smoke reservoir formed by fascias above open fronts of shops

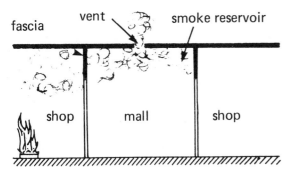

False ceilings and smoke reservoir

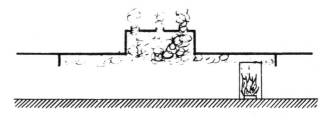

outlets should be at the highest points in a mall roof screen

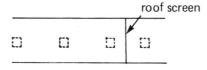

Plan showing ideal distribution of outlets in a mall

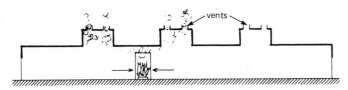

Upstands as smoke reservoirs

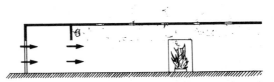

Screen sited a few metres along mall to reduce wind effects

Communication, the control system and security

Next we come to the final ingredient in the shopping centre package, the control system, which consolidates routine day-to-day running and security and emergency action for the whole enterprise. These operations will cover the general protection of the shopping public and the staff, as well as the property and contents of the units and all areas of the centre. There will be a central control room, a nerve centre from which trained security staff will handle equipment which is becoming increasingly sophisticated and correspondingly compact with the opening of each large shopping centre as the microprocessor takes over.

The siting of the control room needs to be considered in relation to construction of the centre and, if the development is to be phased or part occupied, it must be commissioned at the time the first phase is operating. The control room will be working throughout the day, 7 days a week, and must be suitably sited for supervision and for convenience of the security staff.

It is worth a mention that uniformed staff, whether patrolling the centre or engaged on maintenance tasks, are a deterrent to vandalism.

The major elements of control and communication will be:

Fire Safety;

Security (crime, vandalism prevention and accident action);

Monitoring of all mechanical services and equipment for safety, comfort and economic use.

A large centre may have a microprocessor-based data system fed with information from fire alarm and security systems, CO_2 monitoring, heating and ventilating and sprinkler equipment, lighting and car parking. It will have closed circuit television, public address and communication systems with teletype printers and keyboards with video display units, and, of course, indicator lights. Information can be processed for economic running, fault analysis, energy conservation and other factors.

A very large centre may have satellite stations zoned to collect local information to be relayed to the central station control and possibly with certain manual controls for local operation. All systems must of course have standby power and/or battery equipment.

Fire safety is perhaps the dominant factor. In the words of the Department of the Environment Fire Prevention Guide 'A central and constantly manned control room' is needed 'to act as a coordinating point for many forms of fixed communication'. Shopping centre complexes as a whole are not conducive to the efficient use of mobile or personal radio sets as their construction induces poor reception. Telephone heads should therefore be provided at emergency call points throughout the centre connected to the control room and also in any lift car provided for fireman's use.

The control room will be provided with a direct line to the fire brigade; all telephone extensions or call points throughout the centre should be connnected to the control room. There may also be further arrangements for plug-in facilities for the fire brigade and hydrant and staircase points. There may be emergency telephones for use by security staff connected to the control room at suitable points. A public address system can be used as a warning system in case of fire, bomb scares, lost children, etc. and will be zoned for different types of warning, depending on the emergency. The system must be of high quality, clear audibility and subject to frequent testing. The public address system has many other uses; it will broadcast background music, help in promotions, crowd control at the sale times and so on. There will probably be taped programs for use in various eventualities.

Heat and smoke detector and sprinkler systems will be connected to the control room. In a large regional centre there may be subsidiary zoned fire officer's control panels. If these are provided they will be equipped with fire alert indicators, smoke extract ventilation controls, inter-communication for central control rooms and the fire brigade, telephone handset and public address system, selection control; otherwise all these will be operated centrally. The emergency lighting system will also be linked to the control room. Even after the evacuation of any part of the centre affected by fire, the fire brigade will be fighting the fire and will need operation control and communication between fire service units on site and with fire brigade headquarters and with the management of the centre.

Security is frequently at odds with fire safety at least in the context of means of escape; nevertheless security is extremely important. In a closed centre a security system may monitor high security entries such as control room and sub-station as well as major entrances and exits by means of 'keep' or 'lock' monitoring or magnetised controls. Control and communication will be necessary for access to a closed centre out of shopping hours by staff and deliveries, etc. Vehicle delivery service entries are sometimes monitored direct to the control room.

Closed circuit television can be useful as a security aid to cover key points such as escalators, children's play areas and others as the developer requires and a communication network with security and maintenance staff can form part of the system. In a closed centre the police are not involved in routine security

*Queensgate, Peterborough, Control room console
(Peterborough Development Corporation)*

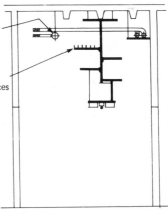

mechanical services
distribution pipe
150 Ø sprinkler supply

two No. 3 compartment trunking
each compartment is 100x100
and shall carry the following services

1 landlord and tenant fire/
   alarm detection
2 landlord and tenant public
   address
3 landlord and tenant
   control system
4 internal telephone and
   call system supplied and
   installed by landlords
   electrical subcontractors
5 P.O. telephone
6 small power

Typical
trolley way
detail

but there may, by arrangement, be a direct communication with a police station. There should be early consultation with a senior crime prevention officer of the local branch of the Police Force who will have useful local knowledge and will advise on security precautions and liaison with the police.

Security within individual units will be the responsibility of the retailers and in the case of open shop fronts, the developers should require the provision of shutters or roller grilles or other protection during closing hours; the developer cannot be responsible for the goods within the retail units. There may however be arrangements for monitoring of the retail units to the central control system out of hours.

There is little doubt that a major crime deterrent is adequate lighting of all areas.

Mechanical and electrical services and plant
It is advisable for all plant and equipment to be controlled, and probably their performance recorded in the central control room where warning will automatically record any malfunction. Thus location can be determined and an immediate response to rectify the fault as quickly as possible. There will be constant monitoring of all mechanical equipment and installations with central control from the control room; this, covering air temperature, ventilation and lighting levels, and performance records will greatly contribute to the economic running of the centre. Within pre-set limits the system can be arranged to react automatically to given conditions. Duplicate cables may be necessary to ensure continuing use in case of fault.

The above description is typical of general matters which may be covered by a control system but these will vary in accordance with the developer's requirements, methods of maintenance, types of equipment

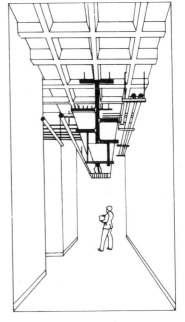

Queensgate, Peterborough, section through service corridor showing trolleyway method of service ducting (Peterborough Development Corporation)

being serviced, the type and extent of mechanical equipment and the quality and number of security staff employed. Each system will be carefully tailored to suit the particular centre requirements. As with all other design elements of the centre this must be considered at the start and the specialist brought in simultaneously with other consultants so that the control system may be integrated with the other services, not as an afterthought.

Chapter 10
Examples

The UK examples, illustrated, demonstrate local characteristics. They tend to be urban redevelopment rather than new sites, usually in or adjoining central areas, sometimes in historic or long developed and well loved settings. They show alternative approaches to this difficult problem of conciliation or contrast with the existing townscape. On the whole they lead away from luxury trading in favour of the familiar multiples and contain supermarket and convenience food outlets. Many for one reason or another fall short of the glamour and excitement and all out shopping/entertainment/relaxation accepted image of the one stop overseas centre, though a number of them have won architectural awards.

Overseas examples give an indication of shopping centre trends elsewhere, and are interesting to compare with UK centres. There are also some examples of both new and rehabilitated smaller specialist developments in key positions.

The references given are selective rather than comprehensive and are listed below:

Nine regional UK centres:

Eldon Square, Newcastle-upon-Tyne.
Brent Cross Shopping Centre, London.
Arndale Centre, Manchester.
Wood Green Shopping Centre, London.
Hempstead Valley Shopping Centre, Kent.
Central Milton Keynes.
Brunel Centre, Swindon.
Queensgate Centre, Peterborough.
Friary Centre, Guildford.

Two UK examples of naturally ventilated closed centres:

Quadrant Centre, Swansea.
The Ridings, Wakefield.

Two smaller UK open centres:

Swan Walk, Horsham, Surrey.
Swan Centre, Leatherhead, Surrey.

Two smaller UK closed centres:

Millburngate Centre, Durham.
West One, Oxford Street, London.

A UK centre in an historic town:

Coppergate, York.

Six foreign centres:

City Deux, Brussels, Belgium.
The Galleria, White Plains, New York.
La Part-Dieu, Lyons, France.
Singapore Plaza, Singapore.
Peninsula Plaza, Singapore.
Eaton Centre, Toronto, Canada.

Four rehabilitation schemes:

Ghirardelli Square, San Francisco.
Faneuil Centre, Boston.
The Market, Covent Garden, London.
London Pavilion, Piccadilly Circus, London.

ELDON SQUARE, Newcastle-upon-Tyne

Architects: Chapman Taylor Partners.
Structural engineers: Felix J. Samuely & Partners.
Services engineers: Steensen Varming Mulcahy & Partners.
Developers: Capital & Counties Property Company Limited and The City of Newcastle-upon-Tyne.
Managed by: Capital & Counties Property Company Limited. G. Allanson, Centre Manager.
Area: 72 500 m^2 (780 000 ft^2), GLA 120 units, Department Store
Enclosed; Multi-storey, air conditioned malls; 2 shopping levels; 1500 car park spaces; Market; Bus Station.
Opened 1976
Other uses: Recreation Centre, offices.

Reference:
Architectural Review (April 1977)
Brick Bulletin (September 1978)
Architect's and Service Engineers Reports.

Urban Development; the site had to be developed in accordance with the planning framework established by the City planning department.

The new shopping malls form part of the new system of city streets and tie in with specific proposals for the central area, e.g. the pedestrianisation of Northumberland Street, the new metro station, car parking and motorway strategy and the need to provide covered vehicular servicing to all adjacent properties which form an integral part of the development site.

The scheme is structured around the pedestrian malls which form the principal arteries of movement, connecting existing established shopping areas of Newcastle with the new bus concourse, car parks, and new underground station. The malls slope to follow the gradients of the site; a radical departure from traditional shopping centre planning.

The project had a profound effect on the City's mains supplies of water gas, telephones and electricity and the disposal systems of surface water and sewage. Major diversions and improvements were effected to all such services before and during the redevelopment, to maintain supplies to users outside the redevelopment area and to serve the new building complex.

The following, taken from a description by Mr. Mackenzie of Steensen Varming Mulcahy & Partners, illustrates the complexity of servicing a large complex project in a city centre.

'The whole area is air conditioned including the malls and concourse. The systems of medium pressure hot water and chilled water are generated in a central plant area and distributed throughout the scheme at service road level'.

Local plant rooms are distributed throughout the development to serve the landlord areas, with individual tenancies providing for their own plant. All air intake and extract routes were predetermined with the systems of louvres forming an integral part of the external cladding system.

Cladding to the buildings around Eldon Square is brick with infill lead panels forming sheltered colonnades and terraces – the set back levels are zinc clad. The external elevational treatment forms a strong unified design. But it seems a pity that planning policy concerning external signing has lost the Centre a splendid opportunity of attracting attention by a really well designed dignified statement, identifying the complex from a distance. It does not proclaim its function by means of any sign above street level. (Photo: Brecht-Einzig)

Service roads and bus concourse areas are fully ventilated to extract the vehicle fumes at both high and low level with the low level extracts located in the roadway acting also as emergency surface water drainage.

Fire fighting and detection systems are extensive with a separate pressurised water main serving the sprinkler systems and wet riser installations. The scheme is completely sprinklered including service roads and malls. Extract fans are automatically switched to high speed, and mall supply fans can be reversed to afford smoke clearance.

Complete security and fire detection systems serve the development incorporating intruder alarms, fire and smoke detection, fire shutters, etc., which are monitored at a central control room manned 24 hours per day.

The main plant consists of three gas fired boilers each rated at 4886 kW supply medium pressure hot water throughout the development.

Chilled water is generated in the same area by three 1000 ton centrifugal machines with cooling towers located on the roof of the office block above.

Tenants obtain heat and chilled water directly from the distribution mains at service road level. Major medium space uses are separately metered with small space users charged by means of an area related service charge.

Variable volume pumps are installed to meet the fluctuating demands in both the heating and cooling distribution mains.

The extensive control systems throughout the development are linked to the central 'Building Automation System' incorporating mini-computer, operators' console and visual display unit, which can be used to effectively monitor and control the various systems.

The electrical requirements are supplied through a system of primary and consumer sub-stations incorporating a system of electrical interlocks to provide for emergency lighting and power. In addition some sub-stations have limited emergency generation.

A system of 11 separate consumer sub-stations providing over 15 000 kVA (approximately 14 000 kW) serves the development with each space user responsible for his own supply agreement direct with the North Eastern Electricity Board. On the landlords supplies the lighting in the malls is designed to a low level of 200 lux with the emphasis placed on the shop fronts for providing sparkle and interest. Both the mall lighting and service road lighting have alternate fittings fed from separate sub-station interlinks affording emergency lighting.

The development has a central TV aerial system, lightning protection, closed circuit TV, public address, etc., the latter being used by the landlord for both information services and providing a facility for the fire service and police to be used in an emergency situation.

Tenants obtain their water supplies directly from the new mains installed in the development, in the normal manner, by agreement with the Newcastle and Gateshead Water Company.

Domestic hot water is not catered for centrally; the larger space users use the primary heating mains to heat water to water calorifiers and all smaller tenancies are provided with electric water heaters. All such tenancies are also provided with toilet facilities and drainage.

Without the interior fitting out work the landlord's services involved the use of some 500 miles of electric cable, 300 tons of sheet metal ventilation ducts and some 20 miles of mains pipework.

The central cooling installation was, at the time, the largest of its type in Britain, and it may still be so, excluding industrial applications.'

Service roads run at a level of 6 m below the malls and feed storage areas on either side that connect with ths shop units above. As the roads approach Northumberland Street and Grey's Monument they fall 6 m below the existing ground levels and provide basement service access to the buildings adjoining the development site.

Internally, the malls present a series of changing views and spaces sloping to follow gradients of the site. This imposes restrictions on shop front design and position of entrances, requiring ingenuity in planning individual units. The malls are divided by a series of concourses where the low level of lighting is contrasted with the introduction of natural lighting from above.

Special features include a double-height water feature and a free-standing circular restaurant, together with play features for children.

The low floor to ceiling height and dark brown slatted ceilings with a lighting level of approx. 200 lux gives a somewhat oppressive feeling in some of the malls. These form a street system allowing the centre to remain a focal point after shopping hours, giving access to a night club, 3 public houses and the Recreation Centre.

Externally, the buildings are carefully designed to present a number of faces according to particular location within the context of the City.

The development was built in two phases.

Rents are, where possible, charged on a turnover basis subject to a minimum figure with periodic review, landlord's management expenditure being recovered by means of service charges.

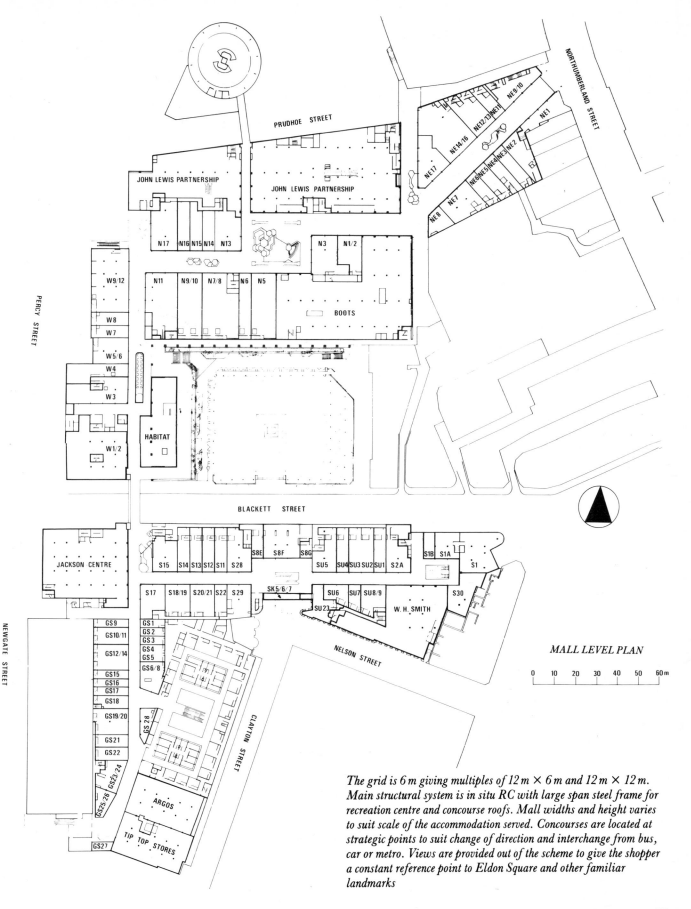

MALL LEVEL PLAN

0 10 20 30 40 50 60 m

The grid is 6 m giving multiples of 12 m × 6 m and 12 m × 12 m. Main structural system is in situ RC with large span steel frame for recreation centre and concourse roofs. Mall widths and height varies to suit scale of the accommodation served. Concourses are located at strategic points to suit change of direction and interchange from bus, car or metro. Views are provided out of the scheme to give the shopper a constant reference point to Eldon Square and other familiar landmarks

BRENT CROSS SHOPPING CENTRE, Hendon, London

Architects: BEP Partnership.
Developers: Hammerson Property and Investment Trust.
Managed by: Donaldsons Property Management.
Michael Brown, Centre, Manager.
Area: 73 000 m² (790 000 ft²), 82 units, 2 Department Stores
Enclosed; Multi-storey, air conditioned malls; 2 shopping levels; 5600 car park spaces; Bus Station.
Opened 1976

Reference:
Developer's Technical Information

Edge of town development; on a virgin site outside an established shopping area, intended to serve the North-West suburbs of London as an alternative to visiting the West End.

It took from 1964 to 1972 to obtain final planning approval, but the project has amply justified itself commercially. It is sited at the centre of three major trunk roads, served by a bus station and has a catchment area of 1¼ million people within 20 minutes drive. It is open normally till 8.00 p.m. (late for a British centre!)

Trading emphasis is on comparison shopping, particularly fashion and consumer durables; the amount of food retailing has been controlled, to be complementary to existing district centres. Certain trades are lacking, e.g. ironmongery and motor accessories shop, garden centre. There is only one pair of escalators, one passenger lift and one set of public toilets! Some of the shops are provided with shared staff toilets. The complex is zoned into six zones for services and servicing, which is by hoist from ground level service areas. Refuse disposal is by private contractor, shop trolleys emptied by management. Road maintenance and cleaning is provided for by management vehicles, with salt and sand stores.

Air-conditioning is from six gas-fired plant rooms on the roof. Shops have fresh air inlets from the malls with air handling at rear.

Sprinkler main is from town mains. Drenchers separate the malls from the courts (now no longer demanded in shopping centres by the authorities).

Internally this is an attractive centre of high quality finish on the American pattern – unremarkable in design, efficiently maintained, with brightly-lit welcoming malls and courts. The shop designs are dominant and varied, and the whole project is commercially highly successful.

Tenants are on long lease, with rent reviews and right to assign after 5 years, with the landlord's option to buy back.

Externally a medley of buildings, set uneasily within a 'spaghetti junction' of approach roads and through routes. Photograph taken before completion of multi-storey car park (Photo: Handford)

Natural light is supplied to malls via self-cleaning skylights and egg-crate type ceilings. Soft water is provided for planting. There is a filtration plant to the fountain and automatic suction for cleaning and water changing. Note upper level bridges across open well to lower floor malls (Photo: James Holmes)

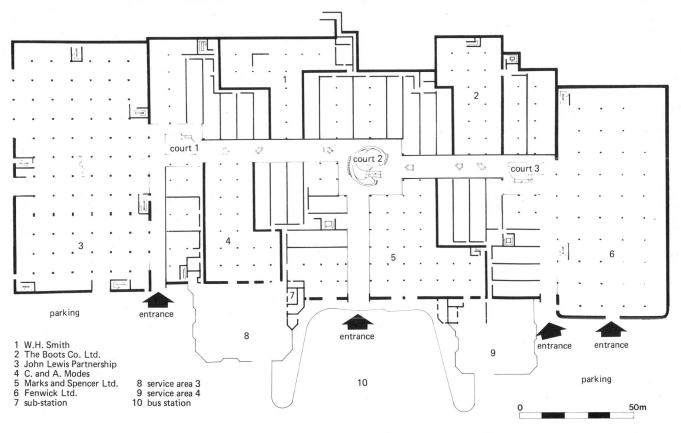

1 W.H. Smith
2 The Boots Co. Ltd.
3 John Lewis Partnership
4 C. and A. Modes
5 Marks and Spencer Ltd.   8 service area 3
6 Fenwick Ltd.   9 service area 4
7 sub-station   10 bus station

Lower ground floor plan

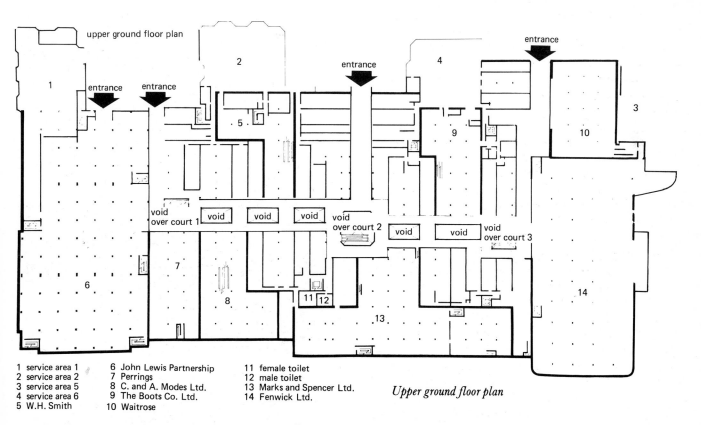

1 service area 1   6 John Lewis Partnership   11 female toilet
2 service area 2   7 Perrings   12 male toilet
3 service area 5   8 C. and A. Modes Ltd.   13 Marks and Spencer Ltd.
4 service area 6   9 The Boots Co. Ltd.   14 Fenwick Ltd.
5 W.H. Smith   10 Waitrose

Upper ground floor plan

Main mall widths 10 m ground floor and 15 m 1st floor. Structural grid 7.5 m × 7.5 m RC construction

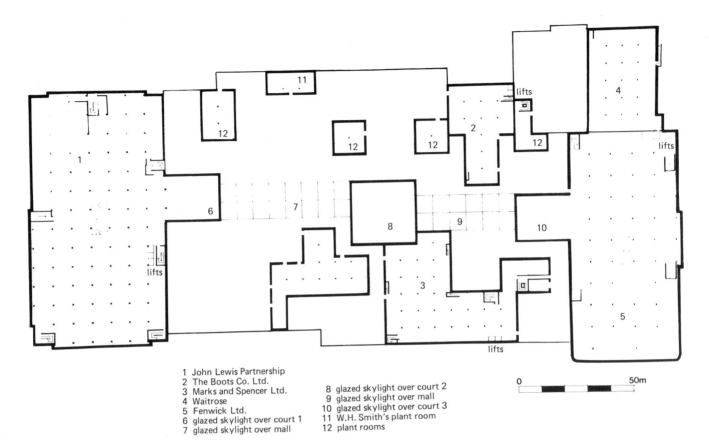

1 John Lewis Partnership
2 The Boots Co. Ltd.
3 Marks and Spencer Ltd.
4 Waitrose
5 Fenwick Ltd.
6 glazed skylight over court 1
7 glazed skylight over mall

8 glazed skylight over court 2
9 glazed skylight over mall
10 glazed skylight over court 3
11 W.H. Smith's plant room
12 plant rooms

0   50m

Second floor plan

The main dome 25 m span, 8 m high, is illuminated through coloured translucent concealed floodlights

ARNDALE CENTRE, Market Street, Manchester

Architects: Sir Hugh Wilson and Lewis Womersley.
Developers: Town & City Properties Limited, jointly with Manchester Corporation.
Managed by: Town & City Properties Limited. Williams, Centre Manager.
Area: 111 000 m² (1 200 000 ft²) 157 units (7 major shops)
Enclosed: Multi-storey; air conditioned malls; 2 shopping levels; 1800 car park spaces; Market; Bus Station.
Opened 1976.

Reference:
Developer's Report

Dominant in design, the elevations form an element striking an almost bullying contrast to the surrounding buildings

Urban development of 15 acres comprising land north and south of two main shopping streets, both bridged by enclosed shopping malls, with a link to the local bus station which holds 1500 buses (30 000 people per day).

This is perhaps the 'flagship' of the Arndale Centre developments and typical of the Arndale style – workmanlike, but unromantic internally, aggressive externally.

There is a basement service core through to all floors – an underground trucking level and basement car park.

The tenant mix is controlled, and an element of segregation introduced – from luxury trading graded down to the Market.

Malls are air conditioned. A dumping main, but not chilled water, is available to tenants. Cooling towers for air conditioning and dumping mains are on the roof.

Communal toilets are provided for shop staff.

There is no natural light, but malls form wide spacious areas, with open wells through two floors; unhappily no promotional activities are permitted in the malls due to rating restrictions. There are 2 restaurants.

Refuse disposal is by means of 1½c yd steel bins housed in refuse rooms in service corridors and collected by management into tractor/trailers for central compaction in two 32c yd containers with a 4 to 1 ratio and a baler for cartons ready for disposal.

The project was carried out in two stages. Rents are fixed. Traders previously on site were decanted and relocated in the new centre.

External view from bridge

Internal view from upper level (Photo: Town & City Properties)

Arndale Centre, Manchester

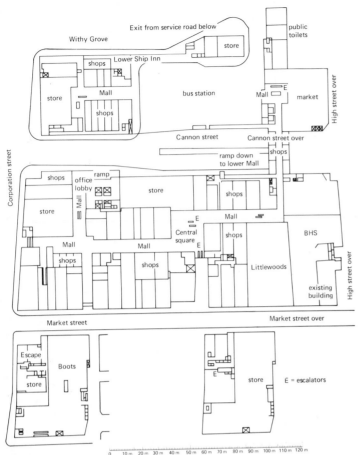

Street level

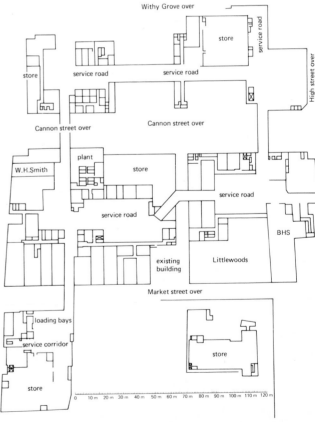

Service level

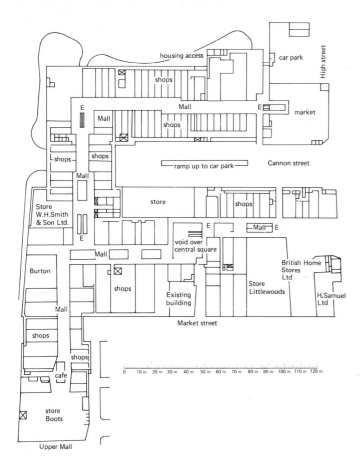

Upper mall level

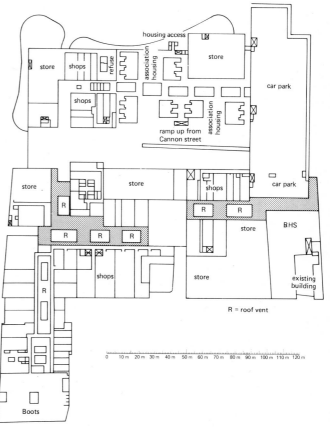

Upper service level

WOOD GREEN SHOPPING CENTRE,
Wood Green, London

Architects: Sheppard Robson & Partners.
Structural & Service Engineers: Ove Arup and Partners.
Developers: Electricity Supply Nominees and London
Borough of Haringey
Managed by: Richard Ellis & Son. (Car park by Local
Authority)
Area: 44 100 m² (475 000 ft²) 108 units Department
store
Enclosed; (but with perimeter shopping); Multi-
storey; 3 other major stores; 2 shopping levels; air
conditioned malls; 1500 car park spaces; Market.
Opened 1980.
Other uses: Offices; crèche; housing (201 flats) ('the
Street in the Air')

Reference:
Developer's brochure
Tenants brief
'Building Design' 13th April 1979
London Borough of Haringey Booklet on *'Redevelop-
ment of Wood Green Town Centre'.*

Urban development in an inner suburb seen as an
extension of the existing High Street trading, designed
as a major shopping centre of strategic importance.

The High Street bisects the development which is
bridged at upper level. A proposed link road will
ultimately divert all but bus traffic but meanwhile the
main traffic route runs through the Centre between
Phases 1 & 2 and perimeter shopping faces this
thoroughfare. Lifts connect the malls directly with car
parks; bus and tube connections are adjacent.

Servicing is at ground level around the perimeter
with eight service yards giving access to shops. Refuse
is compacted, and removed by private contract, operated by developer.

Air conditioning and boiler plant are centrally
located in basement, providing conditioned air, hot
and chilled water to retail areas, servicing a variable
air volume system to each unit, balancing thermally
the heat gains to the unit, from which the tenant must
supply his own variable air volume and low velocity
distribution and duct extract system. Area provided
for plant rooms is approximately 6% of total area.
Cooling towers are in centre of car park.

Smoke prevention in malls is by hydraulically controlled ventilators in detection system. Downstand
beams act as smoke reservoirs, 2½% of floor area
being openable for smoke removal by ducts, where not
directly connected to atmosphere, with breaklight
smoke vents in pavements and basements. The whole

External elevations. (Taken before completion) (Photo: Nicholas Halton)

Internal view. (Photo: Nicholas Halton)

complex is a maximum size building governed by the
'Section 20' GLC Bylaws for Fire Regulations.

Natural light is apparent only at entrances and
sides of the gallery. The malls are artificially lit, to a
low lighting level say 80 lux, the stairs and escalator
malls at a maximum of 180 lux.

Strict control is exercised over design of tenants'
units generally as detailed in a very through 'Tenants'
Brief' (which is almost a dissertation on shop design!)

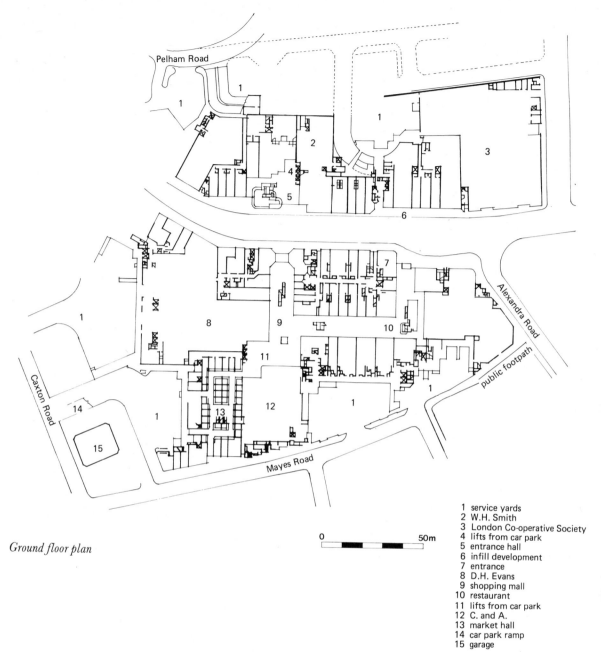

Ground floor plan

1 service yards
2 W.H. Smith
3 London Co-operative Society
4 lifts from car park
5 entrance hall
6 infill development
7 entrance
8 D.H. Evans
9 shopping mall
10 restaurant
11 lifts from car park
12 C. and A.
13 market hall
14 car park ramp
15 garage

An interesting feature is a group of highly special-ised boutiques, specially designed in a high traffic position on the main link between the east and west phases of the development. Each has all-round floor to ceiling windows and is intended to provide high quality retail shopping, each boutique being allocated a speciality field.

The whole development, including the housing over, presents a somewhat overpowering impression to the High Street, dominating by its strength of design and overall scale rather than offering any obvious external invitation to delights within.

Turnover leases are operated. Work was completed in 2 stages.

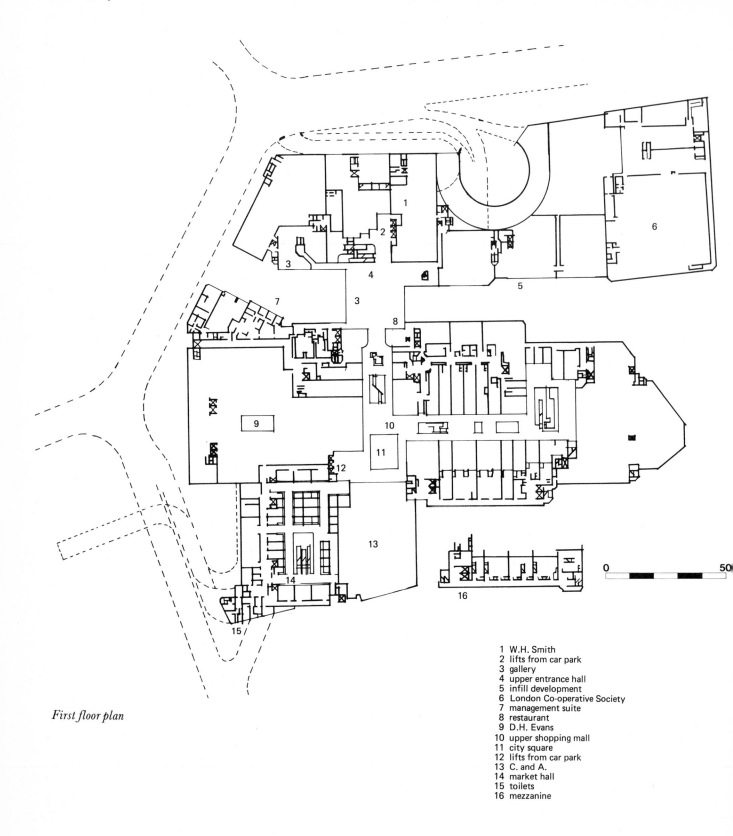

First floor plan

1 W.H. Smith
2 lifts from car park
3 gallery
4 upper entrance hall
5 infill development
6 London Co-operative Society
7 management suite
8 restaurant
9 D.H. Evans
10 upper shopping mall
11 city square
12 lifts from car park
13 C. and A.
14 market hall
15 toilets
16 mezzanine

0   50

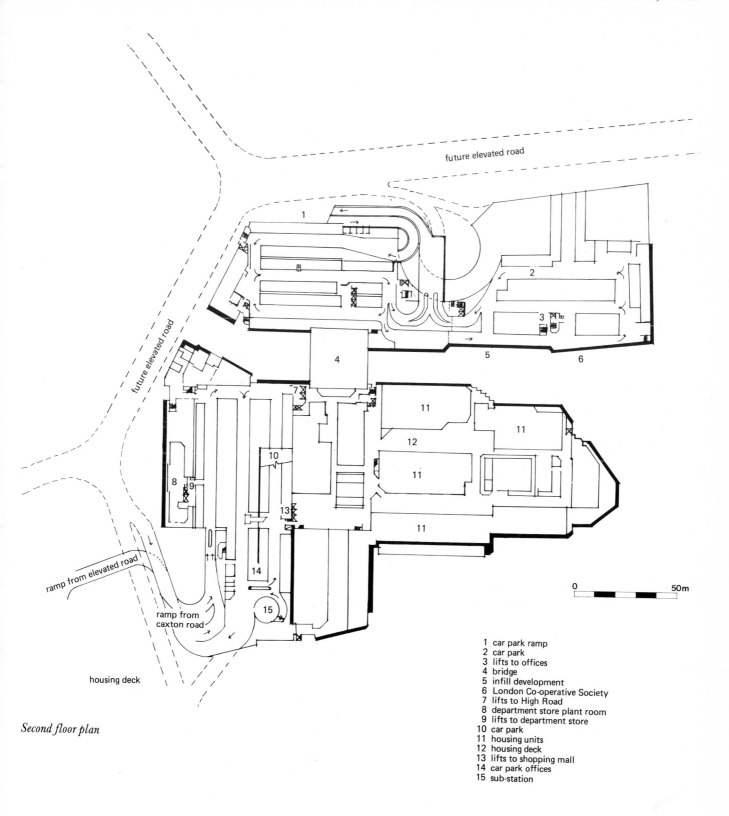

future elevated road

future elevated road

ramp from elevated road

ramp from caxton road

housing deck

0   50m

Second floor plan

1 car park ramp
2 car park
3 lifts to offices
4 bridge
5 infill development
6 London Co-operative Society
7 lifts to High Road
8 department store plant room
9 lifts to department store
10 car park
11 housing units
12 housing deck
13 lifts to shopping mall
14 car park offices
15 sub-station

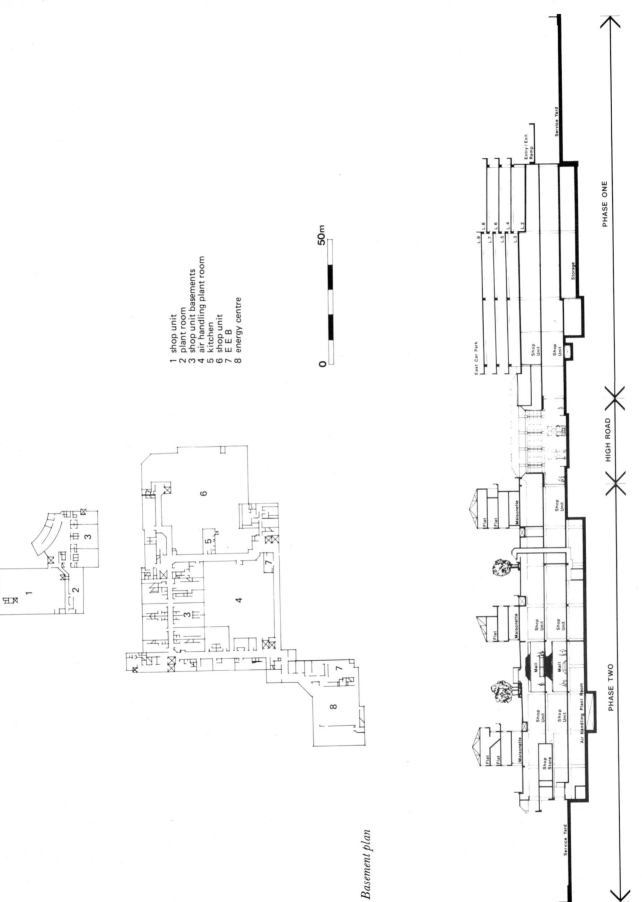

1 shop unit
2 plant room
3 shop unit basements
4 air handling plant room
5 kitchen
6 shop unit
7 E E B
8 energy centre

0   50m

Basement plan

West/East section

HEMPSTEAD VALLEY SHOPPING CENTRE,
Gillingham, Kent

Architects: Stanley Bragg & Associates.
Developers: Federated Homes Limited.
D. J. Peek, Managing Director.
Area: 22 800 m² (244 900 ft²) 47 units plus Hypermarket.
Enclosed; Single-storey; air conditioned malls; 1 shopping level; 2400 car park spaces; Community Hall.
Opened: 1978.

Reference:
Architects report.
Architects Journal June 4th 1980.
'Shopping Centres – from High Street to Hypermarket' E.
Peek, Fire Magazine. UNISAF Publications Limited
December 1979.

Greenfield development. A new 'district' centre, ¼
mile from the M2 motorway which connects London
and the South Coast. At the time of writing perhaps
the only truly out of town 'shopping centre' in the UK.

This is a translation of the 'one-stop greenfield'
shopping centre into UK conditions with a more
'domestic' UK scale than its American prototypes.
Successful in commercial and environmental terms,
and containing a number of innovative features, this
centre caters for the comparison fashion trade of High
Street calibre in an out-of-town location and in association with a Hypermarket. This market store is a
combination of Sainsbury's food and British Home
Stores durable lines into a one store operation.

Great importance was attached to the quality and
extent of natural lighting and internal planting (including trees!) to avoid the oppressiveness that exists
in many centres relying only on artificial light, so that
the public can retain the sense of being outside and yet
be protected from the less desirable effects of our
weather.

The 'fast food' concept has been introduced, with
developers' management of communal eating areas
served by individual selected food concessions. This
was achieved only with perseverance as there was
some difficulty in finding UK fast food concerns who
could broaden the appeal of their operation to suit this
type of fast food centre. This commitment by the
developer extended to his setting up subsidiary

Fast food area (Photo: David Richardson)

Entrance from car-park
(Photo: Colt International)

Hempstead Valley Shopping Centre, internal view. A high level of daylight with natural materials and extensive use of green trees and planting, give the atmosphere of an open market (or 'Parisian side walk') combined with the comfort of a climate controlled environment. Note trading 'carts'. (Photo: Colt International)

businesses as he was not satisfied with the nature of prospective tenants. This venture has proved aesthetically, environmentally and financially viable and has attracted considerable attention from the fast food industry.

Trolleys are prohibited in the malls – a permanent trolley park is sited at mall level alongside the Sava Centre entrance. There is a central storage area for collection by management at car park level, served by two trolley escalators.

The malls are 'air-conditioned' by roof-mounted package units. It is interesting to note that only after commencement of the building contract was the decision made to enclose the mall, with all the attendant requirements for heating, cooling, sprinklers etc., to

the malls and the shops – and the consequent fundamental changes to the design. This courageous decision has been justified by the success of the centre, due also to the continued energetic and positive approach of the centre management.

The estimated catchment area is 500 000 people within 25 minutes driving time.

Tenants are generally on a base rent plus percentage turnover with 25 years leases.

Smaller local traders have been encouraged by the fitting out of smaller units with leases agreed as short as three years, and even opting out of Landlord & Tenants Act in favour of turnover rents, this policy providing flexibility in responding to market situations and giving individual atmosphere.

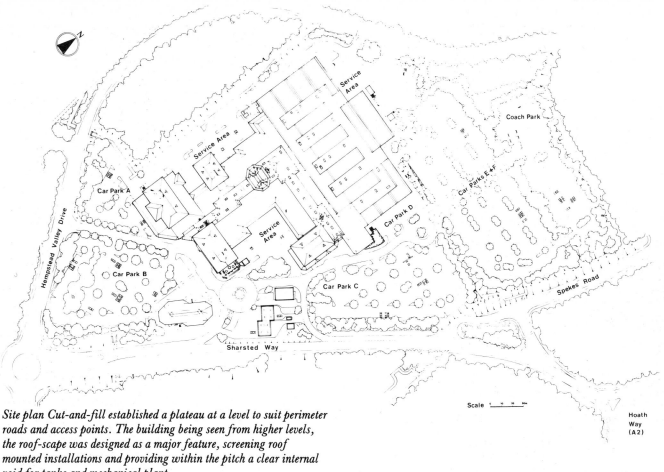

Site plan Cut-and-fill established a plateau at a level to suit perimeter roads and access points. The building being seen from higher levels, the roof-scape was designed as a major feature, screening roof mounted installations and providing within the pitch a clear internal void for tanks and mechanical plant

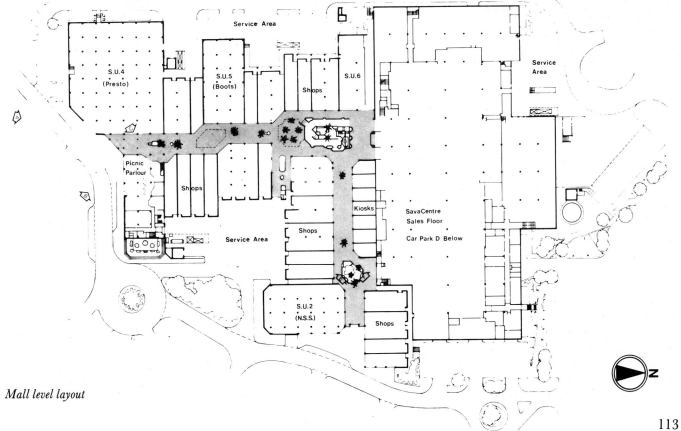

Mall level layout

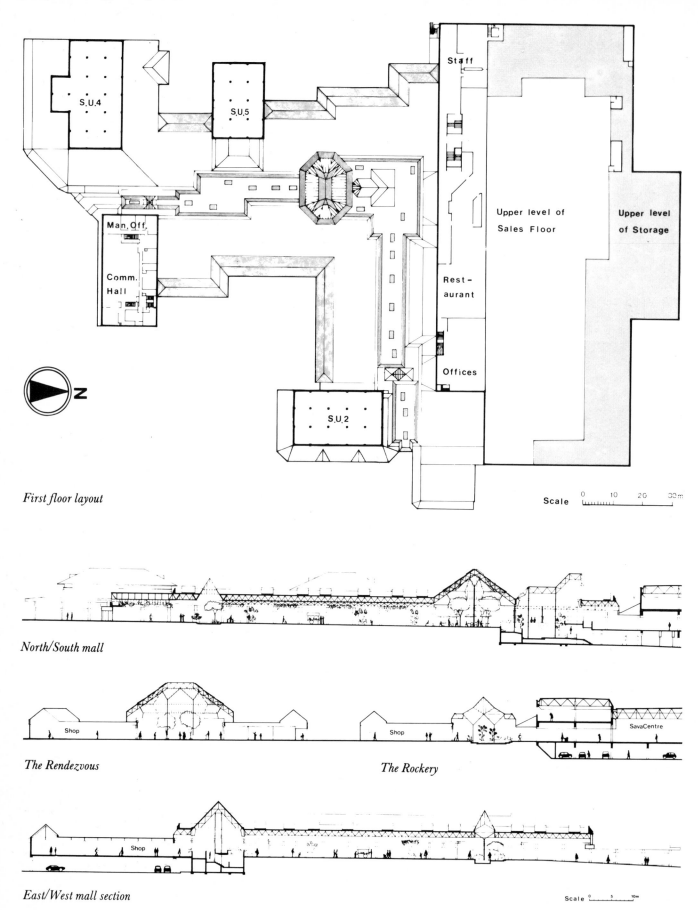

First floor layout

Scale 0 10 20 30m

North/South mall

The Rendezvous

The Rockery

East/West mall section

Scale 0 5 10m

CENTRAL MILTON KEYNES, Milton Keynes, Bucks

Architects: Milton Keynes Development Corporation.
(Finance provided by the Post Office Pension Fund)
Structural & Service Engineers: Milton Keynes Development Corporation.
Developers: Milton Keynes Development Corporation.
Managed by: Milton Keynes Development Corporation.
Area: 102 000 m² (1 100 000 ft²) 125 units
Department store
Partially enclosed but with perimeter shopping; 1 storey; 1 shopping level, 6500 car park spaces; Market.
Opened 1979.

Reference:
'RIBA Journal' May 1979
'Architectural Review' September 1980.
'Architects Journal' 15/22 October 1980.
'Building Services' February 1980.
Developer's Brochure.
Milton Keynes Handbook for Tenants.

Greenfield New Town Development, planned to be, by the 1990's, the main shopping area in the centre of a city with a population of 200 000 – this concept, a part of a town centre, can only be gradually realised as the town grows. It was conceived as a single-level, town centre, covered shopping street complex with roof level servicing – but at present operates virtually as a 'greenfield' centre.

This is one of the largest covered shopping centres in Europe. It is symmetrical in plan, divided into three by two main malls or 'High Arcades' 12 m wide, 14 m high, crossed by eight high subsidiary cross walks at 90 m intervals connecting to car parks and public transport on the perimeter. There are also units facing the Perimeter Arcade, these being let to service units such as estate agents, etc. All the malls are the same width. 12 m. The letting policy has the large stores along the centre band with frontages on to both malls, with smaller units in the outer frontages. Shopping types have been grouped – fashion at one end near the department store, supermarket and food shops at the other, where the emphasis is on convenience shopping. Service units (such as estate agents, etc.) are sited on the perimeter. Catering facilities are distributed around the shopping area to include cafes, restaurants and a 'pub'. There are very large public spaces, – the covered hall, the garden courtyard, the city square and the market square, available for exhibitions, commercial presentations and entertainment.

There is no provision for cooling; a combined ventilation and heating system of ducted warm air from roof mounted gas fired units offer a design temperature of 60°F (16°C) at −1°C (30°F) externally, and a ventilation rate of twelve air changes an hour. Shops draw their air directly through external walls and roofs.

The perimeter entrances were deliberately designed to be permanent openings, approached under 'port cochères' protected by hot air curtains. This was found to have drawbacks due to the strong prevailing winds and high cost of effective hot air curtains. Doors have now been provided to all entrances – not automatic but with one leaf specially designed to be

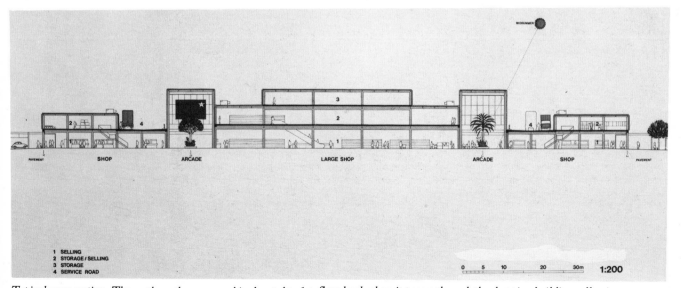

1 SELLING
2 STORAGE / SELLING
3 STORAGE
4 SERVICE ROAD

Typical cross section. The north south access road is elevated to 1st floor level where it passes through the shopping building, allowing vehicular access to the private service road at first floor level which serves the shops (Photo: M.K.D.C.)

There is nothing to indicate from the approaches that this is a shopping centre nor can the activities inside be detected from the outside surroundings. Note porte cochère (Photo: M.K.D.C.)

self-openable by the disabled. It is claimed that this modification will reduce energy cost and consequently service charges and technically this is now an enclosed centre. The Fire Authority was apparently satisfied that due to the large volume of the enclosed single level centre, the existing system could be considered as meeting their smoke exhaust requirements. Provision is made for direct expansion chilling if needed in the future. Would this entail full compliance with further sophisticated smoke control requirements? Will this climatic control become necessary? The philosophy is, I understand, that conditions in the malls as now provided will be substantially more comfortable than those of an outside street.

The main malls are naturally lit, with only a subdued lighting level after dark, the shop fronts being expected to be the main lighting source; the cross malls have predominantly artificial lighting and planting is a major feature of the centre.

A primary factor throughout the design has been provision for the disabled – for instance there are no curbs between car parks spaces and walkways and widths of entrances, changes of level, etc., have been designed with the requirements of the disabled in mind.

This concept of a single level town centre rather than an isolated, self-conscious one-stop shopping centre, is, in its solution, nevertheless the antithesis of the busy 'organic' shopping street, with interesting

The public areas appear to rely mainly on planting for interest – there being no other major foci of special interest. Planting has been designed to use entire plants and trees, taking advantage of the height of the main boulevards and the daylighting and temperature control. Visual evidence suggests that this intention has not yet been wholly achieved! External planting is also a major element in the external design (Photo: M.K.D.C.)

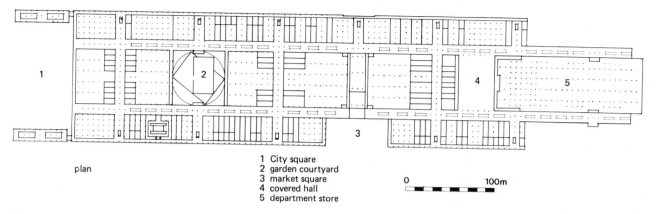

plan

1 City square
2 garden courtyard
3 market square
4 covered hall
5 department store

0   100m

The structure is steel frame supporting precast concrete floors and light-weight roof clad with steel, clear or mirror and glass curtain wall. Steel columns on shop frontages are exposed and painted. The grid is 6 m × 6 m with the middle band 6 m × 12 m

pause points and varied buildings. Milton Keynes Shopping Centre, on the other hand, has a rigid grid, a rigid framework, rigid control over tenants and their designs and trading patterns* to suit an overall design policy giving an impression of immense distances, dignity and grandeur of scale. However, in my mind it lacks spontaneity, fire and glitter and projects an emphatic sense of orderliness. The architecture is 'splendidly' dominant and repetitive, the width of malls and shop bays is constant – scale of spaces and distances is 'vast' – will it work? It has, in its favour, monopoly and position. But what a pity its appeal is not more human and varied and its atmosphere more light hearted!

* The excellently designed but suggestively restrictive 'Handbook for Tenants' tells its own story!

View of mall (Photo: M.K.D.C.)

BRUNEL CENTRE, Swindon

Architects: Douglas Stephen & Partners with Building
Design Partnership.
Developers: Swindon Municipal Borough.
Managed by: Swindon Municipal Borough. B. R. God-
den, Centre Manager.
Area: 60 800 m² (547 000 ft²) GLA 109 units + 4 major
stores
Partially enclosed; Multi-storey; 2 main blocks, one
with air-conditioned malls; 2 shopping levels; 1065 car
park spaces; Market at 1st floor level.
Opened 1973.
Other uses: Offices, housing.

References:
Architectural Review September 1976.
Architects Journal, 18th March 1981
Architect's Report

Urban development blending new elements into the
existing street pattern of the centre of Swindon.

There are two main blocks – the Plaza building and
the David Murray John building.

The Brunel Plaza building, 162 m × 105 m, has a
main mall without gates or doors, roofed with a glazed
vault reminiscent of the town's railway era. The mall
forms a public thoroughfare, connecting to Canal
Walk, which links this building to the other main
block, the David Murray John building. Canal Walk
is a new pedestrian cross-town thoroughfare formed
by filling in the path of an old canal. The 2-storey
Murray John tower which forms the centre focus
contains offices and flats.

The DMJ building is fully enclosed and air conditioned with two levels of shopping, the upper level
being in a central gallery served by a ramped passenger conveyor. The internal gallery is air conditioned,
air entering from suspended ceilings and being drawn
into the shop units. The market is not air conditioned,
but treated with warm air, with natural light and
ventilation. (There appears to be a tendency to a high
temperature due to solar gain.) Automatic doors
retain the treated air. Each shop unit is provided with
electrical, gas and water connection points, drainage,
a feed from the sprinkler system, provision for ducting
air to the roof or external air and obligatory connections to the centre's security system.

Arcaded and open shopping are placed on the
perimeter, the whole development giving varying degrees of shelter from exposure to the weather. A
notable omission is that there are no public toilets in
this 12½ acre development!

In order to have all shopping at natural ground
level, related to existing shops across the streets,

*Brunel Centre, Swindon. Open but roofed with glazed vault: Arcade
leading to David Murray John Building (Photo: Henk Snoek)*

An entrance to the plaza. External view (Photo: Martin Charles)

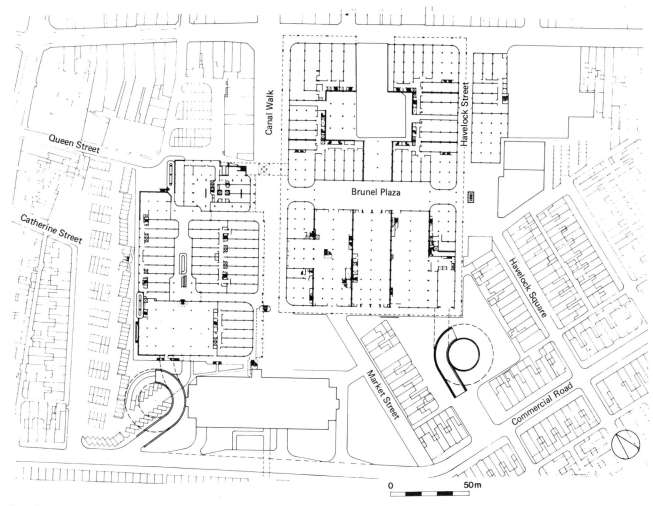

Site plan

servicing is from a rooftop deck. Delivery vehicles climb a spiral ramp beside the DMJ building, cross Canal Walk on a bridge and descend by another ramp from the Plaza building. Shops are served by hydraulic lifts down to corridors behind each unit.

The external silver skin of the building, curving at corners, is of several metals: clear anodized aluminium pressings on the tower, with grey glass; natural anodized aluminium planking inside the arcade; fluted stainless steel panels screening the trucking deck, and black anodized aluminium with bronzed glass to the podium exterior on the street frontages. Blockwork clads the rear.

Trading in this centre seems to concentrate on convenience shopping, there being no apparent 'up-market' accent, letting and management being by the local authority.

The emphasis of the whole complex is firmly that of a strikingly designed architectural concept, both internally and externally, the individual shop designs being subservient to the dominant envelope, and consequently somewhat 'lack lustre' as trading units.

The centre was completed in several phases.

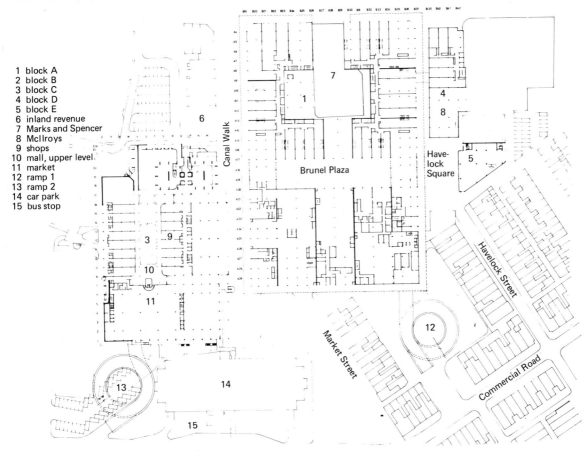

1 block A
2 block B
3 block C
4 block D
5 block E
6 inland revenue
7 Marks and Spencer
8 McIlroys
9 shops
10 mall, upper level
11 market
12 ramp 1
13 ramp 2
14 car park
15 bus stop

Canal Walk

Brunel Plaza

Have-
lock
Square

Market Street

Havelock Street

Commercial Road

First floor plan

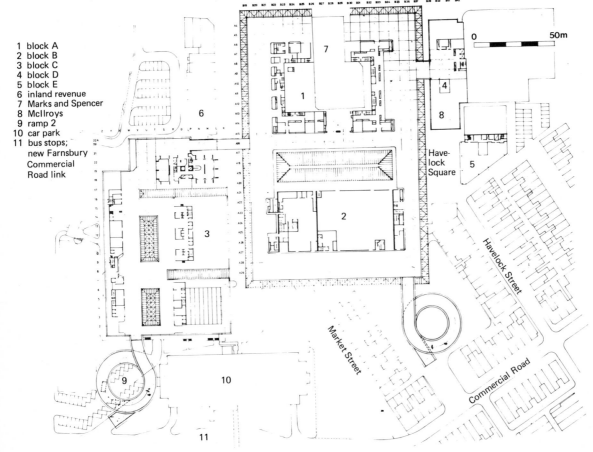

1 block A
2 block B
3 block C
4 block D
5 block E
6 inland revenue
7 Marks and Spencer
8 McIlroys
9 ramp 2
10 car park
11 bus stops;
    new Farnsbury
    Commercial
    Road link

0   50m

Have-
lock
Square

Market Street

Havelock Street

Commercial Road

*Plan of
trucking deck*

120

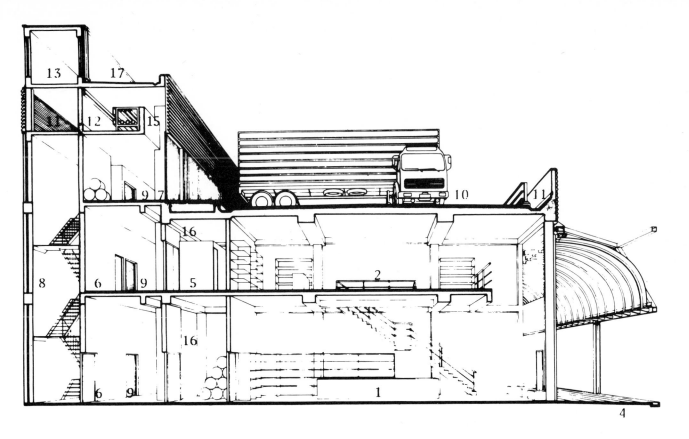

Section

Reinforced concrete construction, frame, floors and roof being of concrete, generally on a 5.5 m bay size. This is doubled to 11 m where clear areas are needed, such as in the market

1 Shop unit – retail space. Staircase position can be varied to suit tenants requirements
2 Shop unit. 1st floor retail or storage space
3 Tenants' shop front. The two storey shopfront option allows views of an upper stairs level. The void can be planked in for addition area
4 Pavement under canopy
5 Shop, toilets and plant area
6 Common service access and escape corridors
7 Loading bay
8 Escape access stairs
9 Goods lifts. Common to groups of shop units

10 Trucking deck. Monitored access for service vehicles only
11 Crash barrier and parapet
12 Service pipe runs. Tenants make their connections at this level as they would to conventional ground run systems
13 Tank rooms
14 Intake louvres. The continuous 'frieze' of louvres allows absolute flexibility in positioning duct terminals
15 Extract louvres. Spent air is dumped on the vehicle side
16 Tenants service duct shafts. Sized to allow full air conditioning of units by the tenants
17 Space for condensers

QUEENSGATE CENTRE, Peterborough

Architects: Peterborough Development Corporation.
Developers: Norwich Union Life Insurance Society and
Peterborough Development Corporation.
Area: 46 000 m² (500 000 ft²) 97 units + 5 major units
Department Store
Enclosed; Multi-storey; air conditioned malls; 2 shopping levels; 2000 car park spaces; Bus Station.
Planned opening 1982.

Reference:
Paper for CIBS Annual Conference 1979 by K. Maplestone, K. Hilton, J. Abraham & W. Lambert.
Peterborough Development Corporation Brochure.

Urban Development; a Regional Centre forming part
of the Greater Peterborough masterplan to enlarge the
city from 80 000 to 160 000 by the late 1980's. Peterborough was designated a New Town in 1968. The
Centre as a whole is to become the shopping capital of
1200 square miles centred on Peterborough. The
Centre's malls link the car parks and bus station to the
principal existing shopping streets. Most existing
buildings fronting the main streets in the eastern half
of the area are retained and some integrated with the
new development. They include several old buildings
on and near Cathedral Square where part of the site is
in a conservation area.

This, on completion, is likely to be one of the largest
and most significant urban Shopping Centres, in the
UK. Amongst its interesting features are the extensive
mechanical and electrical systems and the sophisticated micro-processor-based control system controlling the day to day running of the centre as well as the

1 retail market
2 John Lewis Partnership
3 Waitrose
4 British Home Stores
5 Littlewoods
6 C. and A. Modes
7 Boots
8 Marks and Spencer
9 Woolworth

Site plan

*Central Square in Queensgate
(Photo: Peterborough Development
Coporation)*

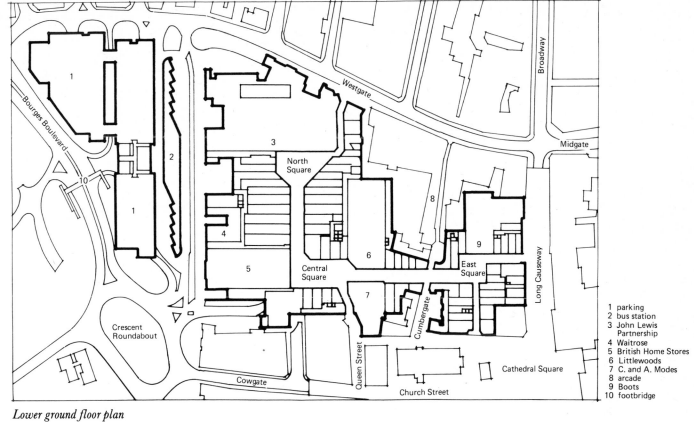

Lower ground floor plan

1 parking
2 bus station
3 John Lewis Partnership
4 Waitrose
5 British Home Stores
6 Littlewoods
7 C. and A. Modes
8 arcade
9 Boots
10 footbridge

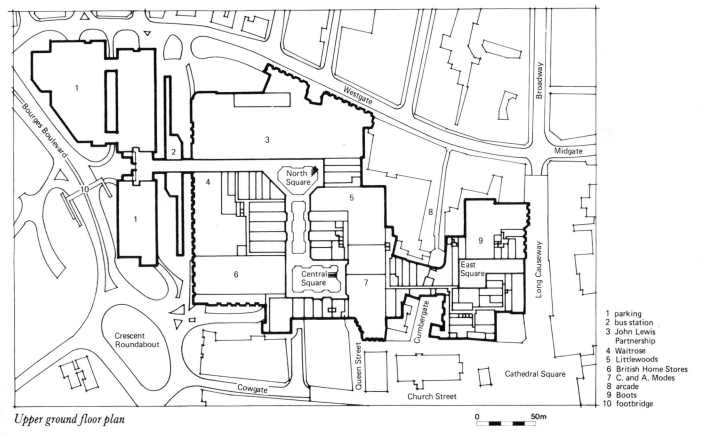

Upper ground floor plan

1 parking
2 bus station
3 John Lewis Partnership
4 Waitrose
5 Littlewoods
6 British Home Stores
7 C. and A. Modes
8 arcade
9 Boots
10 footbridge

0   50m

123

Elevation to Long Causeway. Entrance is on the left

A model of Queensgate Shopping Centre, Peterborough, viewed from the south-east. Long Causeway entrance to East square on foreground (Photo: Peterborough Development Corporation)

emergency operations. The large units will trade on two or three floors, the standard units generally using their upper floors for storage and staff facilities.

Specialist eating places are introduced to provide with the department and variety stores a wide variety of choice. Servicing is in part from ground level road, and part from basement, communal hoists leading to service corridors at the rear of the shops.

Pending the opportunity to judge success, descriptions of some technical features of interest are quoted below: 'A 16 person passenger lift is located in the centre mall, with a fully visible glass car, designed to be a 'fun lift' and a focal point. Four escalators also serve the malls.

The malls are artificially lit. The lighting has variable switching arrangements to produce different lighting effects and by mixing two light sources (MBF & SON) to obtain different results to suit, or contrast with, seasonal and weather changes outside.

Only perimeter shops have gas supply, but gas supply to air handling units is run over the roof from a 260 mm diameter main.

The malls and square are air-conditioned by twelve roof-mounted air handling units. Shops and stores have to provide their own systems as needed, plant areas being provided on the roof, with vertical duct space. Shops take a controlled amount of air from the mall.'

Central mall, looking to central square

FRIARY CENTRE, Guildford

Architects: Sidney Kaye Firmin Partnership
Structural Engineers: Ove Arup & Partners.
Developers: MEPC Limited
Area: 13 400 m² (150 000 ft²) 48 units.
Supermarket, Fashion Store
Enclosed; Multi-storey; air-conditioned malls; 2 shopping levels; 1100 car park spaces; Bus Station.
Opened 1981
Other uses: Housing, Offices, Public House.

Reference:
Developer's Brochure and Schedule of Accommodation and Terms of Letting.
Architect's Report

Urban Development in a town already the major shopping focus of Surrey, this development is to supply the growing retail demand in a town considered to be undershopped.

The mall lay-out is planned to give a vital link between the local authority car park, across a bridge, through the centre to existing shops in central Guildford. A new centralised bus station with covered waiting areas gives direct access to the upper shopping mall and 100 basement car park spaces augment the public car park.

This is a fully enclosed centre with no natural light. Conditioned air is supplied to the shop units as 'bleed-offs' from the conditioned air in the malls, with further cooling via tenants connection to developer's condenser main. The main large units provide their own central plant. Plant rooms and cooling towers are situated on the roof. Servicing is from a covered loading yard, goods being taken via service corridors and lifts to rear of shop units.

The roof of the development, said to be the biggest building in Surrey, is visible from higher ground around Guildford and the roofscape forms an impor-

External view

tant design element, broken up by carefully designed plant rooms, pyramid forms over the squares, and extensive landscaping and planting. This is enjoyed by the occupants of the 3 storey local authority block of flats (61 bed-sitting room units), and also by the offices (30 000 ft²) sited unobtrusively on roof deck for connection to a proposed future office tower block.

Malls use muted colours and subdued lighting, relying for impact on shop fronts. The main square connects levels by escalators, stairs and lift, with decorative features of planning, fountain and special effect lighting.

Tenant mix has been arranged to allow for fashion on the upper floor, other traders, e.g. hardware, stationery, on lower floor, Snack bar, coffee shop, a high class restaurant and a public house are included.

Rents are subject to a 5 year upward review.

Roofscape (Photo: Fox-Waterman)

Internal view of upper level showing suspension of the gallery. Upper level plan. The objective is 'to create an internal environment of high quality, a warm colourful, inviting and stimulating place to enter, to walk around and to sit in – an environment which adds to the pleasure of shopping'

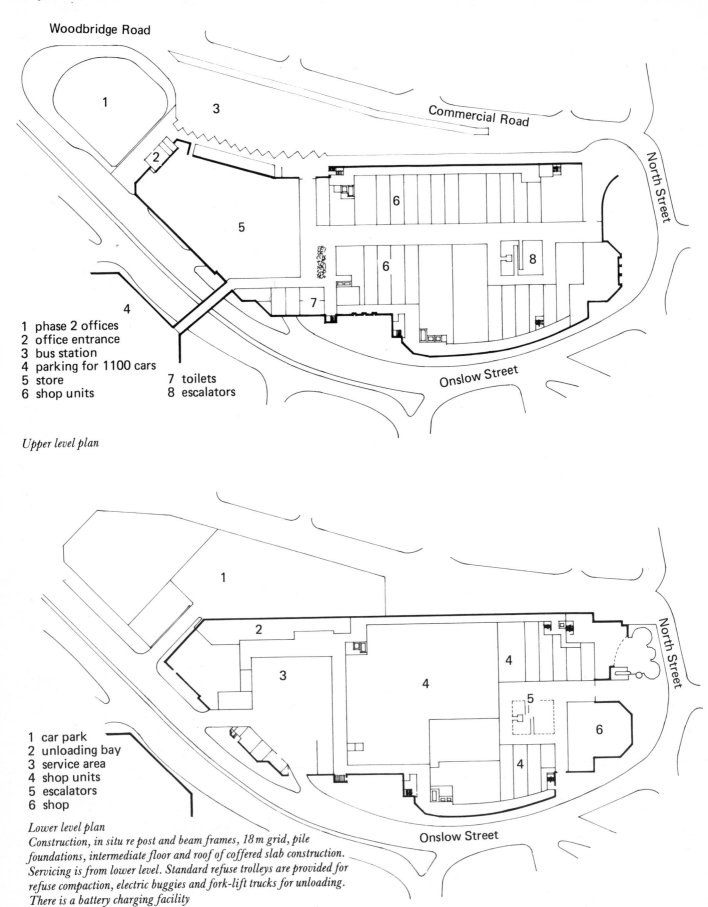

Woodbridge Road

Commercial Road

North Street

1

3

2

5

4

6

6

8

7

Onslow Street

1 phase 2 offices
2 office entrance
3 bus station
4 parking for 1100 cars
5 store
6 shop units
7 toilets
8 escalators

Upper level plan

North Street

1

2

3

4

4

4

5

6

Onslow Street

1 car park
2 unloading bay
3 service area
4 shop units
5 escalators
6 shop

Lower level plan
Construction, in situ re post and beam frames, 18 m grid, pile
foundations, intermediate floor and roof of coffered slab construction.
Servicing is from lower level. Standard refuse trolleys are provided for
refuse compaction, electric buggies and fork-lift trucks for unloading.
There is a battery charging facility

QUADRANT CENTRE, Swansea, S. Wales

Architects: Building Design Partnership.
Developers: Swansea City and CIN Properties.
Managed by: Swansea Corporation.
Area: 27 900 m² (300 000 ft²) GLA 41 units
Department store
Enclosed; 2 storey; 1 shopping level; 1st floor storage;
589 car park spaces; Regional Bus Station.
Opened 1978.

Reference:
'*Building*' 17th October 1980.

Urban development close to a major shopping street
and adjoining the existing market; the department
store was built under a separate contract.

An interesting feature of this centre is the decision
to abandon the 'controlled environment' concept and
to exploit natural lighting and ventilation to the public
areas, to provide a 'low energy' centre. Mall roofs are
designed to provide natural light, ventilation and
smoke control without glare, solar gain or draughts.

This is also an example of general architectural
treatment dominating the mall design. Note the rigid
definition of each shopping level bay by stainless steel
horizontal band and stainless steel faced structural
columns. When a shop stretches across more than one
bay this frame has to be maintained and the tenant
has no option but to repeat his fascia over each bay!

There are no cafés and restaurants within this
development.

External view from North West (Photo: Henk Snoek)

*North mall entrance from Union Street. External wall cladding is
generally in reconstituted slate panels. (Photo: Henk Snoek)*

*Central Square roof supported on a tubular steel space deck with two
levels of roof lighting (Photo: Henk Snoek)*

127

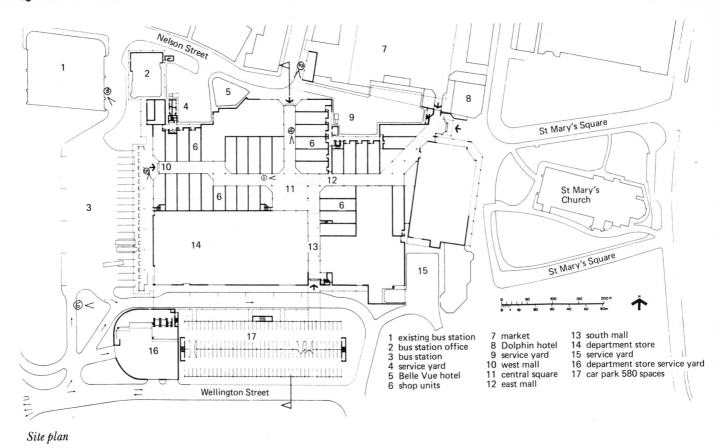

Site plan

1	existing bus station	7	market	13	south mall
2	bus station office	8	Dolphin hotel	14	department store
3	bus station	9	service yard	15	service yard
4	service yard	10	west mall	16	department store service yard
5	Belle Vue hotel	11	central square	17	car park 580 spaces
6	shop units	12	east mall		

fresh air
vitiated air
daylight
solar heat
smoke

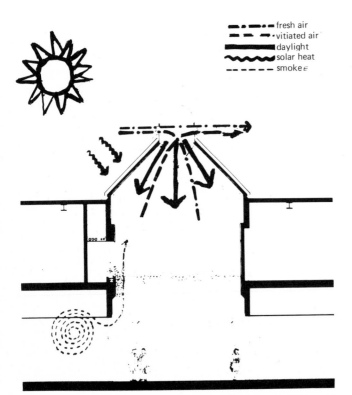

Section through mall in daylight conditions showing entry of natural light and fresh air. Also showing dispersal of vitiated air and smoke

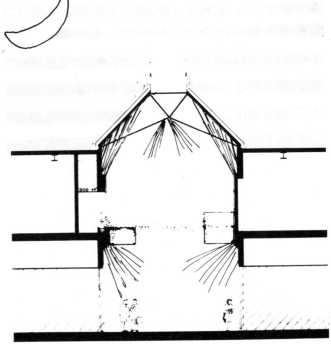

Section through mall at night showing lighting and signs, light is thrown up into the internal roof surfaces. Light to upper level malls and planting is provided by track-mounted spotlights above the shop fronts

THE RIDINGS, Wakefield, Yorkshire

Architects: Chapman Taylor Partners.
Developers: Capital & Counties Property Company Limited jointly with Metropolitan District Council of Wakefield.
Area: 92 900 m² (100 000 ft²) 35–40 units
2 major stores, extensions to 3 existing major stores.
Enclosed; Multi-storey; 3 shopping levels; 1100 car park spaces.
Planned Opening: 1983.

Reference:
Architects' Report
'Building Design', 19th June 1981

Urban redevelopment in an existing City Centre (the largest single building in Wakefield). This is an interesting scheme, interpolating a new enclosed centre into the existing town fabric, and drawing into it existing major stores, some being expanded to open onto the malls. It uses ground slopes to full advantage, and is also of note in its use of three shopping levels, and relying on natural daylighting, without air conditioning and designed to present an atmosphere of covered 'streets'.

The following is quoted from the Architect's description.
The scheme consists of 100 000 ft² department store, a 30 000 ft² supermarket, extensions to Marks & Spencers, British Home Stores and Boots, who have existing units backing on to the development site, a unit for W. H. Smith and also another large unit for Mothercare, plus approximately 35 to 40 standard units of up to 3000 ft².

It is covered and has three levels of mall. Each of these levels relates to a ground level on part of the site. This slopes steeply from the south towards the north and the lower mall starts at the lowest point of Kirkgate, drives through an existing supermarket which will be reformed into standard units, into the lowest level of the main concourse. Here it is at basement level and the mall terminates at this point. From this concourse rises a glass sided wall climber lift, a bank of escalators and a staircase rising up one floor back on to ground level to the middle mall.

This middle mall then runs level from the central concourse up to the highest level of the Kirkgate shopping street. A further upper level mall reflects this, giving a galleried effect to the main length of the shopping mall. On to both of these upper malls all the main units of the scheme open. It is so designed that the magnet traders are positioned to ensure a pedestrian flow throughout all levels of the scheme.

With two (or more!) level mall shopping schemes, the avoidance of a dominant level and consequent weaker areas of mall is important, not only to ensure an attractive shopping flow, but also to ensure that a correct rental income is gained from the scheme. The major space users have entrances on both levels of the mall, the tenant mix being devised to ensure equal interest and retail activities between the two malls. This is helped by the basic planning concept that all three mall levels relate at one part of the scheme or another, to actual ground levels.

The main entrance to the scheme from Kirkgate down Southgate presents the shopper with an equal choice between either going up five feet to the upper level or going down ten feet to the lower mall level. At this point a view of both levels is presented to the shopper, revealing equal interest at both levels. The department store has its two main trading levels on to these malls with 80 ft wide entrances. On the other side is another strong, major space user, W. H. Smith, again presenting entrances at both levels of the mall. These two key traders ensure that the entrance zone is full of interest and will attract a strong shopping flow.

If the first few yards of the scheme were standard units the shoppers might pass them on their way in to the heart of the scheme thus devaluing their positions. By putting strong key traders here, the scheme starts immediately on entering through the glazed entrance screen. The standard units then follow on the lead right round to the far end of the scheme where again there is a very strong unit, the large supermarket.

In conjunction with the supermarket, the lowest level is strengthened by the addition of the restaurant element, placed under the naturally lit large concourse, and planned as a fast-food and take-away area similar to that incorporated in many North American schemes. A very high quality communal eating area will be managed by the Central Management. About fifteen to twenty separate fast-food kiosk and take-away units will be arranged around this area each providing an interesting and varied selection of foods. By combining them together this not only overcomes the problems of food retailers in a shopping mall, but also ensures that by competition, the level of trade will be lifted.

This city centre covered shopping scheme, woven into the complicated site immediately behind the main shopping street, has to support an expensive infrastructure, – lifts, escalators, basement service roads, mechanical ventilation, etc. But, in this energy-conscious age, simplified solutions have been incorporated wherever possible.

The mall will be artificially ventilated and heated but not fully air conditioned, and relying to a large extent on natural daylighting. This helps the design

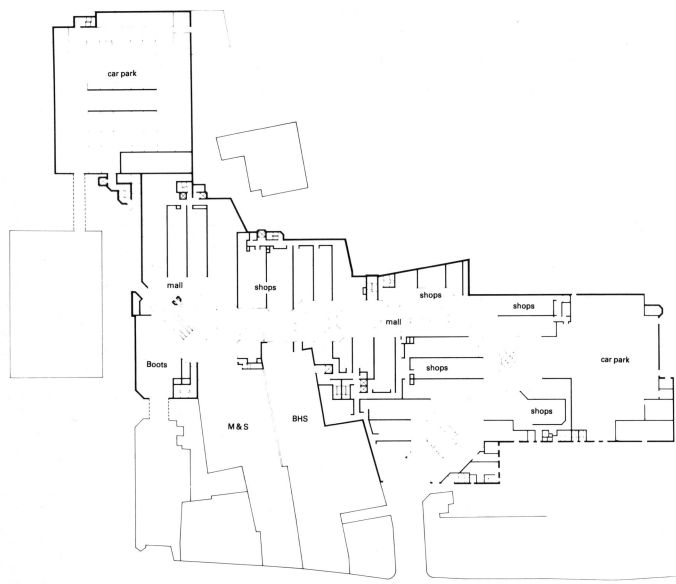

Upper mall level

intent to make the malls into covered streets, with trees, benches, telephone kiosks, lamp standards and the use of brick and tile paving. No rigid architectural discipline will be applied to the design of individual shop fronts in relations to the whole; each tenant will be encouraged to put in exciting and good quality shop fronts in his own style, as happens in the best traditional shopping streets. 850 new car spaces will be provided, the majority at roof and upper levels, designed to feed down into the malls from above.

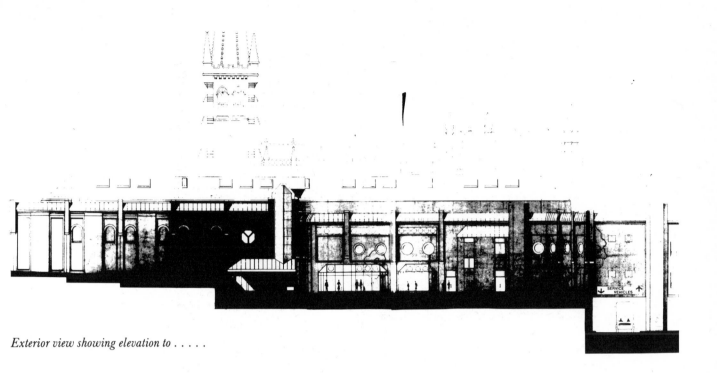

Exterior view showing elevation to . . . . .

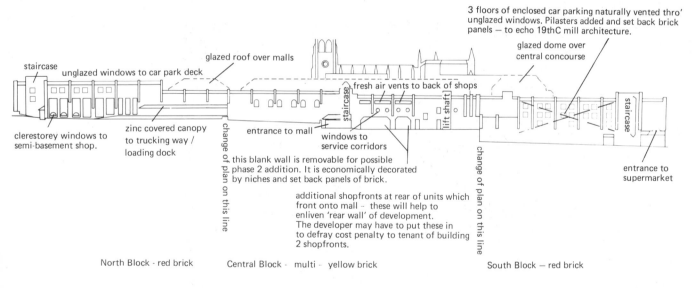

3 floors of enclosed car parking naturally vented thro'
unglazed windows. Pilasters added and set back brick
panels — to echo 19thC mill architecture.

glazed dome over
central concourse

staircase

unglazed windows to car park deck

glazed roof over malls

fresh air vents to back of shops

staircase

lift shaft

staircase

clerestorey windows to
semi-basement shop.

zinc covered canopy
to trucking way /
loading dock

entrance to mall

windows to
service corridors

entrance to
supermarket

change of plan on this line

this blank wall is removable for possible
phase 2 addition. It is economically decorated
by niches and set back panels of brick.

additional shopfronts at rear of units which
front onto mall — these will help to
enliven 'rear wall' of development.
The developer may have to put these in
to defray cost penalty to tenant of building
2 shopfronts.

change of plan on this line

North Block - red brick

Central Block - multi - yellow brick

South Block — red brick

Elevation

SWAN WALK, Horsham, Sussex

Architects: Clifford Culpin & Partners. Fitzroy Robinson & Partners.
Developers: Norwich Union Insurance Group and Horsham District Council.
Managed by: Norwich Union Insurance Group.
Area: 11 200 m² (121 000 ft²) 40 units
Open; Multi-storey; 1 shopping level; 2 major stores; 585 car park spaces.
Opened 1977.
Other uses: Offices.

Reference:
Developer's Brochure.

Urban development in a North Sussex market town. The development is in the heart of the town centre.

An 'L' shaped shopping mall links the prime positon of West Street with the Carfax, the historic shopping area, which includes a new Head Post Office and the Bus Terminus.

The scheme comprises two major retail stores, J. Sainsbury Limited 34 740 ft² and The Boots Company Limited 33 850 ft² respectively, 33 shops, offices of about 14 000 ft² gross, a multi-storey car park served by two 13-person and three 20-person lifts, public toilets and a new entrance to the long established Capitol Theatre.

The architecture features mansard roofs and tile hung elevations and canopies in order to conserve the historic and picturesque character of the town. The shopping malls are canopied and the shops have rear service access at ground level, so that the malls are traffic free. West Street has also been pedestrianised to coincide with the completion of this scheme.

The little open centre echoes the scale and materials of the existing town, but unhappily is dwarfed by a monster car park which makes no concession to the centre or the existing town character

Open mall with canopies. Note low canopy height

1 retail unit
2 multi-storey car park
3 toilets
4 service area
5 Capitol theatre
6 existing development

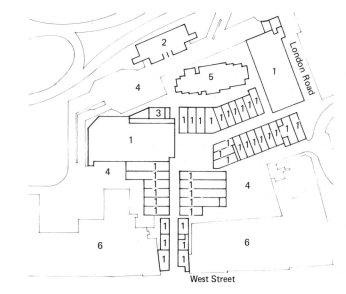

Site plan

SWAN CENTRE, Leatherhead, Surrey

Architects: Building Design Partnership.
Developers: Mole Valley District Council jointly with
Federated Estates.
Managed by: Federated Property Service
Area: 8280 m^2 (90 000 ft^2)
Open; 2 levels, one shopping level, 3 major stores and
23 smaller units; 430 car park spaces.
Opened: 1981
Other uses: Offices, Old Peoples' Day Centre.

Reference:
Leatherhead Town Centre 1st Development Brief.
'Shopfitting International' April/May 1981.

Urban development; a District Centre serving an
immediate catchment area of 40 000. The population
has an above-average income and car-ownership level.

Leatherhead was losing a share of its potential trade
to alternative, better served, shopping centres, due to
inconvenient and inadequate shopping facilities. The
existing shopping streets are narrow, the High Street,
in part only 30 ft wide, serves not only the main
shopping function, but as a traffic through route and
service road for the existing shops. The existing town
centre buildings are mostly two storey, maximum
three storey, in height, and include a number of listed
buildings and others of townscape value.

The new development provides modern shopping
facilities in conjunction with a new relief road removing traffic from the High Street. It is an open centre
with generous canopies as weather protection, and its
design is intended to be in sympathy with the traditional scale and character of the town. The profile has
been kept low, with local brick facings, clay tile roofs
and timber windows.

Pedestrian access to the new centre, is through
existing openings from the High Street. The shops and
stores face the open mall, giving a circular pedestrian
flow from the High Street through a central square,
back to the High Street passing all the new shops and
some existing High Street shops. The High Street,
though partially pedestrianised, will allow very limited servicing to those existing shops with no rear
access. A secondary mall connects to the link road and
residential area beyond. Lavatories are provided in
the mall including facilities for the disabled.

Car parking is on three main levels located over the
shops, reached from the new link road and connected
to the Centre by staircase and three 20 person lifts,
located close to the supermarket.

Delivery access is from the roof top service areas.
The majority of the shops have first floor storage
directly served from this service deck. The remainder
are connected to the deck by goods lifts and stairs,
which also serve some existing High Street shops. The
supermarket has its own unloading area.

The centre is designed to rely more on convenience
than durable goods, with a 30 000 ft^2 supermarket as a
major customer attraction.

Central concourse

Main concourse

(above, left) South west mall
(above, right) Covered mall
(left) View towards Sainsburys. Note trolleys

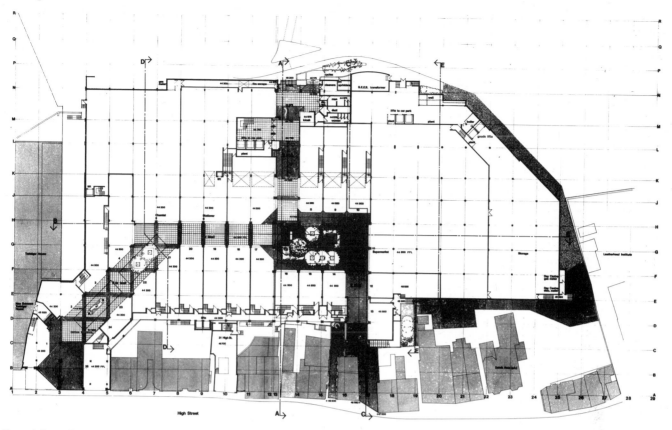

Ground floor plan

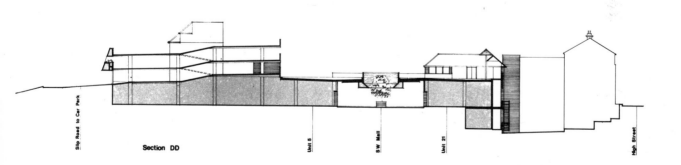

Section
The re-routing of traffic round the Town Centre by the new ring road has not yet been wholly successful. Clearer identification of shopping routes by adequate directional signing, both to the Swan Centre and the existing pedestrianised High Street will be needed to revitalise the existing shopping and draw attention to the new Centre.

MILLBURNGATE CENTRE, Durham

Architects: Building Design Partnership.
Developers: City of Durham & Bovis Property Division.
Managed by: The City of Durham
Area: 6040 m² 31 units.
Partially enclosed; Multi-storey; one shopping level;
260 car park spaces on 3 levels.
Opened 1976.
Other uses: Offices, Maisonettes.

Reference:
'*Architectural Review*' February 1977.
Developer's Brochure.
Architect's Report.

Urban development in a medieval city with a magnificent cathedral, as seen from across the river. Its main interest is its architectural appeal as a sensitive contribution to the existing townscape on a prominent riverside site, which was the only area available for new shopping facilities.

The centre is on the edge of the town, forming the end of a pedestrian shopping route from the market place and over the river bridge, integral with the mainly pedestrian heart of Durham, and facing the old town across the river.

The scheme was the successful submission in a limited competition between eight developers (and their consultants); the Royal Fine Arts Commission were involved in the final design approval.

The retail layout varies between major units in the air conditioned mall, perimeter units facing North Road and units in preserved properties adjacent to the bridge. These, built on medieval bridgehead foundations, have been restored.

A second phase, 7000 m², linked to the existing, is proceeding. Developers of this are Teeside Investment and Architects are BDP.

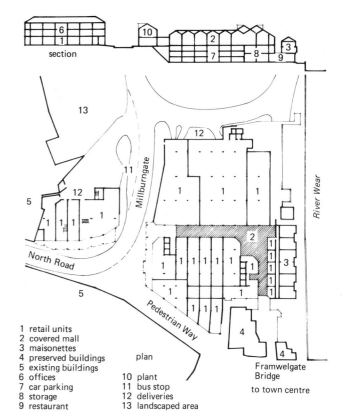

1 retail units
2 covered mall
3 maisonettes
4 preserved buildings   plan
5 existing buildings
6 offices   10 plant
7 car parking   11 bus stop
8 storage   12 deliveries
9 restaurant   13 landscaped area

The steep fall of the site has allowed car parking and covered servicing below mall level, and to provide pedestrian routes at various pening onto roof terraces

The slope of the site has allowed the provision of stepped riverside terraces with views of the city.

The mall is small scale with day-lighting and a vaulted square and 'warm-brown' tile finishes (Photo: Keith Gibson)

WEST ONE, Oxford Street, London

Architects: Chapman Taylor & Partners.
Developers: MEPC.
Centre Manager: Walter Williams
Structural Engineers: Ove Arup & Partners.
Area: (48 500 ft²) GLA.
Enclosed; Multi-storey; air conditioned malls; 3 shopping levels; 27 units and major store; interconnection with Underground station.
Opened: 1981
Other uses: Offices and residential.

Reference:
Developer's Brochure.
Architect's Report.

Urban development; integrated into the heart of one of the world's most famous shopping streets, this redevelopment incorporates shops, offices and residential uses.

The shopping is planned on three levels – underground concourse, ground level and first floor level, forming an integral part of the pedestrian movement through Bond Street Station. The three levels are connected by glass-enclosed escalators and the ground level and first floor public areas are fully air-conditioned.

West One, Oxford Street, London (Photo: Chapman Taylor)

The roof areas are landscaped for the benefit of office and residential occupants. A 'two building' approach, reducing the apparent mass of the development, gives sympathy to the differing, existing character. Elevation to Oxford Street has faceted anodised aluminium glass curtain walling, while the return elevations are in modelled brick work with lead clad mansards and recessed windows. (Photo: Chapman Taylor)

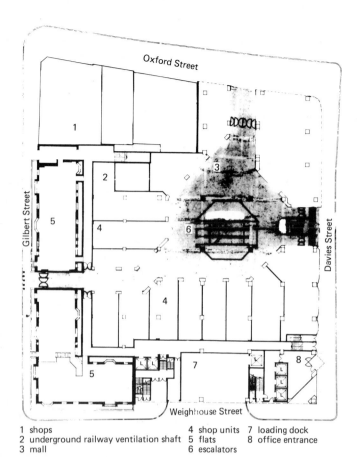

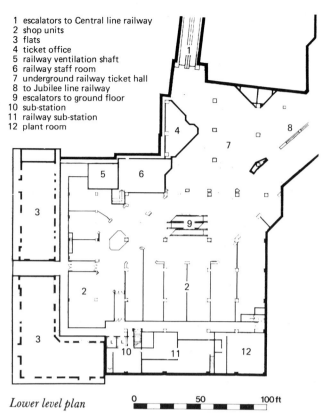

1 escalators to Central line railway
2 shop units
3 flats
4 ticket office
5 railway ventilation shaft
6 railway staff room
7 underground railway ticket hall
8 to Jubilee line railway
9 escalators to ground floor
10 sub-station
11 railway sub-station
12 plant room

Lower level plan

0   50   100 ft

1 shops
2 underground railway ventilation shaft
3 mall
4 shop units
5 flats
6 escalators
7 loading dock
8 office entrance

Ground floor plan

1 shops
2 railway ventilation shaft
3 flats
4 planting
5 escalators to ground floor
6 shopping
7 shopping centre management

Shopping integrated with London Transport Tube Station with glazed ventilated escalator shaft. These shop fronts are fire shuttered

Second floor plan

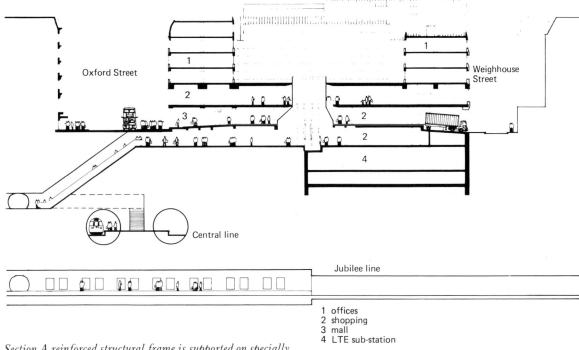

Oxford Street

1

2

3

4

Weighhouse Street

1

2

2

Central line

Jubilee line

1 offices
2 shopping
3 mall
4 LTE sub-station

Section A reinforced structural frame is supported on specially designed sub-structure integrated into design of the tube station

A glass enclosed central shaft rises from the concourse through the shop levels to the upper courtyard and this shaft absorbs the positive and negative pressures and associated air movement generated by the

tube trains underground. Thus the air-conditioned environment at ground and first floor levels is maintained and the shops can open into a quiet and controlled environment (Photo: Chapman Taylor)

COPPERGATE, York

Architects: Chapman Taylor and Partners.
Developers: Wimpey Property Holdings Limited.
Area: (130 000 ft^2) 23 shops units
Department Store
Open; 300 car park spaces.
Planned opening 1984.
Other uses: Museum for York Archaeological Trust;
residential.

Reference:
'Building Design', 20th June 1980
Architect's Report

Urban development; an outstanding conservation
area where the established character of York with its
particular scale and enclosure has been taken as a
major determinant. The mainmaterial to fit in with
the established York vernacular is a soft textured red
brick.

Square from shopping walk

The car parking is located above the department
store, enclosed in brick elevations with pitched roofs
echoing the forms of the main development. All ramp
access and egress points have been concealed from
general view and blended into the overall architectural concept. A unique feature of this shopping centre is
the subterranean archaeological museum, the result of
the discovery during excavation of the best preserved
remains in Europe of a Viking village. York City
Council negotiated with the shopping centre developers for the provision, funded by the York Archaeological Society, of the re-erection, as found, of this
village; the whole being accurately reconstructed as an
exhibition of Viking life of 1000 years ago. It will be
approached through a shop unit, acting also as a gift
shop, descent being by lifts and staircases, progress
through the museum being by 'time car' with provision for easy access by the handicapped and is designed for a maximum input of 400 people per hour.

Servicing is concealed from general view and the
main servicing areas give the maximum flexibility of
use avoiding complicated goods handling systems and
mechanical ventilation. The new urban square comprises paved landscaped areas which retain the majority of the existing trees. Public lavatories are designed
as a separate building within the scheme.

This project demonstrates a positive solution to the
integration of a new open shopping centre into an
historic city.

Shopping walk

Riverside walk

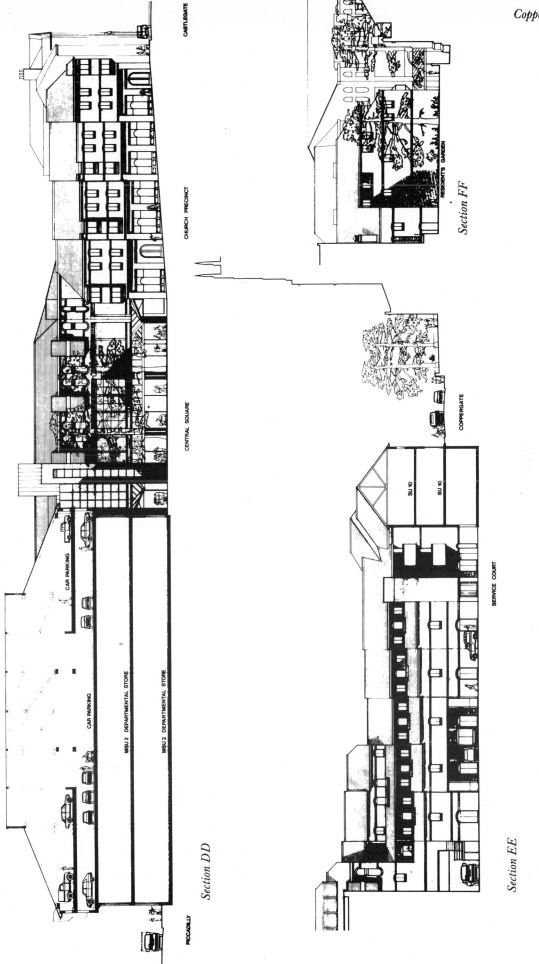

CHURCH PRECINCT

CENTRAL SQUARE

CAR PARKING

CAR PARKING

MSU 2 DEPARTMENTAL STORE

MSU 2 DEPARTMENTAL STORE

PICCADILLY

Section DD

RESIDENT'S GARDEN

Section FF

COPPERGATE

SU 10

SU 10

SERVICE COURT

Section EE

Coppergate, York. Sectional views

141

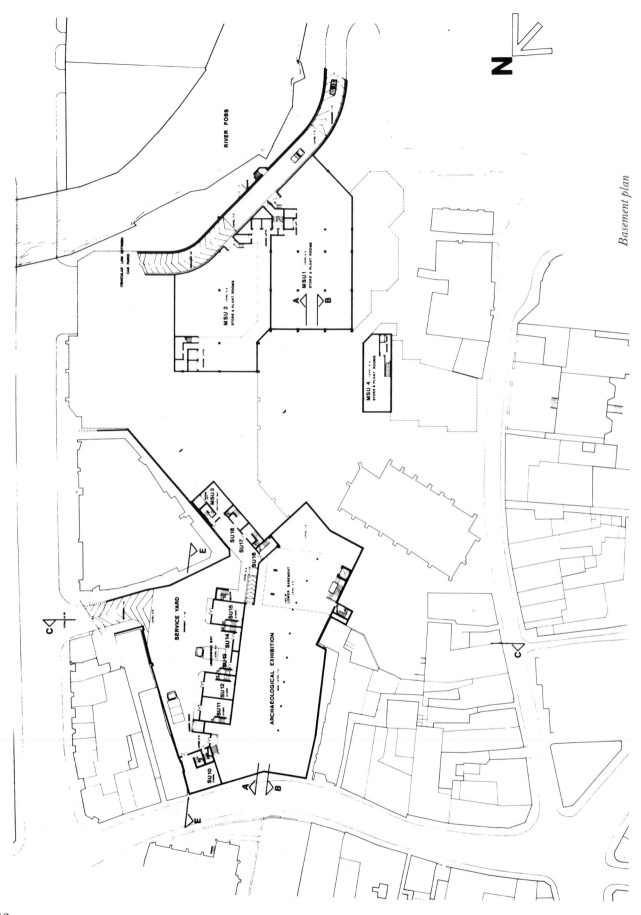

Basement plan

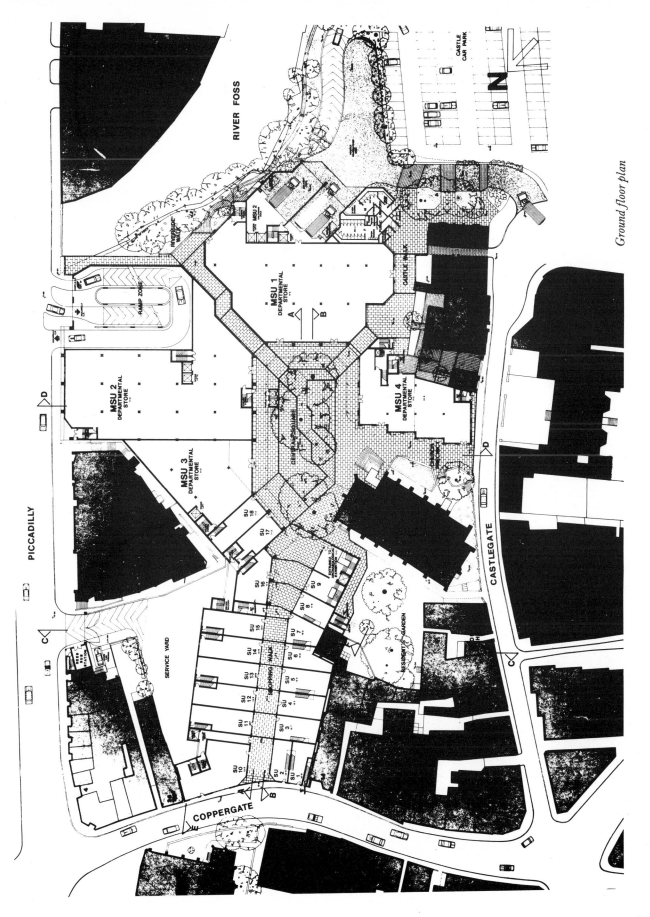

Ground floor plan

RIVER FOSS

CASTLE CAR PARK

N

MSU 2

MSU 1
DEPARTMENTAL
STORE

A

B

RAMP ZONE

RIVERSIDE WALK

CASTLE PARK

MSU 2
DEPARTMENTAL
STORE

D

MSU 4
DEPARTMENTAL
STORE

MSU 3
DEPARTMENTAL
STORE

CHURCH

CENTRE SQUARE

D

PICCADILLY

SU 18

SU 17

C

SU 16

SU 9

SU 15

SU 8

SERVICE YARD

SU 14

SU 7

SU 13

SU 6

SHOPPING WALK

RESIDENT'S GARDEN

SU 12

SU 5

CASTLEGATE

SU 11

SU 4

C

SU 10

SU 3

SU 2

SU 1

B

COPPERGATE

CITY 2, Brussels, Belgium

Architects: Aaron Chelouche associated with Lathrop-Douglass.
Developers: La Société des Centres Commerciaux de Paris.
Managed by: La Société des Centres Commerciaux de Paris.
Area: 22 000 m^2; 145 units
2 Department Stores.
Enclosed; Multi-storey; 3 level shopping; air conditioned malls; Metro; 4000 car park spaces.
Opened: 1979.

Reference:
Developer's Brochure.

Urban development. An impressive Regional Centre in the centre of Brussels, giving onto the main pedestrianised shopping thoroughfare Rue Neuve, directly linked to the metro and integrated into surrounding streets and shopping areas. The catchment area is estimated at 1 785 000, 18% of the whole Belgian population!

A bridge link across a main road to the main Department Store passes from one Plaza to another and contains retail units, maintaining continuity at all levels.

Tenant mix is controlled. On the lowest floor are food shops, supermarket, restaurants. On the intermediate floor, fashion accessories, gifts, household goods, cinemas. Fashion and clothing generally are on the upper floor. There is an innovative 'gourmet' fast food 'picnic' area. Internal finishes are of luxury quality, with landscaping, planting, fountains, seating. Shops are provided with communal toilets.

Restrictions on this very central site have caused some problems on goods deliveries – the goods delivery area being small in relation to the centre.

The external elevations present an uncompromising statement to the street, but with sufficient vertical emphasis to relate to the street scale.

Natural light is provided to the main plaza (Photo: Nigel Woolner)

Staircase court (Photo: Nigel Woolner)

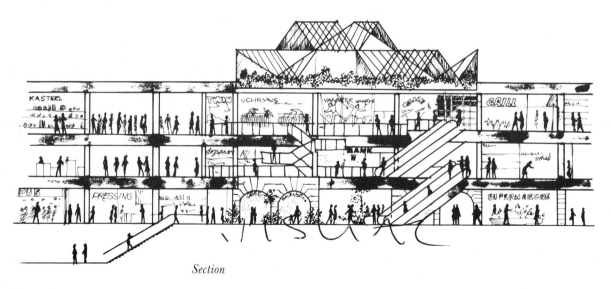
Section

144

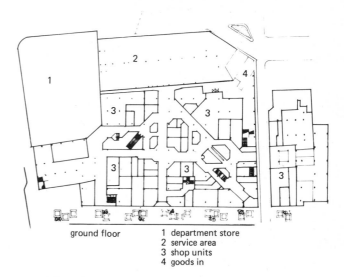

ground floor   1 department store
2 service area
3 shop units
4 goods in

Ground floor plan

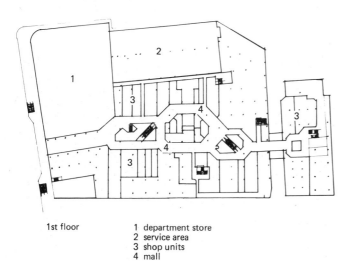

1st floor   1 department store
2 service area
3 shop units
4 mall

First floor plan

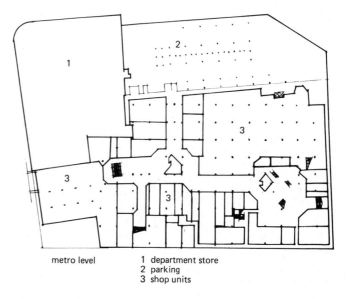

metro level   1 department store
2 parking
3 shop units

Metro level

THE GALLERIA, White Plains, New York, USA

Architects: Copeland, Novak and Israel.
Owner/Developer: The Cadillac Fairview Shopping
Centers (US) Limited.
Area: 850 000 ft^2
Closed; air-conditioned malls; 150 units; 4 levels
2 department stores; 2850 car park spaces (5000
additional spaces nearby); Cinema.

Reference:
Developer's Brochure and Information

Urban redevelopment in an older district of the City of
White Plains, a 10 acre central location in Westchester
County, New York. Expressways and Thruways make
the city easily reached from all parts of Westchester,
Putnam and Fairfield Counties. A bus stop is inte-
grated into the Centre to accommodate 360 daily
buses connecting all communities in Westchester
County.

The primary catchment area is estimated at
750 000, Secondary at 1.5 million. Two levels of the
four-level shopping span a four-lane street in the
centre. The focus of the centre is a multi-dimensional,

The animals are a temporary display mounted by students

An elegantly designed wall-climber lift forms an interesting feature

full height atrium containing at lowest 'garden' level
an interesting fast food area with seating for 1000 and
more than twenty eating establishments. This food
court, overlooking pools, rock formations and exotic
planting, is an attractive feature, drawing people into
the Galleria and encouraging them to stay, devised as
an integrated entertainment and recreation zone.

The tenant mix is controlled, providing a broad
range of retail outlets attracting a variety of income
levels. The 'garden' level contains gourmet foods,
bakery, cookware, candy shop and other specialist
shops as well as the restaurants. The main street level
houses banks, a twin cinema and shops and service
traders. The two upper levels are devoted to fashion
shops. Servicing is from main street level. Chilled
water is provided to tenants. Two sets of escalators
and a glass-enclosed lift provide vertical circulation.

The mall design has offered considerable scope for
individual treatment of shop units and shop design
generally is interesting, varied and of high quality.

The project has revived activity in the dormant
urban renewal area of White Plains.

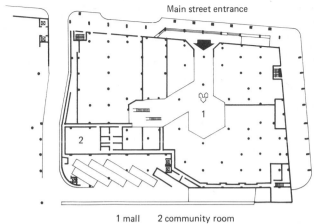

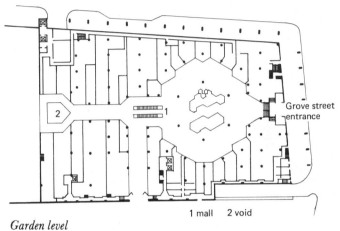

Two views of shopping mall

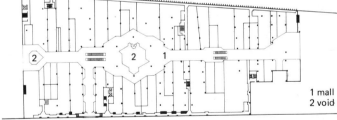

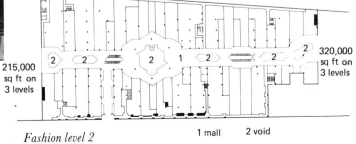

View from centre court upper level. (Note flexibility of shop front treatment)

LA PART DIEU, Lyons, France

Architect: (for conceptual design) Copeland Novak Israel.
Developers: La Société des Centres Commerciaux with Crédit Lyonnais.
Area: 110 000 m² (1 200 000 ft²)
2 department stores, 250 units.
Enclosed; Multi-storey; air-conditioned malls; 5 shopping levels; 4300 car park spaces; metro station, railway station.
Opened: 1975.
Other uses: Hotel, offices, apartments complex.

Reference:
Developer's Brochure 'La Part Dieu'.
ICSC European Conference Paper by Jean Louis Solal 'Development of La Part Dieu' 1977.

Urban development; a regional centre in down-town Lyons. Part of a megacomplex on the site of the largest cavalry barracks in Europe, purchased by the City from the Secretary of Defence, for the purpose of extending the city centre to strengthen the down-town area and ensure the city's economic activity, the basic principle being segregation of all pedestrian and automobile traffic. Pedestrian paths and elevated walkways are located on a plaza, a concrete slab 16 ft above street level, 7½ acres of land being devoted to this 1 200 000 ft² shopping centre.

There is natural smoke extract from malls and corridors into the roof space by a combination of ducting and voids. There is a system of smoke and heat detectors, large shops being equipped with fire shutters and similar techniques.

Wells in wider main malls give visual link between shopping levels. (Photos: Nigel Woolner)

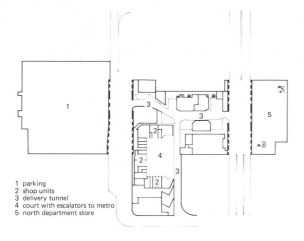

Basement

1 parking
2 shop units
3 delivery tunnel
4 court with escalators to metro
5 north department store

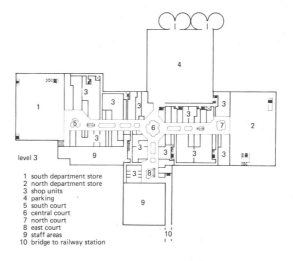

Level 3

1 south department store
2 north department store
3 shop units
4 parking
5 south court
6 central court
7 north court
8 east court
9 staff areas
10 bridge to railway station

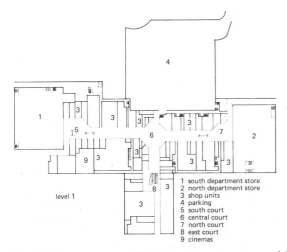

level 1

1 south department store
2 north department store
3 shop units
4 parking
5 south court
6 central court
7 north court
8 east court
9 cinemas

Level 1. Department store linked to main centre at ground floor level bridging over road with court and malls. Wells in wider main malls give visual link between shopping levels

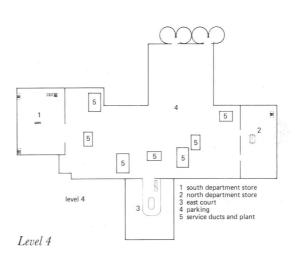

level 4

1 south department store
2 north department store
3 east court
4 parking
5 service ducts and plant

Level 4

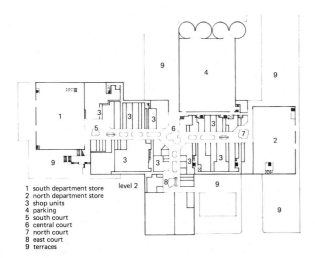

level 2

1 south department store
2 north department store
3 shop units
4 parking
5 south court
6 central court
7 north court
8 east court
9 terraces

Level 2

PLAZA SINGAPURA, Singapore

Architects: BEP Akitek (Pte).
Owner/Developer: The Development Bank of Singapore Limited.
Area: 400 000 m² (1 000 000 ft²) rentable floor space.
Covered centre; air-conditioned; 7 storeys; 2 basements; 9 storey car park for 752 cars.
Other uses: Bank, offices.
Completed 1975.

Reference:
Architect's Report.
Developer's Brochure.
'Building Materials & Equipment' January 1975.

As this is an interesting example of a centre operating in a different climate and different conditions from most of the other examples, a fairly full description is given below. The climate is one of high temperature and high humidity, with temperature varying only between 27°C and 28°C.

The Plaza Singapura site is one of the commercial centres of Singapore where some of the foremost hotels, offices, shopping centres and entertainment theatres are located.

Due to its proximity to the Republic's Presidential residence, the approval was subject to certain restrictions, viz, the building height limit of 100 ft above Orchard Road level, the prohibition of any openings, windows or accesses along the western facade and security measures to be built into the building design. The architects have attempted to break this monotony by a mural relief treatment consisting of solid panels at various planes of different colours and materials with the introduction of planting at 2nd and 3rd floor levels in the form of planting boxes. Other conditions for planning approval were a 120 ft pedestrian underpass across Orchard Road linking this landscaped forecourt with the gardens on the opposite side of the road, ensuring speedy and safe discharge of pedestrian traffic across a busy intersection. This is built with its ceiling at 6 ft under Orchard Road, in order to avoid the major services which run under the road. The tunnel is well lit and mechanically ventilated and provides access also to the 2nd basement of the Plaza Singapura building. The whole subway was constructed by the 'cut and cover' method to avoid interruption of the traffic flow along the road.

The building comprises 7 storeys above ground level with 2 basements and a 9 storey car park building, with 460 000 ft² rentable floor space, making the Plaza Singapura the largest shopping complex in the Republic.

Landscaped lobbies with decorative glazed external walls on 2nd and 3rd floors allow natural light into the building. Strategically placed seating is provided in these internal courts and lobbies.

A landscaped courtyard at 1st floor, open to the external air, separates the car park building at the rear of the site from the main building; a dry form of landscaping with reticulating fountain relieves the utilitarian monotony of the car park building.

The three upper floors are let for non-retail use. The whole of the 4th floor is occupied by the offices of the Telecommunication Authority of Singapore whilst the 5th floor has been leased as offices and medical clinics. Provision for restaurants and entertainment is on 6th floor with intermittent areas for coffee and snack bars on the lower floors.

The major front facade on the ground floor is occupied by the Orchard Road branch of the Development Bank of Singapore, their offices extending to the 1st basement through an internally linked staircase.

The exterior of the building is clothed in vitreous glass mosaic with special accent at the 2nd and 3rd floor levels. A dominant feature of the external wall treatment is the fibreglass decorative mural which surrounds three sides of the building at the 4th floor level. Special lighting at the 5th floor level highlights this mural at night

*Diagrammatic view of a 130 ft × 60 ft 6 storey high court at 1st floor
roofed with a 230 ft × 100 ft glazed skylight which also extends over
the 6th floor lobbies.*

The 2 basements and the prime area on the ground floor are occupied by Hachan Department Store and Supermarket, a Singapore/Japan joint venture which commenced business in mid-September 1974.

Unit shops occupy remaining floors.

Delivery and goods handling facilities are located in the 1st basement with an access and exit ramp separate from the access and exit ramps servicing the car park. The 10 000 ft^2 loading bay which is capable of handling 8 delivery trucks simultaneously is served by a 9 ft wide service corridor running the whole length of the building and off which 3 large service lifts are strategically located to serve all floors in the building.

Refuse collected from each floor is discharged to a central collection area in the 1st basement via one of the service lifts. Here it is mechanically compacted and stored for removal from the building under a private system independent of the Republic's Public Health Department.

Drinking fountains dispensing chilled water are provided at every floor for the convenience of the public and tenants. There are 'Pantry rooms' on each floor for the communal use of tenants.

Building finishes

Wall and ceiling finishes are by tenants. Ceramic floor tiles are used throughout the lobbies, internal courts and concourses. Note that glazed aluminium shop-fronts are installed by developer, punctuated with Dekoral copper laminate panels.

Due to the non-uniform nature of the foundations, steel sheet piling with pre-stressed ground anchors was used around the perimeter of the building with the exception of the area around the car park exit ramp. The substructure consisting of two basements and including the ground floor slab is of conventional reinforced concrete flat slab design on bored pile foundations. The superstructure is prestressed concrete. Provision has been made for a future ten storey tower block over the main building and two additional floors in the car park building.

28 sets of 44 in width escalators travelling in both directions connect all floors from the second basement to the 5th floor. There are 6 passenger lifts of 3000 lb capacity and 300 fpm speed with provision for 2 extra lifts in the future. 3 freight lifts also of 3000 lb capacity and 300 fpm speed on the opposite side of the building, with provision for extra 2 lifts in the future serve all floors. One of these lifts and the 1200 lb 200 fpm

passenger lift in the car park building are provided with firemen's operation for emergency use.

A central air-conditioning system with several multi-zone air handling units located on each floor, assures shoppers and tenants of a constant comfortable atmosphere. Thermostat controls in each tenancy allows the tenant to regulate the temperature to suit his comfort. Precooled air at 72°F and 55% R.H. is ducted to each tenancy with allowance in the shop-front design for return air to escape into the corridors and back to the A.H.U. rooms via their return air wall grilles which are equipped with sound attenuation boxes.

The main air conditioning plant and switch room is in the 1st basement housing 3 sets of centrifugal water chilling sets of 1000 T.R. each and 1 set of 500 T.R. capacity complete with chilled water and condensing water pumps. Provision has been made for 2 additional chiller sets in the future.

Cooling towers are located at the topmost floor of the exit ramp. Chilled water is reticulated through a vertical riser to each floor.

Fresh air supply to the airhandling units is from five sets of primary air handling units all of which are located on the 6th floor. All toilets, plant rooms and enclosed staircases and fire lobbies are mechanically ventilated. In addition a separate exhaust system is provided for the medical clinics on 5th floor and the kitchen areas in the building.

The main PUB transformer switch rooms are located at the ground floor. Owner's and tenants transformers and switchrooms are distributed over several floors in the car park building. Two 600 kVA diesel-alternator sets supplied from an underground 2000 gallon bulk fuel tank, with provision for automatic switching ensure continuity of power supply for emergency lighting and essential services in the building in the event of power failure in the mains.

An integrated indication and control system located in the central control room in the 1st basement provides efficient surveillance, control and maintenance of all services and equipment in the building.

The entire complex including the car park is protected with an automatic sprinkler system.

The building is served by ten hosereel risers in the main building and three in the car park. Two dry riser inlet connections along Oldham Lane enable the Fire Brigade to pump water into the equipment installed in the building.

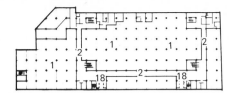

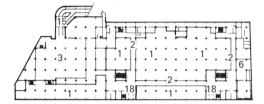

1	shopping	13	Deck A (48 cars)
2	arcade	14	Deck B (45 cars)
3	loading bays	14A	Deck B1 (40 cars)
4	water storage tank	15	ramps
5	pump room	16	internal courts
6	reception	17	exit
7	entrance	18	passenger lifts
8	Post Office	19	restaurant
9	bank	20	Deck H (32 cars)
10	plaza	21	Deck I (36 cars)
11	pool, sculpture and landscape garden	22	cocktail lounge
		23	Decks C & D (52 cars)
		24	Decks CI & DI (44 cars)

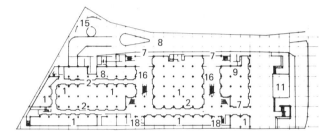

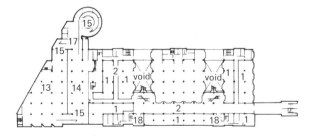

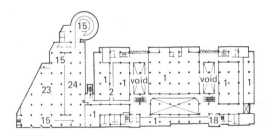

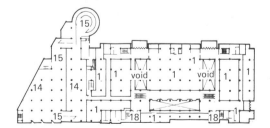

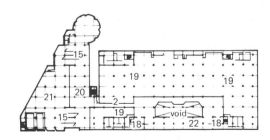

Floor plans
Five strategically located and completely fire-isolated escape staircases in the main building with two similar staircases in the car park ensure quick evacuation of the building in emergencies. Further fire precautions are provided in the form of the automatic switching over to the emergency diesel generators to supply power to a basic level of lighting and other vital equipments in the building in the event of

power failure. In such an emergency all lifts have also been designed to automatically return to the ground floor. Two smaller internal courtyards on ground floor with landscaped areas under the escalators open off the large glazed entrances from Oldham Lane. These courtyards can be viewed from the voids which extend up to 3rd floor. The building's public address system and information counter is also located at internal court nearer to Orchard Road

PENINSULA PLAZA, Singapore

Architects: Alfred Wong Partnership.
Developers: Consolidated Hotels Limited.
Area: 34 000 m^2 (366 000 ft^2) net rentable area.
Gross built-up area: 50 000 m^2 (538 000 ft^2) including
department store.
Enclosed; multi-storey; air conditioned; 4 shopping
levels; 600 car park spaces.
Other uses: Offices in 32 storey office tower above 4
level shopping podium.

Reference:
Developer's Brochure
Architect's Information.

Urban development; strategically located in the heart
of the 'choicest shopping district' in Singapore.

The centre will be linked to the City Centre station of
the new Mass Rapid Transport system. 50 bus routes
converge here and pedestrian traffic is strong – drawn
by hotels, theatres, churches, public and other offices.

22 escalators serve the basement to 4th floor and 2
passenger lifts, ground to 8th floor (shopping floors,
offices, car showrooms and car park) and a heavy duty
goods and service lift. Shop unit size offers range from
31.0 m^2, (360 ft^2) to 340 m^2 (3660 ft^2).

Tenant mix caters for a wide retail range. Corner
units are provided with special water supply for
special service units, such as pharmacy, and four have
been specifically allocated for hairdressing salons with
special exhaust fans.

This centre is significant in providing fully finished
units, shop fronts, signs, interior lighting, floor and
ceilng finishes, all being of standard design – though
by arrangement specially designed units may be permitted. This system, while facilitating speed of competition and simultaneous opening by allowing blank-
et approvals for all units, shifts the design emphasis,
from a necessarily standard shop unit design, to the
public concourses and imposes restrictions in the
retailers' methods of trading, though with economic
advantages in fitting out costs.

Air-handling units generally serve shop units. Communal toilet facilities are provided for staff and there
are toilets for public use.

Letterboxes with letter mailing chutes are provided
in the basement for all units.

The Management is responsible for refuse removal
from refuse areas at ground level.

Three open wells give views of all levels to shoppers from the central mall (Photo: Alfred Wong)

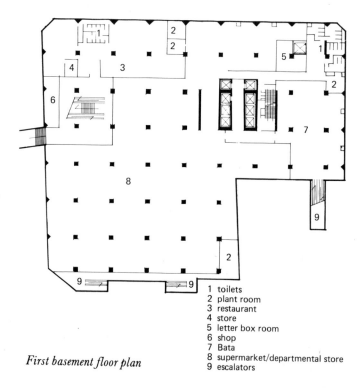

First basement floor plan

1 toilets
2 plant room
3 restaurant
4 store
5 letter box room
6 shop
7 Bata
8 supermarket/departmental store
9 escalators

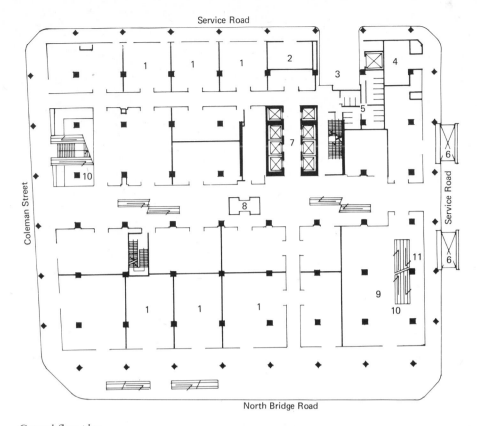

Ground floor plan

1 shops
2 bin centre
3 loading and unloading bay
4 switchroom
5 toilet block
6 car lifts
7 lift lobby
8 information counter
9 Bata
10 escalators to basement
11 escalator to 1st floor

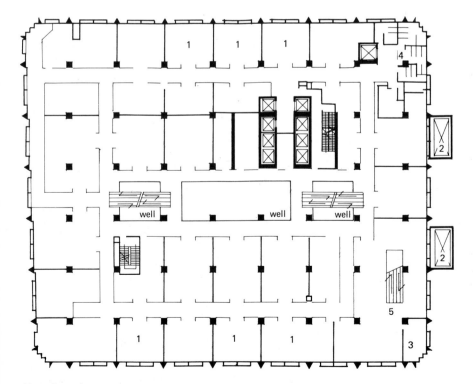

First floor plan

1 shops
2 car lifts
3 plant rooms
4 toilets
5 Bata

EATON CENTRE, Toronto, Canada.

Architects: Bregman & Harann and Zeidler Partnership. (For Eatons Store E. L. Hankison)
Owner/Developer: The Cadillac Fairview Corporation Limited.
Area: (Phases 1 & 2) 250 800 m² (2 700 000 ft²)
Closed; air condtioned mall; 270 units; 4 levels
2 department stores; 1700 car park spaces, (2 parking garages; 1 surface parking area for 200 cars); Cinema complex; 2 subway stations.
Retail area completed: 1979.
Other uses: Offices completed 1981.

Reference:
RIBA Journal, July 1980.
Architectural Review, February 1978 and May 1980.
Chain Store Age Executive, May 1977.
Urban Land Institute Project Reference File, October–December 1978.
Bauen und Wohnen, November 1977.
Developer's Information Sheet.

Urban development; an exciting 'giant size' mixed use development for retail, office and future residential uses. The site adjoins the new City Hall, is near government and university buildings, hospitals, theatres and hotels. The subway system connects directly with the development at three points. Two stations were widened, a third planned. A set of two-level escalators were built at the Dundas end. Four streets had to be closed. Circulation allows free pedestrian movement within the Centre and into the surrounding City core.

The catchment area has 2 million persons within ½ hour travelling time (all types of transport), 200 000 office workers within easy walking distance. It is estimated that 78% Eaton Centre shoppers walk or use public transport (only 22% by automobile), and already annual sales volume exceeds the cost of the project.

The 'Galleria' or main mall is 860 ft long, with width 28 ft to 68 ft and its arched glass roof, reminiscent of the Milan Galleria, rises 93 ft above the highest shopping level, 127 ft above the lowest; the mall concept is of a four-level shopping street, open wells revealing other levels to the shoppers. Ducts and lifts are exposed and treated as part of the design, and the mall is landscaped with trees, fountains, sunken courts, large paintings. The glass walled offices above the shopping levels offer views of the centre to the occupants and large plazas punctuate the mall, which is naturally lit in daylight hours.

The life of the centre is almost round the clock; the retail mall leads to Holy Trinity Church, which by agreement was integrated into the scheme and to the Salvation Army Building, which is never closed. Most stores stay open from 10 a.m. to 9 p.m. and some of the 23 restaurants and cafés stay open till 1 a.m.

There is control of the tenant mix intended to appeal to a broad range of shopper rather than high income groups. First level is for service units, e.g. drug stores, banks, fast food. A farmers' market offers fresh produce, beverages and gourmet foods. Level two is for middle to upper middle priced fashion, for men and women. Third level, connecting to Eaton Store main level, is for European high fashion international shops and local independents. Level four, 'The Mews', is for the most part devoted to artists, artisans and restaurants. Shop units are fully air-conditioned from a central system.

The ground slope allows pedestrian traffic to be pulled through the malls at three galleria levels from subway stations and street levels, the new 1 million ft², Eaton Department Store being at the north end of the main galleria. Simpson's 957 000 ft² store, renovated inside and out, is connected to the centre by a bridge and underground walkway.

Goods delivery is below ground level, with 39 trucking bays and 13 freight elevators. Waste is compacted and collected by private contract, cardboard being separated by tenants for recycling.

Built in two phases, with 4.5 acres reserved for further development (hotel and residential). The centre is said to have already recouped its capital cost.

The two major stores one at each end of the site, are tied together by three powerful shopping levels. The Eaton Centre is claimed to be the largest in Canada

General view of main mall

A prominent glass walled rotunda at the entrance forms the Yonge Dundas junction, gives a view from outside, promising excitement within

View of side mall

1 Simpson's department store   8 future development
2 bridge   9 Trinity Square
3 old city hall   10 Holy Trinity Church
4 office tower   11 Eaton's department store
5 Woolworths   12 car park
6 Salvation Army building   13 office tower
7 delivery ramp

Site plan

Eaton Centre, Toronto

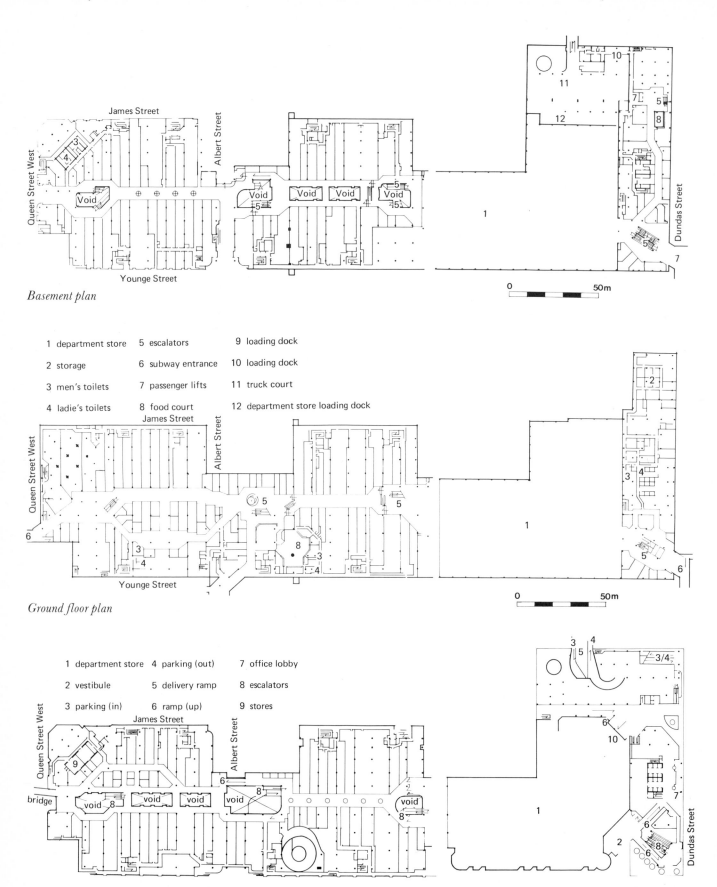

Basement plan

1 department store 5 escalators 9 loading dock

2 storage 6 subway entrance 10 loading dock

3 men's toilets 7 passenger lifts 11 truck court

4 ladie's toilets 8 food court 12 department store loading dock

Ground floor plan

1 department store 4 parking (out) 7 office lobby

2 vestibule 5 delivery ramp 8 escalators

3 parking (in) 6 ramp (up) 9 stores

Second floor plan

158

GHIRARDELLI SQUARE, San Francisco, California, USA

Architects: Wurster Bernardi & Emmons Inc.
Developers: William M. Roth.
Area: (187 000 ft²)
Terraced multi-level shopping
Multi storey; covered and open malls; 75 shops; 16 restaurants; 300 car park spaces.
Opened: 1964.

Reference:
Louis Redstone 'New Dimensions in Shopping Centres & Stores'
Keith Scott and Roger Gammell 'Speciality Centres' Estates Gazette July 1979.

Urban Development on the waterfront. Rehabilitation of block of historic buildings, formerly a chocolate factory.

This is a specialist centre with obvious tourist attraction, comprising mainly cafés, restaurants and speciality boutiques; these offer distinctive merchandise – clothes, jewellery, gifts, fine prints, ethnic imports and unique one-product goods, the accent being on quality, diversity and speciality. New structures are integrated into the existing, and full advantage has been taken of the contours in the arrangement of the various levels of shops and plazas. Ramps connect the terraces for the benefit of the handicapped. The City's earthquake code has been met, even while retaining the timber frame of existing buildings.

This is an aesthetically exhilarating and commercially successful venture, famous as a landmark in retail development and successful rehabilitation.

The multi-deck stepped levels of the subterranean garage create a series of terraces in the central plaza. Designed into and around the plazas are gardens, fountains, balconies, stairs, railings, lights, banners and cupolas. New elements, e.g. glass domes, clere-stories, bay-windows and gutters, were designed to be compatible with the existing buildings and exposed structural features were left exposed and intact wherever possible

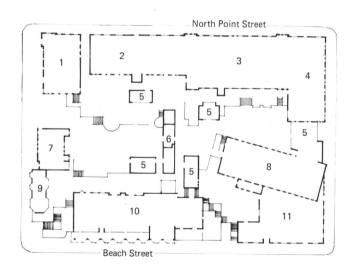

1 the clock tower	7 restaurant
2 Mustard building	8 The Woolen mill
3 Cocoa building	9 The Carousel
4 Chocolate building	10 Wurster building
5 shops	11 power house
6 plaza shops	

Site plan

FANEUIL CENTRE, Boston, USA

Architect: Benjamin Thompson
Developer: Rouse Company of Columbia, Maryland.
Area: (221 000 ft²) GLA 50 Speciality shops, 4 restaurants.
Other uses: offices
Opened: 1976 (1st phase)

Reference:
'Speciality Centres' by Keith Scott and Roger Gammell, Estates Gazette, July 1979.
Architectural Record, December 1977.
Chain Store Age Executive, December 1977.

Urban redevelopment, in three existing Greek revival buildings, which were built on landfill facing Boston Harbour between 1824 and 1826.

It consists of three long market buildings, each 535 ft long by 50 ft wide. Quincy Market, built in 1826, is flanked by the North and South markets, of slightly later date. After 30 years of decline in the state of the buildings they have been rehabilitated and redeveloped as a very successful commercial venture.

Quincy Market*, the central building, the first to be opened, is mainly devoted to food and food related products as well as a variety of restaurants and places in which to eat.

South Market contains 2 malls: the 'Arcade', a three level vertical series of jewellery and gift shops, connects with the 'Gallery' at third floor where fashion and imported furnishings shops line a wide zig-zag mall. There is also a third element of 19 shops, each with a separate external entrance. North Market, the last to be completed, is also a fashion centre, but includes such items as sporting goods and children's wear.

It is interesting to compare the Faneuil Centre, Boston, with Covent Garden, London. The motivation was different – Faneuil Centre was a commercial enterprise to realise the potential of neglected buildings by obtaining a suitable return on investment. Covent Garden was a conservation exercise by a Public Authority anxious to preserve the buildings by finding a suitable use for them.

(Quincy Market)
* *'Food from the Stalls is served on paper and is intended for taking out. Oak tables and booths beneath the Rotunda provide seating places, but real uncluttered quiet can be found one floor up on old park benches directly under the building's great dome.'*
'Through the ramps and glassed-in porches that flank the ground floor of this market are cobblestone pedestrian walkways with stone wheels for siting and more park benches.'
Quotes from New York Times, June 3rd 1981 (Sheryl Julian)

Faneuil Hall marks the entrance to the restored market place (Photo: Gerry Wrighter)

Retail space has been extended into the open plazas by glass canopies (Photo: Nigel Woolner)

Push carts for small entrepreneurs who test their products for a week, a month, or more, and many graduate to a permanent shop (Photo: Gerry Wrighter)

160

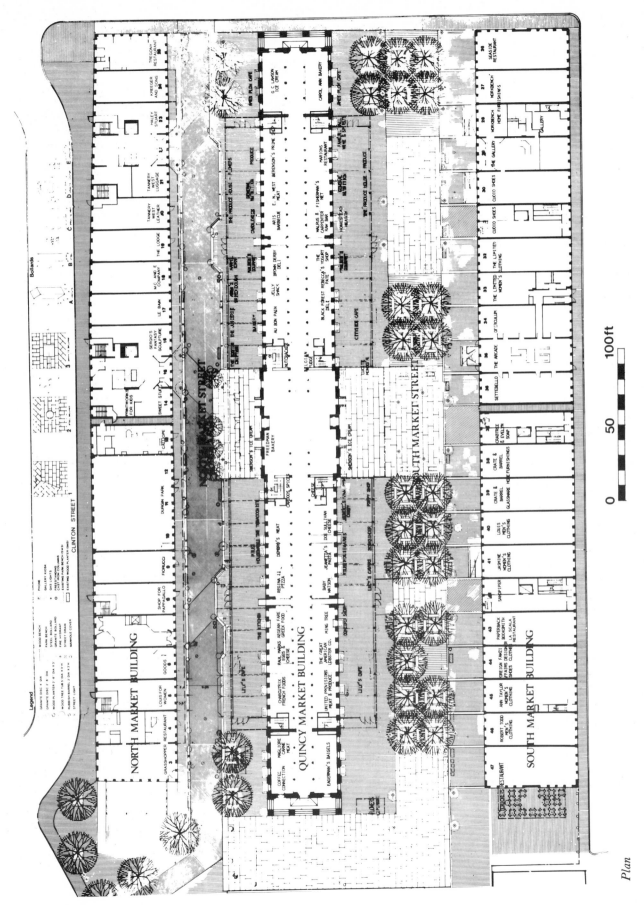

Plan

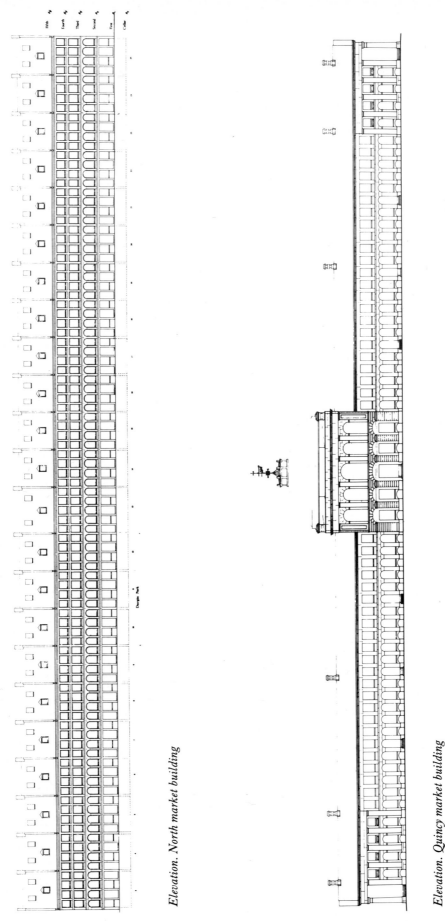

Elevation. North market building

Elevation. Quincy market building

The above diagrams show simple elevations. For interest see pages 165 and 167

Aerial view

THE MARKET, Covent Garden, London

Architects: GLC Architects Department.
Developers: Greater London Council.
Managed by: Mr. Turner, Centre Manager for GLC.
Area: 3716 m² (40 000 ft²)
Covered malls; multi-storey; 2 level shopping.
Opened 1980.
Other uses: studios, offices.

Reference:
Architect's Journal 27th May 1981.
RIBA Journal June 1980.
Tenants' Handbook Part A.
Developer's Brochure.

Urban development in a highly signficant central district of London with a catchment area within 10–15 minutes walk of 300 000 residents and workers, and 13 000 hotel bedspaces. When the Covent Garden Markets moved to a new site, the market building designed by Charles Fowler, and opened in May 1830, was left vacant. As a building of historic and architectural interest the Local Authority decided to

Shop fronts restored to their original designs. Basement areas opened up to new courtyards. Amongst the problems were to revise rainwater disposal systems which previously used the columns as rainwater pipes, and to provide fire-proofing treatment to the columns (Photo: Nicholas Halton)

Artificial lighting is solar switched. Special light fittings were designed to simulate the original gas lighting by tungsten halogen lamps. Cast iron stands recovered from the Flower Market and restored and re-erected in the North Halls are let on a weekly or monthly basis (non-combustible goods only).

Open well and staircase (Photo: Nicholas Halton)

retain and restore it, and adapt it to a suitable new function, the adopted solution being a specialist shopping centre. Thus the motivation for this development, unlike other examples of rehabilitated shopping centres, was not primarily commercial, but a political commitment to a use, as a conservation policy, a desire to preserve the building and enhance the local environment.

The complex consists of three parallel ranges of buildings, joined at the east end by a colonnade, the two courtyards covered by cast iron roofs, a Victorian addition to the original building.

Fire regulations have exerted a major influence on the basic planning of the whole conversion scheme, to safeguard means of escape, the fire-resistant qualities of new and existing construction and fire-fighting measures. Thus the two main halls have not been fully enclosed, the ends and clere-storeys being left open. Fire Brigade access is from the perimeter and shop uses have had to be limited.

Two courtyards have been excavated at lower level to open up the basement and give ready access by staircases to lower level shops. These have been ingeniously constructed out of the labyrinth of small brick vaulted spaces; their use being possible only in those areas which can gain access to an escape route. Breakable smoke vents are provided at ground level into basement shops.

The shop fronts have been restored to their original designs by the developer, only the shop interiors being fitted out by the tenants. The very detailed tenants handbook lists the design restrictions on colour, lettering, etc. The original colour scheme of the main halls has been restored.

The Piazza outside the market building has been pedestrianised.

There are no public toilets provided by the developer within the scheme; communal toilets are provided for retailers use.

Waste is collected by management, compacted and collected from one of the two loading bays.

The units are let to give a controlled mix, covering broadly artistic and leisure interests, also wine bars, coffee shops, restaurants, a pub. No 'high fire risk' users can be allowed and there is also a physical limitation on type and quantity of goods delivery, vehicular being only as far as the perimeter loading bays.

Where central heating is installed to offices, the boiler flues are taken into existing stacks, with chimney pots purpose-made to match the original.

The naturally lit main halls are not heated and consequently only in the summer can they be used as sitting out areas for cafés and restaurants. 'Buskers'

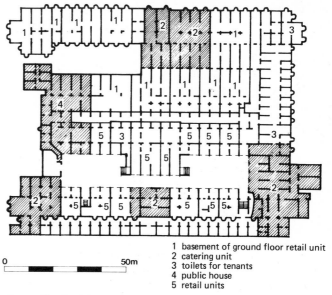

1 basement of ground floor retail unit
2 catering unit
3 toilets for tenants
4 public house
5 retail units

0   50m

Covent Garden Market, London. Basement plan

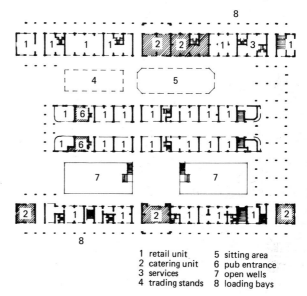

1 retail unit   5 sitting area
2 catering unit   6 pub entrance
3 services   7 open wells
4 trading stands   8 loading bays

Covent Garden Market, London. Ground floor plan

are auditioned by the market manager before being allowed to play on a specially allocated pitch for the entertainment of visitors to the centre.

The scheme can be criticised for its self-conscious 'period' restoration and rigidity of control, stemming perhaps from its non-commercial origin, and also for its limited tenant 'mix', but it has certainly achieved its object, to renovate an important area of the centre of London and renew interest and commerce in the area. It is estimated that the centre attracts 14 000 visitors daily.

Rents are generally on a 3 year rent review and related to capital investment and service charges.

LONDON PAVILION, Piccadilly Circus, London

Architects: Chapman Taylor Partners.
Structural Engineers: R. T. James & Partners.
Developers: The London Pavilion Company Limited.
Area: 1100 m² (12 400 ft²)
Enclosed; air-conditioned; Multi-storey; 3 shopping levels.
Interconnection with underground station.
Planned Opening: 1982
Other uses: Leisure (2 cinemas 500 seats each, 3rd, 4th floors); Restaurant 220 seats, 2nd floor.

Reference:
Architect's Report

Urban development in the heart of Piccadilly Circus, London ('the hub of the Universe'?)

The scheme provides new retail floor space and associated leisure facilities within the framework of an existing building. The existing facade of the 'London Pavilion' is retained with careful insertion of new shopping and leisure facilities behind. The shopping is planned round a three-storey open mall connected by glass-sided escalators.

A system of interlocking staircases has been designed which provides exits from all levels with a minimum of impact on the ground level retail floorspace.

The detailed design of a building of this type with its mixture of uses and structures is of necessity complex including the integration of the many statutory requirements in relation to means of escape, fire regulations, compartmentation, etc.

The retained elevations have necessitated servicing the building directly from Shaftesbury Avenue and therefore there are no loading bays as such but there is access to service lifts through the existing arches in the retained facade.

Two cinemas/foyers and bars each of 500 seats rising above the height of retained elevations. Note architectural integration – a new stucco frieze incorporates full size figures from world of theatre, above which a curved glass roof spans back to the upper auditorium walls with a balustraded promenade for patrons to view Piccadilly Circus.

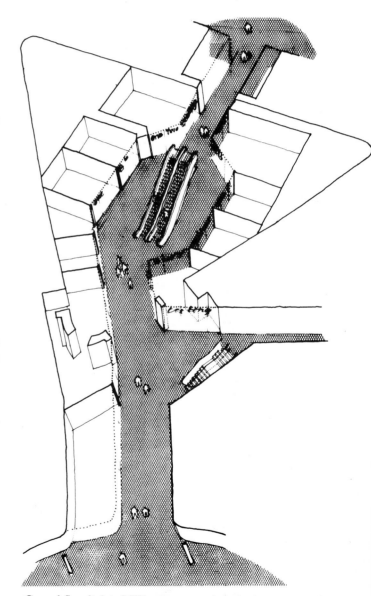

Ground floor link to LTE concourse, underground concourse and shops

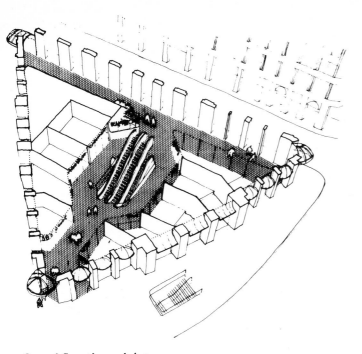

Ground floor plan and shops

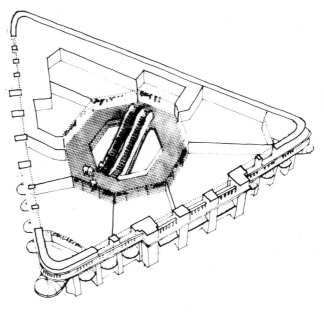

First floor plan and shops

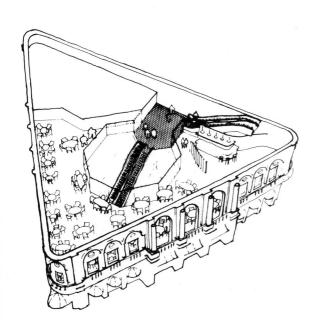

Second floor restaurant, using existing facade with views into Piccadilly Circus

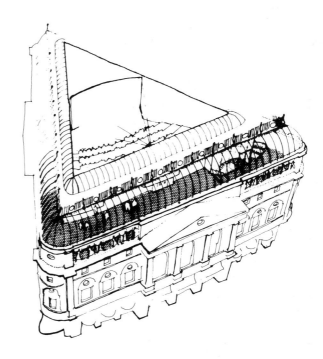

3rd and 4th floors

Bibliography and source material

1. Books

Architects' Journal, *Shop Building Design Guide*, Architectural Press (1966)

Clive Darlow BSc. ARICS (ed), *'Enclosed Shopping Centres'*, Architectural Press, London (1972)

Victor Gruen & Larry Smith, *'Shopping Towns, USA: The Planning of Shopping Centres'* Reinhold Publishing Corporation, New York, Progressive Architecture Library (1960)

Gosling & Maitland *'Design & Planning of Retail Systems'* Architectural Press, London (1976)

Ernst Neufert *'Architects' Data (Handbook of Building Types)'* 2nd International English Edition, Granada Publishing (1980)

R. Northen FRICS & M. Haskoll FRIBA, ARIAS, FFB *'Shopping Centres: A Developer's Guide to Planning and Design'*. Centre for Advanced Land Use Studies. College of Estate Management (1977)

Louis G. Redstone FAIA *'New Dimensions in Shopping Centers and Stores'* McGraw Hill, New York (1973)

Edward D. Mills, ed. *'Planning: Buildings for Habitation Commerce and Industry'* 9th Edition, Butterworths, London (1977)

2. Technical reference, papers, journals and other publications

'Guidelines for Shopping', British Multiple Retailers Association (1980)

'Shopping Centres in North West Europe', Multiple Shops Federation (1967)

'Car Parking for Shoppers', Multiple Shops Federation

'The Planning of Shopping Centres', Multiple Shops Federation (1963)

'Standards for Service Areas in Shopping Centres', Multiple Shops Federation (1968)

'Development of Shopping Centres in Major Downtown Metropolitan Areas', Jean-Louis Solal, ICSC European Conference, 1978

'Percentage Rents, Minimum Guaranteed Rents and Indexation' ICSC European Conference, Panel Session I (1978).

'Report on the Census of Distribution and Other Services (1966–1971) HMSO (1970)

'The Future for Shopping Centres' International Council of Shopping Centres. Centre for Advanced Land Use Studies (1978)

'Kirkgate Arndale Centre, Bradford, Shopping Centre Air Conditioning Case Study' by B. Bradshaw, of Haden Young Limited published by Lennox Industries Limited (1975)

'Shopping Precincts. The Queensgate Centre, Peterborough' Paper at CIBS Annual Conference 1979 by K. Maplestone, K. Hulton, R. Abraham, W. Lambert.

'Energy Effective Lighting Manual' Philips Electronic and Associated Industries Limited (1979)

'Vibrations in Buildings 1 & 2' Building Research Station Digest 1970.

'The Architect and Building Maintenance' Nadine Beddington, FRIBA, FSIAD, Institute of Building Maintenance Information Service paper, Building maintenance-present and future' (1977)

'Institute of Building Maintenance Management – A guide to good practice' Institute of Building (1975)

'Planning for Fast Foods: Report of an URPI Conference' URPI U20 December 1980

'Register of Managed Shopping Schemes' URPI P3 June 1980.

'Managed Shopping Centres Bibliography' URPI B4 December 1979.

Housewives Mobility and Travel Pattern Digest LR97 Technical Information Library Services Transport and Road Research Laboratory.

3. Fire prevention

'Access for Fire Appliances' Home Office Fire Department, Fire Prevention Note No. 1/70 and letter to Chief Officers dated 30.1.76

'*Design of roof-venting systems for single-storey buildings*',
*P. H. Thomas MA PhD, & P. L. Hinkley HMSO Fire
Research Technical Paper No. 10 (1964).*
'*Fire Precautions in Town Centre Redevelopment*' Fire Prevention Guide No. 1 HMSO (1972)
'*Guide for Smoke and Heat Venting*' NFPA No. 204
National Fire Protection Association (1968)
'*Investigations into the Flow of Hot Gases in Roof Venting*' P.
H. Thomas MA, PhD, P. L. Hinkley, C. R. Theobald
& D. L. Simms BSc, AInst P, Fire Research Technical
Paper No. 7. HMSO (1963)
'*Precautions against Fire. Part 2: Shops and department
stores*' British Standards Code of Practice CP3, Chapter IV Part 2 (1968)
'*Rules for the Construction of Buildings*' Grades 1 & 2 Fire
Offices' Committee and Fire Offices' Committee of
Ireland (1978)
'*Rules for the Construction of Buildings*' Standards I–V
Fire Offices' Committee and Fire Offices' Committee
of Ireland (Reprint 1979)
'*Smoke Control Methods in Enclosed Shopping Complexes of
One or More Storeys: a design summary*' H. P. Morgan,
BSc., Fire Research Station. Department of the Environment Building Research Establishment. HMSO
(1979)
'*Smoke hazards in covered, multi-level shopping malls: a
method of extracting smoke from each level separately*' H. P.
Morgan & N. R. Marshall. Department of the Environment Building Research Establishment. (1978)
'*The Effect of a Sprinkler on the Stability of a Smoke Layer
Beneath a Ceiling*' M. L. Bullen, Fire Research Note
1016 Fire Research Station. Department of the Environment and Fire Offices' Committee. Joint Fire
Research Organization (1974)
'*Shopping Centres – from High Street to hypermarket*'. A
special survey by E. Peek. Fire Magazine. UNISAF
Publications Limited 1979.
'*Smoke Control in Large Stores connected to extensive Covered
Shopping Malls*. Design of "Slit-Extraction" Systems
for Openings on to the Mall (Provisional)' Fire Research Station (1978).
'*Smoke control measures in a covered two-storey shopping mall
having balconies as pedestrian walkways*' H. P. Morgan
BSc & N. R. Marshall Building Research Establishment Information Paper (1979).
'*The Fire Problems of Pedestrian Precincts – Part 5 A Review
of Fires in Enclosed Shopping Complexes*' H. G. H.
Wraight. Fire Research Note No. 1012 Fire Research
Station. Department of the Environment and Fire
Offices' Committee Joint Fire Research Organization
(1974).
'*Fires in Shopping Malls*' P. L. Hinkley, G. Butcher & A.
Parnell. Heating & Ventilating Research Association
(1974).

4. UK Legislation

'*Health and Safety at Work etc. Act 1974*' HMSO (Reprint
1975)
'*Offices, Shops and Railway Premises Act 1963*', Under
which are also: '*Sanitary Conveniencies Regulations 1964*';
'*Washing Facilities Regulations 1964*'.
'*Food Hygiene Regulations 1970*', Made under the Food &
Drugs Act 1955.
'*Weights and Measures Act 1963*' HMSO.
'*Licensing Act 1964*', HMSO.
'*Fire Precautions Act 1971*', HMSO.
'*London Building Acts 1930–1939*',Under which are made
'GLC London Building (Constructional) By-Laws
1972. Amended 1979'. GLC.
'*Highways Acts 1959, 1961–1971*' HMSO.
'*Building Regulations 1976 with amendments*', HMSO.
'*Large New Stores*' Circular from Department of Environment & Welsh Office, HMSO (1976).
'*Large New Stores*' Circular from Department of Environment & Welsh Office HMSO (1977).
'*Large New Stores*' Development Control Policy Note 13
Department of the Environment & Welsh Office
HMSO (1977).

5. Relevant Bodies and Institutes

The Unit for Retail Planning Information Limited,
Victoria House,
26 Queen Victoria Street,
Reading. RG1 1TG.

International Council of Shopping Centres,
665 Fifth Avenue,
New York 10022,
USA.

British Multiple Retailers Association, (Formerly
Multiple Shops Federation)
Commonwealth House,
19 New Oxford Street,
London. WC1.

Building Research Establishment,
Fire Research Station,
Borehamwood,
Hertfordshire, WD6 2BL.

Fire Offices' Committee,
Aldermary House,
Queen Street,
London. EC4.

Fire Protection Association,
Aldemary House,
Queen Street,
London. EC4.

National Economic Development Office,
21 Millbank,
London. SW1.

British Standards Institution,
2 Park Street, London. W1.

Article Number Association (UK) Limited,
6 Catherine Street,
London. WC2.

Centre for Advanced Land Use,
College of Estate Management,
Whiteknights Park,
Shinfield Road,
Reading. RG6 2AW.

Appendix: A list of managed shopping centres in the UK

(Minimum area: 100 000 ft^2)

Town	Name of centre	Town	Name of centre
Aberdeen	Aberdeen Market	Brighton	Churchill Square
Abingdon	The Bury Precinct	Bristol	Broadmead S.C.
Aldershot	Wellington Centre	Bristol – Kingswood	King's Chase
Aldridge	The Square	Bristol – Knowle	Broadwalk
Andover	Chantry Way	Bristol – Nailsea	Shopping Centre
Ashford	Tufton Centre	Bristol – Yate	Yate Shopping Centre
Aylesbury	Friars Square	Burnley	Burnley Shopping Centre
Banbury	Castle Centre	Burton	Dame Paulet Square
Barnsley	Metropolitan Centre	Bury	Bury Shopping Centre
Basildon	Town Square	Camberley	Town Square
Basildon – Pitsea	District Centre I	Cambridge	Lion Yard Precinct
Basildon – Pitsea	District Centre II	Cambridge – Barr Hill	District Centre
Basingstoke	Porchester Square	Cannock	Cannock S.C.
Bath	Southgate Centre	Canterbury	White Friars
Bedford	Harpur Centre	Chatham	Pentagon Centre
Billingham	Queensway	Chatham (Gillingham)	Hempstead Valley Centre
Birkenhead	Grange Precinct	Chelmsford	High Chelmer Centre
Birkenhead	The Pavements	Clydebank	Clyde Shopping Centre
Birmingham	Birmingham S.C.	Coalville	Broadway
Birmingham	Bull Ring	Coatbridge	Main Street
Birmingham	Corporation Square	Colchester	Kingsway Centre
Birmingham	New Street Centre	Colchester	Lion Walk
Birmingham – Aston	Newtown Shopping Centre	Corby	Queens Square
Birmingham – Castle Vale	Shopping Centre	Craigavon	Shopping Centre
Birmingham – Chelmsey Wood	Shopping Centre	Cramlington	Shopping Centre
		Crawley	Queens Square
Birmingham – Northfield	Grosvenor Centre	Croydon	St. George's Walk
Birmingham – Yardley	Tivoli Centre	Croydon	Whitgift Centre
Bishops Stortford	Jackson Square	Cumbernauld	Phases I and II
Blackburn	Blackburn S.C.	Cumbernauld	Phase III
Bletchley	Brunel Centre	Cwmbran	Gwent Square
Bolton	Arndale	Dartford	Arndale
Bournemouth – Queens Park	Hampshire Centre	Derby	Eagle Centre
		Doncaster	Arndale
Bracknell	Charles Square	Dudley	Churchill Precinct
Bracknell	Charles Square	Dudley	Trident Centre
Bradford	Kirkgate Market/Arndale Centre	Dundee	Wellgate Centre
		Dundee	Overgate Centre
		Dunstable	The Quadrant

Town	Name of centre	Town	Name of centre
Eastbourne – Langney	District Centre	Leeds – Crossgates	Arndale
East Kilbride	Plaza Centre	Leeds – Seacroft	Queens Court
Eccles	The Mall	Leicester	Haymarket
Edinburgh	St. James Centre	Leicester – Oadby	District Centre
Edinburgh – Wester Hailes	Shopping Centre	Letchworth	The Letchworth Centre
Edmonton	Edmonton Green	Liverpool	St. Johns Centre
Ellesmere Port	Marina Walk	Liverpool – Belle Vale	Shopping Centre
Exeter	Guildhall Centre	Liverpool – Bootle	New Strand
Fareham	Fareham Shopping Centre	Livingston	Almond Vale Centre
		London	Elephant & Castle Shopping Centre
Farnborough	Queensmead		
Farnborough	Kingsmead	London – Hendon	Brent Cross
Feltham	The Centre	London – Kensington	High St. Station
Gateshead	Trinity Square	London – Lewisham	Riverdale
Glasgow	Anderston Cross	London – Shepherds Bush	Shepherds Bush Centre
Glasgow	Sauchiehall St. Centre	London – Stratford	The Stratford Centre
Glasgow – Drumchapel	Phases I and II	London – Waltham Cross	Pavilion
Glasgow – Easterhouse	District Centre	London – Wandsworth	Arndale
Glasgow – Rutherglen	Shopping Centre	London – Wood Green	Shopping Centre
Glasgow – Pollock	Shopping Centre	Luton	Arndale
Glenrothes	Kingdom Centre	Macclesfield	Grosvener Centre
Gloucester	Eastgate	Maidenhead	Nicholson Walk Phases I and II
Grays	Main Square		
Great Yarmouth	Market Square Gates	Maidstone	Stoneborough Centre
Greenock	Hamilton Way	Manchester	Walkden Shopping Centre
Grimsby	Riverhead Centre		
Grimsby	Freeman Centre	Manchester	Market Place
Halesowen	The Precinct	Manchester – Altrincham	Altrincham S.C.
Hamilton	Regent Way	Manchester – Middleton	Arndale
Hammersmith (London)	Kings Mall	Manchester – Moss Side	Shopping Centre
Harlow	Harvey Centre	Manchester – Salford	Shopping Centre
Hartlepool	Middleton Grange	Manchester – Wythenshawe	The Birtles
Hatfield	White Lion Square		
High Wycombe	The Octagon	Mansfield	Four Seasons Centre
Horsham	Swan Walk	Merthyr Tydfil	St. Tydfil Square
Huddersfield	Princess Alexandra Walk	Middlesborough	Cleveland Centre
Hull	Prospect Centre	Middleton	Arndale Centre
Hull – Bransholme	District Centre	Milton Keynes	Shopping Centre
Huyton	Shopping Centre	Morecambe	Arndale
Ipswich	Greyfriars	Motherwell	Brandon Street Centre
Irvine	River Walk	Nelson	Arndale
Jarrow	Viking Centre	Newark	St. Marks Place
Keighley	Rombalds Square	Newcastle	Eldon Square
Kettering	Newborough Centre	Newport	Kingsway Centre
Kidderminster	Swan Centre	Newton Abbey (N.I.)	Abbey Centre Phase I
Killingworth	Shopping Centre	Newton Abbott	Shopping Centre
Kilmarnock	Kilmarnock Centre	Newton Aycliffe	Town Centre
Kings Lynn	Vancouver Centre	Northampton	Grosvener Centre
Kingston	Eden Walk Phase I	Northampton – Weston Favell	District Centre
Kirkby	St. Chads I and II		
Kirkby	St. Chads III	North Shields	North Shields Centre
Leeds	Bond Street Centre	Norwich	Anglia Square
Leeds	Merrion Centre	Nottingham	Victoria Centre
Leeds	Trinity Street	Nottingham	Broadmarsh

Town	Name of centre	Town	Name of centre
Oldham – Chadderton	Shopping Centre	Sunderland	Shopping Precinct
Orpington	The Walnuts Precinct	Sutton Coldfield	Gracechurch Centre
Oxford	Westgate	Sutton-in-Ashfield	Idlewells Centre
Oxford – Cowley	Cowley Centre	Swansea	The Quadrant
Paisley	River Cart S.C.	Swindon	Brunel Centre Phases I and II
Peterborough	District Centre		
Peterborough	Queensgate Centre	Swindon	Brunel Centre Phase III
Peterlee	Yoden Way Phases I and II	Swinton	Shopping Centre
		Telford	Shopping Centre
Plymouth	Drake's Circus	Thornaby	Thornaby Town Centre
Poole	Arndale	Urmston	Shopping Precinct
Portsmouth	Tricorn Centre	Uxbridge	Uxbridge Centre
Portsmouth – Porchester	District Centre	Wakefield	Kirkgate Precinct
Port Talbot	Aberafan Centre	Walkden	St. Ouen Centre
Preston	St. Georges Centre	Wallasey	Liscard Road Centre
Reading	The Butts	Wallsend	The Forum
Redditch	Kingfisher Phases I and II	Walsall	Old Square
Rochdale	Rochdale S. Centre	Walsall	Town End Square
Romford	The Liberty	Warrington	Golden Square
Runcorn	Shopping City	Washington	The Galleries
St. Helens	Market Centre	Watford	Charter Place
Sale	Shopping Centre	Wellingborough	Arndale
Salford	Shopping City	West Bromwich	Sandwell Centre – Queens Square
Salisbury	Old George Mall		
Scunthorpe	Southgate	West Bromwich	Sandwell Centre – Kings Square
Skelmersdale	Concourse		
Slough	Queensmere	Widnes	Widnes Centre
Solihull	Mell Square	Wigan	Wigan Centre
Southend-on-Sea	Victoria Circus	Windsor	King Edward Court Shopping Centre
Spennymoor	Arndale		
Staines	Elmsleigh Centre	Winsford	Fountain Court I
Stevenage	Queensway	Woking	Woking Centre
Stirling	Thistle Centre	Wolverhampton	Mander Centre
Stockport	Merseyway	Wolverhampton	Wulfrun Centre
Stockton-on-Tees	Castle Centre	Worcester	Blackfriars
Stoke – Hanley	Motson Island	Worcester	Lychgate Centre
Stourbridge	Ryemarket	Workington	St. John's Precinct
Stretford	Arndale	Yate	Yate S.C.

The above list, based on information supplied by the Unit for Retail Planning Information is for interest only and is not intended to be fully comprehensive.

Index